"Baptists are (in)famous for their participation in American politics, but exploration of their variegated political views is relatively thin. Obbie Tyler Todd addresses this gap in his latest book, *Let Men Be Free*. This is an important work for understanding the philosophies and theologies that led Baptists to champion particular political solutions for the young republic."

—MATTHEW Y. EMERSON
Oklahoma Baptist University

"This fascinating book shows how religious freedom shaped both Baptist churchmanship and Baptist citizenship during the early years of the Republic. Deeply researched and well written, *Let Men Be Free* is a superb contribution to Baptist history and American studies. Enthusiastically recommended!"

—TIMOTHY GEORGE
Samford University

"*Let Men Be Free* is an impressive work of historical scholarship. Obbie Tyler Todd ably demonstrates how the historic Baptist commitment to soul freedom animated Baptist political engagement during the Early Republic. Along the way, white Baptists moved from the periphery of persecuted dissenters to the center of antebellum American evangelicalism. This is the sort of monograph that will inspire a flurry of scholarly articles and doctoral dissertations. Highly recommended."

—NATHAN A. FINN
North Greenville University

"Obbie Tyler Todd effectively documents both the central concerns of Baptist politics in the early American republic and the diversity within the movement. I particularly appreciated his treatment of the Baptist Federalists. This is an important book for understanding not just Baptist history, but American history, as Baptists did much to shape the nation, from its founding through the nineteenth century."

—JONATHAN DEN HARTOG
Samford University

"Working within the long tradition of scholar-pastors, Obbie Tyler Todd shows in this well-researched and elegantly written book that from the earliest decades of US history, Baptists have been all over the place politically. There were patriots and loyalists, elitists and populists, (Jeffersonian) Republicans and Federalists, supporters of slavery and abolitionists, Christian nationalists and dissenting prophets, outsiders, insiders, and everything in between. This is a good read and a welcome contribution to Baptist history."

—BARRY HANKINS
Baylor University

"While Baptists agree on the importance of religious liberty, they have not always agreed on how this principle should be implemented, or on a host of other political and social issues. *Let Men Be Free* is an engaging book with a wealth of detail drawn from a wide range of sources which describes the intricacies of the political and religious contexts in which Baptists sought to engage their cultures and the diversity of their views."

—LLOYD A. HARSCH
New Orleans Baptist Theological Seminary

"A cohesive history of a group as varied as Baptists may seem like an oxymoron. But Obbie Tyler Todd has done it in *Let Men Be Free*, the first comprehensive history of Baptist politics in the early United States. Anchored in a central theme of religious liberty, Todd illuminates the kaleidoscope diversity of Baptists in the new nation. A go-to resource for anyone reading or writing on religion in the early American republic!"

—BRIAN FRANKLIN
Associate director, SMU Center for Presidential History

"Obbie Tyler Todd combs carefully through the lives and writings of early American Baptists, tracing their political and social theology. Despite such profound disagreements (and many more besides), Todd argues one issue, a 'polestar,' united Baptists as they moved from the dissenting margin into cultural establishment: religious liberty. This rising scholar offers both an important introduction to a neglected phase of American history and a gripping and compelling read."

—MALCOLM B. YARNELL III
Southwestern Baptist Theological Seminary

Let Men Be Free

Monographs in Baptist History

VOLUME 25

SERIES EDITOR
Michael A. G. Haykin, The Southern Baptist Theological Seminary

EDITORIAL BOARD
Matthew Barrett, Midwestern Baptist Theological Seminary
Peter Beck, Charleston Southern University
Anthony L. Chute, California Baptist University
Jason G. Duesing, Midwest Baptist Theological Seminary
Nathan A. Finn, North Greenville University
Crawford Gribben, Queen's University, Belfast
Gordon L. Heath, McMaster Divinity College
Barry Howson, Heritage Theological Seminary
Jason K. Lee, Cedarville University
Thomas J. Nettles, The Southern Baptist Theological Seminary, retired
James A. Patterson, Union University
James M. Renihan, Institute of Reformed Baptist Studies
Jeffrey P. Straub, Independent Scholar
Brian R. Talbot, Broughty Ferry Baptist Church, Scotland
Malcolm B. Yarnell III, Southwestern Baptist Theological Seminary

Ours is a day in which not only the gaze of western culture but also increasingly that of Evangelicals is riveted to the present. The past seems to be nowhere in view and hence it is disparagingly dismissed as being of little value for our rapidly changing world. Such historical amnesia is fatal for any culture, but particularly so for Christian communities whose identity is profoundly bound up with their history. The goal of this new series of monographs, Studies in Baptist History, seeks to provide one of these Christian communities, that of evangelical Baptists, with reasons and resources for remembering the past. The editors are deeply convinced that Baptist history contains rich resources of theological reflection, praxis and spirituality that can help Baptists, as well as other Christians, live more Christianly in the present. The monographs in this series will therefore aim at illuminating various aspects of the Baptist tradition and in the process provide Baptists with a usable past.

Let Men Be Free

Baptist Politics in the Early United States
1776–1835

Obbie Tyler Todd

Foreword by Thomas S. Kidd

PICKWICK *Publications* • Eugene, Oregon

LET MEN BE FREE
Baptist Politics in the Early United States (1776–1835)

Monographs in Baptist History 25

Copyright © 2022 Obbie Tyler Todd. All rights reserved. Except for brief quotations in critical publications or reviews, no part of this book may be reproduced in any manner without prior written permission from the publisher. Write: Permissions, Wipf and Stock Publishers, 199 W. 8th Ave., Suite 3, Eugene, OR 97401.

Pickwick Publications
An Imprint of Wipf and Stock Publishers
199 W. 8th Ave., Suite 3
Eugene, OR 97401

www.wipfandstock.com

PAPERBACK ISBN: 978-1-6667-4376-0
HARDCOVER ISBN: 978-1-6667-4377-7
EBOOK ISBN: 978-1-6667-4378-4

Cataloguing-in-Publication data:

Names: Todd, Obbie Tyler, author. | Kidd, Thomas S., foreword.

Title: Let men be free : Baptist politics in the early United States (1776–1835) / by Obbie Tyler Todd; foreword by Thomas S. Kidd.

Description: Eugene, OR: Pickwick Publications, 2022 | Series: Monographs in Baptist History | Includes bibliographical references and index

Identifiers: ISBN 978-1-6667-4376-0 (paperback) | ISBN 978-1-6667-4377-7 (hardcover) | ISBN 978-1-6667-4378-4 (ebook)

Subjects: LCSH: Baptists—United States—History—18th century | Baptists—United States—History—19th century

Classification: BX6237 T63 2022 (paperback) | BX6237 (ebook)

VERSION NUMBER 11/01/22

To Roman & Ruby

"If government can answer for individuals at the day of judgment, let men be controlled by it in religious matters; otherwise, let men be free."

−John Leland *(The Rights of Conscience Inalienable, 1791)*

Contents

Foreword by Thomas S. Kidd | ix

Introduction | xiii

CHAPTER 1
The Baptist Quest for Religious Liberty | 1
   Baptist Jeffersonianism | 7
   "We are the Poor of the World" | 16
   Revolution as Reformation | 25
   Protestant Pluralism | 28
   Politics of Optimism | 33

CHAPTER 2
Baptism Patriotism | 35
   Patriotism Questioned | 38
   Joining the Cause | 42
   American Exceptionalism | 47
   Faith in the Founders | 53

CHAPTER 3
Baptist Republicans | 60
   The Party of Jefferson | 62
   God and the Individual | 71
   Checks on Power | 74

CHAPTER 4
Baptist Federalists | 82
   "Infidelity" and the French Revolution | 85
   The Divinity of the Constitution | 91
   Entities and Education | 96

CHAPTER 5
Race and Removal | 102
"The Negro Question" | 103
Freedom on the Frontier | 115
Friends of Humanity | 117
"Civilizing of these Indians" | 120

CHAPTER 6
Missions, Nationalism, and Foreign Policy | 129
"We are a World within Ourselves" | 132
An Emergent Religious Nationalism | 136
The War of 1812 | 153
War and Missions | 159

CHAPTER 7
Ecumenism, Education, & the Birth of a "Respectable" Denomination | 163
Two Kinds of Ecumenism | 166
Education and Political "Respectability" | 172
Learning and Liberty | 178
Rallying Around Education | 183

CHAPTER 8
Religious Outsiders No Longer | 187
Greater Wealth and Influence | 193
Establishing Disestablishment | 202

Bibliography | 209

Index of Subjects | 227

Index of Names | 231

Index of Scripture | 235

Foreword

by Thomas S. Kidd

BAPTISTS HAVE ALWAYS BEEN a politically combative people. Political advocacy by Baptists hardly began with Jerry Falwell, Sr. and the Moral Majority. Nor did it begin with Martin Luther King, Jr., one of the most famous Baptist pastors in American history who many forget was a Baptist. Although the Baptists' Continental Anabaptist cousins sometimes argued for an entire Christian separation from politics, Baptists in the English-speaking world have tended to engage rather than withdraw from the political sphere. Their political causes have included slavery (whether pro- or anti-), temperance, evolution or prayer in public schools, civil rights, and more. But there has always seemed to be a natural affinity among Baptists for politics, especially in the United States.

As Obbie Tyler Todd's excellent and much-needed book *Let Men Be Free* explains, religious liberty has consistently been the lodestar of Baptist politics in America. This was primarily because Baptists were scarred by government-sponsored harassment and persecution, dating back to their emergence from the English Separatist movement in the 1600s. Early Baptists often ended up banned, harried, and/or reviled in the English colonies in America. As late as the eve of the American Revolution, colonial governments were fining, beating, and jailing Baptists, especially in Massachusetts and Virginia. It was in Virginia that up-and-coming Patriot leaders James Madison and Thomas Jefferson watched Baptist ministers being jailed in the late 1760s and early 1770s, mainly for refusing to obey government strictures on where and when they could preach. Madison and Jefferson had already imbibed John Locke's philosophy of religious toleration, but in the persecution of the Baptists they encountered a flesh-and-blood example of what happened when an established church and its state-backed authority did not tolerate spiritual dissent and diversity.

This signaled the beginning of one of the oddest but most consequential political partnerships in American history: the union of evangelical Baptists with Jefferson. Jefferson had already become skeptical about traditional Christianity by the time of the Revolution. Yet his commitment to disestablishment and religious liberty made him a favorite of many Baptists, such as those of the Danbury Baptist Association of Connecticut. This was the association to whom Jefferson addressed his famous "wall of separation" letter in 1802, in which he assured the Baptists that he stood with them in their state-level fight to eliminate established churches. Jefferson, Madison, and dissenting evangelicals had won that fight in Virginia in 1786, but most of the New England states maintained an established status for the Congregationalist Church after the passage of the First Amendment to the Constitution in 1791. The First Amendment prohibited Congress from creating a national church, but left it up to the states to decide how to handle church-state relations.

Thus far the traditional story of Baptists and religious liberty tends to assume that virtually all Baptists in politics were Jeffersonians. But as Todd shows, there was far more political variety among early national Baptists. Many prominent Baptist leaders, especially well-connected Baptists in educational and benevolent institutions (such as missionary societies) were Federalists, and political opponents of the Jeffersonians. As Todd astutely reveals, the fact that religious liberty was the Baptist lodestar did not determine the specific political allegiances and priorities of individual Baptists. In a lesson that we need to relearn today, the idea that "Baptists" or "evangelicals" behave as a monolithic bloc in politics has usually been an ideological mirage. It would be hard to imagine any Baptist not supporting religious liberty in general, but what was the greatest threat to religious liberty? Was it government involvement with the church *per se*? Then you'd probably end up as a Jeffersonian. Was the greatest menace to religious freedom the "infidelity" associated with the French Revolution and aggressive skeptics such as Thomas Paine? If you believed that, you'd probably vote for Federalists. Baptists in early national and antebellum America were divided over theology and by ethnicity, and they were also divided politically, despite the general Baptist commitment to religious liberty.

These early national divisions between Baptists in politics should perhaps have been more obvious to scholars, given the titanic Baptist rifts that emerged in the antebellum period. The first of these schisms resulted from the anti-mission controversy of the 1820s, which played out along lines that were reminiscent of the Jeffersonian-Federalist split of the early

1800s. The anti-mission Baptists recoiled at the panoply of benevolent and missionary societies sprouting in the 1810s and '20s, societies often enjoying the support of political, ecclesiastical, and business insiders of the northeastern elite. (Not coincidentally, these were mostly sons of Federalist Party stalwarts.) Should Baptists cozy up with wealthy northeasterners of a range of denominations, in order to exercise Christian "influence" on society and government? Or were Christians meant to operate exclusively within the God-given structure of the local church for evangelism and discipleship? Pro-missions Baptists took the former position, the anti-mission folks the latter.

Nothing would damage Baptist unity more than the slavery controversies from the 1840s to the Civil War. Again, old political divisions echoed through the fights over slaveholding that led to the fateful Baptist sectional schism and the formation of the Southern Baptist Convention (SBC) in 1845. Regional divisions were the most obvious ones in that controversy, but many in the SBC also saw abolitionists as elitist, bossy northerners who wanted to impose an extrabiblical political agenda on the church. Baptist antislavery advocates were disproportionately northern, of course, but they also tended to see opposition to slavery as a means of exercising Christian influence against one of the nation's most besetting sins. Proslavery Baptists accused the antislavery group of unduly injecting politics into the spiritual sphere, but the founders of the SBC were not exactly being apolitical, either. Refusing to act against slavery, or supporting slavery's extension into new states like Texas (admitted to the Union the same year as the formation of the SBC), was a different kind of (proslavery) Baptist politics.

Baptist history writers have often championed various ideas or doctrines as the "traditional" Baptist view of a subject. And surely there are some topics - such as religious liberty, congregational autonomy, or believer's baptism - where there really is a "traditional" view, or one that virtually all Baptists have held. But on the political applications of Baptist beliefs, there has always been a spectrum. That spectrum changes over time, but it has also produced enduring themes of division over the proper relations between church and state, the biblically-mandated agenda of God's people in the world, and the moments in which believers should seek to influence the laws and mores of society. As *Let Men Be Free* shows, the general principle of religious liberty has rarely provided uniform answers to such questions. This goes a long way toward explaining why Baptists have been so adept at fighting over politics.

Introduction

BAPTISTS ARE VERY PARTICULAR about their history. They're also prone to disagree over politics. For these two reasons, this was a somewhat difficult book to write. One cannot attempt to parse and present the politics of Baptists in the early republic without inevitably confronting the political issues they face today. Baptists in the United States have always been political creatures, one might say. But this is also why such a book is so important. There is scarcely a question of political significance that could be posed to Christians in the twenty-first century (i.e. war, education, taxes, race, gender, states' rights, etc.) that was not considered, in *some* form, by Baptists in the eighteenth and nineteenth centuries, most especially that of religious liberty. Therefore, as the first comprehensive treatment of Baptist politics in the new American nation, this book offers a window into the past as well as to the present.

However, much like today, Baptists in the infant nation were a diverse bunch. This is almost certainly one of the reasons why a book of this sort has not been attempted, at least in this way. Between 1776 and 1835, the United States was home to Separate Baptists, Regular Baptists, United Baptists, General Baptists, Particular Baptists, Calvinist Baptists, Free-Will Baptists, African Baptists, Primitive Baptists, Anti-Mission Baptists, Missionary Baptists, Two-Seed-in-the-Spirit Baptists, Landmark Baptists, and others. In turn, as one might expect, Baptist politics was a kaleidoscopic reflection of Baptist life itself. For example, various styles of Calvinism and revivalism had a significant impact upon the way Baptists expected the state to promote religion. But what has not always been explored is the way that Baptist politics shaped Baptist doctrine. For instance, Missionary and Anti-Missionary Baptists were divided on much more than evangelism. The controversy also centered around the nature of ecclesiastical power, the church-state separation, and relations with Britain. Baptist education was not just about training young men for the work of the ministry. Colleges were erected to promote republican virtue against rising French "infidelity," to inculcate the next generation in the importance of religious liberty, to compete with other denominations in the new religious marketplace, and to establish Baptists as a "respectable" denomination in order to participate in the public square. And all of this took place in the shadow of the Revolution. In June 1831, when Englishman Henry Caswall was traveling through Gambier, Ohio, he met a Baptist who was not particularly pleased with the new Episcopal college. The man grumbled,

> I have fought the British in the revolutionary war; I have again encountered them in the last war; and I know something of their character. I know they would not contribute so many thousands to build a college in Ohio without a sinister object. I am, therefore, convinced that Bishop Chase is an agent employed by them to introduce British domination here. The college is in fact a fortress, all you students are British soldiers in disguise, and when you think you have an opportunity, you will throw off the mask, and proclaim the king of England.[1]

In a nation that separated church and state, religion and politics were still inextricable. Therefore, the story of Baptists in the early United States cannot be told without accounting for the theological convictions that propelled them to action *and* the political consciousness that animated their decisions. And in such a diverse community of faith, the one political thread tying Baptists together was the greatest gift they believed the American Revolution had bequeathed to the church: religious liberty.

The title to this book is *Let Men Be Free* because religious freedom was, in the words of John Leland, the "polar star" of Baptist politics.[2] The founders knew this well. When James Madison wrote to Virginia Baptist George Eve in 1789, just sixth months after Virginia ratified the Constitution, he assured the minister that he was still "a friend to the rights of Conscience" and "particularly, with respect to religious liberty." Madison had not forgotten the Baptists. The First Amendment was coming. After all, it was the Baptists who had helped Madison vote down Patrick Henry's religious assessment bill in 1785 (in effect, a plural establishment) and enact Virginia's Statue for

---

1. Caswall, *America and the American Church*, 45–46. Diana Hochstedt Butler explains, "In the minds of some Ohioans at least, the Episcopal Church was antidemocratic and an anti-American front for British interests. The combination of a shortage of ministers and Yankee suspicion put Episcopalians in a difficult evangelistic position in relation to their Protestant neighbors" (Butler, *Standing Against the Whirlwind*, 65).

2. Leland, "Speech Delivered in the House of Representatives of Massachusetts, on the Subject of Religious Freedom, 1811," 354.

Religious Freedom.³ As historians have shown, the Baptist quest for religious liberty became, in some sense, *America's* quest for religious liberty. But what has not been examined in great detail is the diversity of the Baptist program. To borrow a biblical analogy, in their pursuit of the "polar star" of religious freedom, Baptists did not always arrive in the same Bethlehem. And they were often following different stars. Similar to their spiritual ancestors today, Baptists did not always define religious liberty in quite the same way. The state of Massachusetts offers the starkest of contrasts. Whereas John Leland was a "thoroughgoing Jeffersonian," his Republican counterpart Isaac Backus "never qualified his belief in a Christian commonwealth."⁴ While Backus did not object to the teaching of the Westminster Confession in New England schools or compulsory attendance at public worship, he *did* repudiate the idea that citizens should pay taxes to a local parish church, regardless of the denomination. Further still, Backus did not always see eye-to-eye with his friend and pastor of First Baptist Church of Boston, Samuel Stillman, a Federalist who was much more prone to maintain good relations with the Congregationalists.

Like Thomas Jefferson, Baptists in the early republic were both idealists and pragmatists, envisioning a brave new world freed from the cords of state religion yet often willing to lock political arms with those who opposed their most basic religious convictions, be they Deists or Dwightians.⁵

---

3. James Madison to George Eve, January 2, 1789. Madison was familiar with the Baptists in Virginia. According to Jay Cost, the combination of Madison and Baptists and Quakers in 1785 "proved an insuperable alliance" against Patrick Henry's religious assessment bill. "Not only did the assessment fall to a decisive defeat, but the House of Delegates, under Madison's careful leadership, also enacted Virginia's Statute for Religious Freedom. Penned by Jefferson as part of the revisal, this landmark piece of legislation enshrined both the disestablishment of religion and tolerance for all believers, two principles that would eventually be established for the nation by the First Amendment" (Cost, *James Madison*, 61).

4. Eric C. Smith explains, "Leland embodied the rise of liberal individualism that marked American society in the latter eighteenth century. As a thoroughgoing Jeffersonian, he wished to unshackle himself from the tyranny of the past, as well as from the present control of the wealthy and educated, that he might simply think for himself" (Smith, *John Leland*, 5). McLoughlin, *Isaac Backus and the American Pietistic Tradition*, 150.

5. This is essential to what Jon Meacham calls Jefferson's "art of power." Meacham reflects, "Jefferson had a remarkable capacity to marshal ideas and to move men, to balance the inspirational and the pragmatic" (Meacham, *Thomas Jefferson*, xx). By "Dwightians" I am referring to Timothy Dwight (1752–1817), the President of Yale who was often regarded as the leading political voice for the Standing Order, the alliance between New England clergymen and the civil government. In 1800, Dwight warned a friend, "The introduction of Mr. Jefferson will ruin the Republic; the postponement of his introduction will . . . save it" (Fitzmier, *New England's Moral Legislator*, 62).

In this too it might also be said that Baptists have not changed much over the course of the last two centuries. Baptists today are often accused of yoking themselves with political leaders who diverge significantly from their beliefs, but such coalitions have always been a mainstay in Baptist — and American — politics. Indeed, without these coalitions the First Amendment would not have been possible.

In *America: A Sketch of Its Political, Social, and Religious Character* (1855), German Reformed scholar and Mercersburg theologian Philip Schaff described the United States to his fellow Europeans as "a world of the future" due to the "general prevalence of freedom of conscience and religious faith, and of the voluntary principle, as it is called: that is, the promotion of every religious work by the free-will offerings of the people."[6] With the eyes of an immigrant, Schaff saw many ills in American society, including slavery. But he also saw progress. If indeed the American nation came to represent the "world of the future" with its emphasis on voluntary religion, those Christians who championed religious liberty in the earliest days of the republic might now be considered ahead of their time. Contending for the very ideals that virtually every twenty-first century American takes for granted, Baptists in the early United States were, in one sense, a denomination of the future. And with a combination of political savvy and millennial optimism, they certainly saw themselves as such. "Civil and religious liberty have spread with astonishing rapidity," boasted the Georgia Baptists in 1804. "What grand events have taken place in half a century past? And we believe still more great, more good, more glorious things are just at the door."[7] Indeed, Baptists had good reason to be optimistic. By 1983, Lutheran historian Martin Marty seemed to confirm these grand expectations and the fulfillment of Schaff's political prophecy when he identified something he called the "Baptistification" of America.[8] *Let Men Be Free: Baptist Politics in the Early United States (1776-1835)* is therefore not just an examination of how America shaped Baptists, but how Baptists shaped America.

Due to the complex nature of Baptist politics, the book is structured both thematically and chronologically. Before exploring the major divisions and controversies that arose in the Baptist quest for religious liberty, the

---

6. Schaff, *America*, 93, 98.
7. In Ray, *Daniel and Abraham Marshall*, 230.
8. Marty, "Baptistification Takes Over," 33–36. Even former Congregationalist clergymen occasionally celebrated the dissolution of the Standing Order. Lyman Beecher once confessed that the disestablishment of religion in 1818 was "the best thing that ever happened to the State of Connecticut. It cut the churches loose from dependence on state support. It threw them wholly on their own resources on God" (Beecher, "Downfall of the Standing Order," 252–53).

work begins with principles, patriotism, and partisanship. In chapter one, I establish religious liberty as the guiding aim of Baptist politics in the early republic and explore the Jeffersonian (and anti-Jeffersonian) nature of the Baptist project. In chapter two, I seek to show how Baptists viewed their new nation and how that new nation viewed Baptists, during the Revolution *and* in the years following. Chapters three and four are committed to elucidating the basic commitments of Baptist Republicans and Federalists, with the latter contributing a brand-new field of research in Baptist and American historical studies. Even though these two parties were dissolved by the time of Andrew Jackson's election to the presidency in 1828, as Daniel Walker Howe has shown, "Both Whigs and Democrats claimed to be heirs of the Republican party of Jefferson though both in fact contained some former Federalists."[9] The nation's first two political parties were therefore critical in the development of Baptist politics in the United States and are thus indispensable to this book. In chapter five, I pivot the conversation to examine the way that Baptists did or did not contend for the liberties of others, particularly African Americans and Native Americans. This is an essential part of the Baptist story, as it throws light upon the strengths and shortcomings of the entire quest for religious freedom. Finally, the last section of the book is devoted to policies, programs, and progress. In chapter six, I tell a familiar Baptist story, the mission movement, but in a more political and diplomatic context than has traditionally been presented. In chapter seven, I do the same with Baptist education, examining the political movements and motivations that lay behind the push for schools and colleges. Finally, chapter eight is an analysis of the political, economic, and social rise of Baptists in the Jacksonian era, the period which I identify as the end of the "early United States."

As a Baptist, I am not unaware of the potential for blind spots when recounting the history of my own denomination. Therefore, in order to maintain the highest degree of objectivity in my research, I have sought a wide range of primary sources from a host of different voices in the early republic. In all eight chapters, I have labored to show more of the *breadth* of the American Baptist political tradition than has typically been explored during this epoch of history. Therefore, in addition to sources, I have also concentrated on groups. Black Baptists, Native American Baptists, female Baptists, Free-Will Baptists, Landmark Baptists, and others have been included in this work. Finally, in order to avoid the temptation to do Baptist history inside a denominational vacuum, I have situated Baptists in the larger context of American religious and political history, something that

---

9. Howe, *Political Culture of the American Whigs*, 90.

I believe is sometimes lacking from Baptist historiography. These three aspects of the book — sources, groups, and context — comprise a safeguard against an overly rose-colored narrative of Baptist politics. With regard to the relationship between theology and politics, my approach has been similar to historian Mark A. Noll's in his *Princeton and the Republic (1768–1822)*: "a focus on the role of religion also enriches the more comprehensive story of American republicanism."[10] By accounting for the deeply rooted beliefs that energized the political life of early American Christians, and by investigating how these theological ideas took political form, we can gather a better sense of the American experiment, warts and all.

---

10. Noll, *Princeton and the Republic (1768–1822)*, 9.

Chapter 1

The Baptist Quest for Religious Liberty

Baptists in America have always been a motley group of people, and in the aftermath of the American Revolution, their politics were no different. From the necessity of standing armies to the power of the judiciary to Native American policy, Baptists were nearly as diverse politically as they were theologically. Yet, in a world where civil government and religion were inextricable, and in states where citizens were still born into the local parish church, the doctrine of believer's baptism—and with it the concept of a believers' church—was an inescapably political idea. As a result, Baptist politics was defined not by a candidate or a party or even a single issue, but by its goal: religious liberty. In fact, when Baptists divided on critical issues like slavery, tariffs, banks, colleges, the ratification of the Constitution, and the War of 1812, they often did so under the same banner of religious liberty. Therefore, for instance, the consensus among scholars that Methodism was a largely "apolitical" denomination in the earliest years of the republic could not be said of Baptists, a people whose very beliefs seemed to demand participation (and persecution) in the public square.[1]

James Manning, the first president of Rhode Island College, and his circle of Baptists provide an excellent example of this diversity and unity within Baptist politics. With four separate parcels of land in Pennsylvania and Ohio, Manning's Hopewell Academy classmate David Jones was a "Jeffersonian agricultural economist" who lobbied for generous western land distribution as a means of "civilizing" Indians, teaching them the gospel,

---

1. Wigger, *American Saint*, 155. According to Russell E. Richey, "Doubtless it was just that prescribed political passivity that made Methodists relatively uninterested in the nature and meaning of the American political experiment" (Richey, *Early American Methodism*, 41).

and combatting English tyranny on the frontier.² However, Manning opposed large tracts of land for similarly Baptist reasons. He endorsed a "well-regulated agrarian law" to "prevent monopolies of land" and to protect America from "countries under the unmerciful dominion of the two beasts of tyranny."³ Manning's dear friend Isaac Backus belonged to a new Baptist faction known as Separate Baptists. In the wake of the Great Awakening, this radically evangelical group broke away from the Congregationalists after objecting to the impurity and spiritual decline of the state church. Although Backus eventually reversed his antifederalist position and voted in favor of ratification, Separate Baptists exhibited a suspicion of government power that led them to side with the party of Jefferson.⁴ Unlike Backus, who was a Republican due to his support of religious liberty, Manning was in fact a Federalist who believed that the Constitution actually *protected* religious liberty.

Religious liberty also became the backdrop for the battle over Baptist education. According to John Leland, Baptist colleges were merely aping the "bookish knowledge" of the Standing Order and forsaking the simple gospel. "Religion and education," he insisted, "do not, therefore, stand on the same ground; for education is an article which natural men can legislate upon with understanding." Conversely, Manning, who Leland mocked as a profiteer of the gospel, believed that Baptist colleges "greatly disseminated the knowledge of civil and religious liberty through this country."⁵ The assortment of political views held by Baptists were as diverse as any other denomination in America, but they were bound together by a fundamental belief in the inviolability of the individual conscience in matters of faith.

In short, freedom of religion was the polestar of Baptist politics. For this reason, as scholars have thoroughly shown, white Baptists were also unified in their mutual adoration for Thomas Jefferson, the man whom John Leland called "The Apostle of liberty."⁶ More than any single Ameri-

---

2. Wolever, *Life, Journal and Works of David Jones, 1736–1820*, 169, 110–13, 116, 91.

3. "Granville Sharp to James Manning, 21st Feb., 1785," in Guild, *Life, Times, and Correspondence of James Manning*, 359. While these were Sharp's words, Manning later replied to Sharp and said, "I concur with you in sentiment exactly concerning the importance of a mediocrity in the proportion of landed possessions in the hands of freeholders. It is the real strength of a nation, and most agreeable to the dictates of reason and the rights of man" ("James Manning to Granville Sharp, July 26, 1785," in Guild, *Life, Times, and Correspondence of James Manning*, 362).

4. "Introduction," in McLoughlin, *Isaac Backus on Church, State, and Calvinism*, 15.

5. Leland, "Miscellaneous Essays: Number Thirteen," 430; John Leland, "Which Has Done the Most Mischief in the World, The Kings-Evil or Priest-Craft?," 491, 495; Manning, "To Thomas Llewelyn, LL.D., London, November 8, 1783," 318.

6. Leland, "Events in the Life of John Leland," 36. For an excellent biography of John

can other than Washington, Jefferson represented to Baptists the natural marriage of republican and Baptist ideals and the willingness of the new nation to preserve "liberty of conscience, the greatest and most important article of all liberty."[7] Even more than Washington, Jefferson became the Baptists' supreme political ally in their sacred quest to obtain religious liberty in all thirteen states. After quoting from Jefferson's inaugural address in his speech before the Massachusetts Assembly in 1802, Thomas Baldwin, the pastor of Second Baptist Church of Boston, recognized that his audience was not as sympathetic to the newly elected President. "I am not insensible," Baldwin acknowledged, "that, considering the divided state of public opinion, I am here venturing on a point of very great delicacy; and yet to pass wholly unnoticed the Federal Administration, which has been constantly mentioned on all similar occasions, might be deemed disrespectful to the constituted authorities of our country." Nevertheless, he added, "It is but just to observe, that our present *Chief Magistrate*, as well as his predecessors, was among the first asserters of our freedom and independence." Baldwin then showed his Republican colors when he concluded, "It will not be denied that the present administration differs in some important points from the preceding; and that a new order of things in some respects is taking place . . . I will only add, our religious as well as our political sentiments, oblige us to 'give custom to whom custom, and honor to whom honor is due.'"[8] Baldwin certainly spoke for most white male Baptists, the majority of which had voted for Jefferson in 1800.[9] His text encapsulated the heart of Baptist politics in the new nation: "As free, and not using your liberty for a cloke of maliciousness; but as the servants of God." (1 Peter 2:16)

Black Baptists were also animated by a desire for religious freedom, but their concept of "freedom" and their view of Jefferson were obviously much different than Baldwin's. As slaves in Jefferson's so-called "empire of liberty," blacks inhabited a nation in which they were neither citizens nor people (according to the notorious 3/5 Compromise).[10] Therefore, even in a church that offered the spiritual equality of a believer's baptism, the Afro-Baptist community became, in the words of Donald G. Mathews, "a movement

---

Leland, see Smith, *John Leland*.

7. Isaac Backus, in McLoughlin, *Soul Liberty*, 171.

8. Thomas Baldwin, *A Sermon, Delivered Before His Excellency Caleb Strong* (Boston: Young & Minns, 1802), 29–30.

9. McLoughlin, *Soul Liberty*, 2.

10. At the 1787 Constitutional Convention, delegates reached a compromise to determine how many seats that each state would receive in the House of Representatives. The result was that 3/5 of a state's slave population would be counted toward the state's total population.

within a movement, a community within a community, a society within a society."[11] The anti-slavery forces that emerged in the Baptist church in the earliest years of the republic were not potent enough to produce a culture of emancipation nor to eliminate the stigma of abolitionism, especially in the South. In Virginia, a petition from Cumberland County to the House of Delegates in 1777 complained about Baptist mischief and their tendency "to alienate the affection of slaves from their masters."[12] In the first decades of the new American nation, enslaved blacks and the Baptist church found common cause in the liberty of conscience. However, this same liberty could also betray such a fragile unity. By 1793, the General Committee of Virginia Baptists had reversed their original anti-slavery position from 1785, recasting slavery as a political issue that belonged *outside* the church and leaving black Baptists to pursue liberty on their own terms. Just as the non-elitist Baptist faith helped breathe meaning into the experience of slavery, it also created troubling contradictions, as many Baptist churches began to place white preachers over black preachers and denied the right to gather without white supervision.[13] Not surprisingly, black Baptists defined religious liberty in a much less Americanized sense, albeit with Jeffersonian ideals they adopted from their white brethren.[14]

George Liele, for example, helped found the First African Church of Savannah, Georgia, a congregation that historians have called "the center from which the black Baptist movement spread" and "the linchpin in the international black Baptist movement."[15] Liele left Savannah for Jamaica not as a missionary, but as a refugee. When the city was evacuated during America's War for Independence, Liele, whose former master and current patron was a loyalist, sailed with other British loyalists to Jamaica in 1783. Liele understood that once the mainland colonies had severed ties with the mother country, Britain's slave policy and growing abolitionist movement would be uprooted in North America.[16] As John W. Catron has noted, "the

---

11. Mathews, *Religion in the Old South*, xvii.

12. Scully, *Religion and the Making of Nat Turner's Virginia*, 77.

13. Tyler-McGraw, *African Republic*, 18.

14. Black Baptists sang spirituals with political undertones. According to one historian, the hero behind the spiritual "Go Down Moses" is Francis Asbury, the abolitionist Methodist Bishop. For another scholar, the "Moses" figure is Denmark Vesey, the leader of the failed Charleston slave insurrection in 1822 (Pitts, *Old Ship of Zion*, 80).

15. Frey and Wood, *Come Shouting to Zion*, 131; Catron, *Embracing Protestantism*, 200.

16. John Saillant explains, "Some of the black abolitionists became British loyalists in the era of the American Revolution, since they believed that the power of Parliament an the authority of the Crown were likely to be leveled against the slave trade and slavery" (Saillant, *Black Puritan, Black Republican*, 47).

black Protestant diaspora" most certainly "occurred as a result of the American Revolution."[17] Black Baptists were as zealous for freedom as white Baptists, but their quest for religious liberty took a much different path, one that often led them *away* from white Baptist churches and from the United States. When African American Baptist Lott Carey was ordained in 1821 to serve as a missionary to Africa, his sermon at First Baptist Church of Richmond, Virginia was a "powerful exposition on the liberty of the believer in Christ," leading scholars to suggest that he was implying much more than spiritual freedom.[18] Soon after arriving in what became the colony of Liberia, Carey contended with agents of the African Colonization Society, reminding the board that it had not been his intention to unite Baptist missions with the ACS. Lott had departed from America only to find that blacks in Africa had been turned into "laborers and mechanics" for housing construction.[19] Religious liberty was still a struggle, even across the Atlantic.

Nevertheless, black Baptist preachers in Africa still brought with them many of the principles of the Revolution. Soon after the war, British officials in Sierra Leone were concerned that ministers like Baptist David George were too "American" and "republican" in their preaching and thus subversive to the political and religious establishment.[20] During the Revolution, George had escaped with the British to Nova Scotia, eventually transporting to Freetown, Sierra Leone. Such stories of black Baptists were ironic on a number of levels. In the case of Liele and George, even those blacks who fled the Revolution still possessed the spirit of 1776 in their ministries. And although Thomas Jefferson's vision of white hegemony pushed black Virginians like Carey *out* of the country, Jefferson's revolutionary ideas about liberty and the church-state separation remained with Carey overseas, aiding his Baptist cause. Indeed, Jefferson's influence did not just propel black Baptists to become international missionaries. In late August 1831, lay Baptist preacher (and self-proclaimed prophet) Nat Turner led one of the largest slave revolts in the history of the United States in Southampton County, Virginia.[21] Due to illness and indecision, the rebellion had been postponed. Turner's initial choice was July 4.[22]

---

17. Catron, *Embracing Protestantism*, 200.

18. Sobel, *Trabelin' On*, 156.

19. Tyler-McGraw, *African Republic*, 131.

20. Catron, *Embracing Protestantism*, 218–19.

21. Sobel calls Turner's Baptist faith "a most unorthodox type, unconsciously reflecting influences of the Voodoo that Turner consciously rejected" (Sobel, *Trabelin' On*, 165).

22. Nat Turner's *Confessions* do not detail why the rebels settled on this date. It was a holiday, and most likely when slaves were given the day off. However, Patrick H.

In his defense of religious liberty and the First Amendment, the man who had become a stumbling block to the Standing Order had become to white Baptists their political cornerstone and to black Baptists a source of political inspiration. When the Danbury Baptist Association wrote to Jefferson in late 1801, they proudly concluded, "we have reason to believe that America's God has raised you up to fill the chair of State out of that good will which he bears to the Millions which you preside over."[23] Jefferson had been appointed by God to deliver America from religious tyranny. Months after their letter was sent to Jefferson, and just months before Baldwin's address to the Massachusetts House and Senate, Baptists gave Jefferson their largest thank offering: a giant cheese. On New Year's Day, the White House welcomed John Leland and a 1,235-lb. cheese wheeled from Cheshire, Massachusetts. On the massive cheese bore the Jeffersonian motto: "Rebellion to tyrants is obedience to God." Indeed, if any Baptist in America embodied the political principles of Thomas Jefferson, it was the enduring and ever-colorful John Leland, who obsequiously referred to his fellow Virginian as "my hero."[24] It was Leland's own resolution that the Virginia Baptist General Committee had adopted in 1790 stating "that slavery is a violent deprivation of the rights of nature and inconsistent with republican government."[25] In some ways, Leland was more Jeffersonian than Jefferson. In 1824, an aging Leland reflected upon his career and resolved, "here is an arm seventy years old, which, as long as it can rise to heaven in prayer, or wield a pen on earth, shall never be inactive, when the religious rights of men are in jeopardy. Was there a vital fibre in my heart, that did not plead for rational religious liberty, I would chase the felon from his den, and roast him in the flames."[26] At times, Leland even seemed to parrot Jefferson himself. Echoing Jefferson's controversial thoughts in his *Notes on the State of Virginia*, Leland insisted, "If a man worships one God, three Gods, twenty Gods, or no God—if he pays adoration one day in a week, seven days, or no day—wherein does he

---

Breen explains, "The rebels also understood the ideological significance of the date. The prophet may have seen this revolt as part of a religious war that would lead to the second coming, but the other rebels understood that this struggle coincided with the principles laid out by Thomas Jefferson in the Declaration of Independence" (Breen, *Land Shall Be Deluged in Blood*, 27).

23. "From the Danbury Baptist Association," 407–9.

24. John Leland, "Blow at The Root," 255. Leland preached in Virginia from 1776 to 1791.

25. Scully, *Religion and the Making of Nat Turner's Virginia*, 110.

26. Leland, "Address Delivered at the Request of the Republican Committee of Arrangements, at Pittsfield, on the Anniversary of American Independence, July 4, 1824," 507.

injure the life, liberty or property of another?"²⁷ In Leland's view, "Government has no more to do with the religious opinions of men, than it has with the principles of mathematics."²⁸ When Jefferson wrote to the Danbury Baptists on New Year's Day in 1802 and famously vowed to erect a "wall of separation" between church and state, he had in mind Baptists like Leland, who, coincidentally, had just delivered his "mammoth" cheese to the White House that same day.²⁹ Two days later, Jefferson invited the so-called "Mammoth Priest" to preach before a joint session of Congress. The President attended Leland's sermon himself. Leland's text was Matt 12:42 "And behold a greater than Solomon is here"—an allusion to both Jesus Christ *and* the President.

Baptist Jeffersonianism

However, as Daniel Walker Howe has noted, "it is not easy to make generalizations about the Baptists."³⁰ Just as they disagreed on seemingly everything else, Baptists did not always define religious liberty in quite the same way. For some, it was simply the lack of preferential treatment of any one Protestant denomination over another. For others, it was the free exercise of religion without *any* support from the state whatsoever. If virtually all Baptists welcomed Jefferson's support for the First Amendment and adopted his vision of disestablishment in America, Baptist politics was an ongoing debate over just how "Jeffersonian" they intended to be.³¹ Whereas Leland was a self-professed "dyed in the skin" Republican, most white Baptists were not willing to remove religion from government in the same way that Jefferson wished to extricate government from religion.³² For instance, even the Republican Isaac Backus believed in the "sweet harmony" between church and state.³³ Not only did Backus agree with most state constitutions against Roman Catholics holding office, he did not object to compulsory

---

27. Leland, "Yankee Spy," 221. See Jefferson, "Query XVII," 166.

28. Leland, *Rights of Conscience Inalienable*, 184.

29. For a helpful analysis of these events, see Dreisbach, *Thomas Jefferson and the Wall of Separation Between Church and State*, 9–24.

30. Howe, *What Hath God Wrought*, 180.

31. At the state level, however, the First Amendment may not have been as influential as previously believed. Carl H. Esbeck and Jonathan J. Den Hartog observe, "No state modeled its constitution after the First Amendment, or even considered the amendment when making state religion" (Esbeck and Hartog, "Introduction: The Task, Methodology, and Findings," 9).

32. Leland, "To the Hon. R. M. Johnson, June 9, 1834," 648.

33. McLoughlin, *Soul Liberty*, 195.

attendance at public worship and strict observance of the Sabbath.[34] He was, as Stanley Grenz has called him, "Puritan and Baptist."[35] Most rank-and-file Baptists did not seem to share Leland's position that government-funded military chaplaincy was "unconstitutional" and a "species of religious establishment."[36] John Gano, who was alleged to have baptized George Washington, was nicknamed "The Fighting Chaplain."[37] Baptist Silas Mercer likewise served as a chaplain during the Revolutionary War, obtaining the rank of Major.[38] During the Indian Wars of 1790–95, the ardent Republican David Jones boasted that he was the only chaplain in the United States Army.[39] Jones served almost sixteen years as military chaplain, including during the War of 1812 when he was seventy-six years old![40]

Views of religious liberty could sometimes divide families and even marriages. In 1803, at First Baptist Church of Providence, Rhode Island, pastor Stephen Gano (John Gano's son and James Manning's nephew) was accused of heresy—by his very own wife. For more than two hours, in front of the entire church, Joanna Gano charged her husband, an avowed freemason, with "worshipping Idols" and "perverting the Scriptures." Mrs. Gano accused Rev. Gano of "holding himself in connection with a Society which in her view was the 'Mystery of Iniquity.'" The latter was a reference to the man of lawlessness in 2 Thessalonians 2, a figure often associated by Baptists with a political ruler or a nation state. For Joanna, Stephen's freemasonry was not only unbiblical but hostile to the very nature of the church. In a somewhat revealing outcome, Joanna, not Stephen, was convicted by the church of "disorderly conduct" despite not being present at her own trial. Two weeks later, she was excommunicated for her "hard and unchristian language and conduct."[41] Even inside the home, Baptists did not always

---

34. McLoughlin, "Editor's Introduction," 399; McLoughlin, *Soul Liberty*, 194, 239. McLoughlin identifies *Policy As Well As Honesty* as significant for Backus's insistence that he believed as strongly as the Standing clergy that Massachusetts should be a Christian state (McLoughlin, "Editor's Introduction," 369).

35. Grenz, *Isaac Backus, Puritan and Baptist*.

36. Leland, "Extract of a Letter to Col. R. M. Johnson, Dated Janaury 8, 1830," 561; Leland, "Elective Judiciary," 293.

37. William Wade Burleson explains, "He received his nickname 'The Fighting Chaplain' due to his unflinching willingness to minister to the dying on the front lines of the war" (Burleson, "Preface," 3). For Gano's own account of Washington and his service, see Gano, *Biographical Memoirs of the Late Rev. John Gano*.

38. Ray, *Daniel and Abraham Marshall*, 21.

39. Wolever, *Life, Journal and Works of David Jones*, 123, 174.

40. Wolever, *Life, Journal and Works of David Jones*, 27.

41. Record Book, First Baptist Church of Providence, August 3, August 9, and August 15, 1803, Rhode Island Historical Society. Joanna did not speak before the

agree upon the extent of the church-state separation. Whether those views were acceptable, however, depended upon other social factors.[42]

In the early republic, nonestablishment and religious liberty were not necessarily synonymous in the Baptist mind. Many Baptists who contended vigorously for liberty of conscience and the free exercise of religion were not necessarily opposed to a religious establishment of some kind. Although some like Richard Johnson and Obadiah Brown would later contend with Leland that Sunday mail prohibition was a form of state religion, the majority of their Baptist cohorts did not see a postal day of rest as a violation of religious liberty, some even going so far as to accuse Leland of renouncing Christianity.[43] In contrast with Leland and Jefferson's opposition to national thanksgiving and fast days, Federalist and Charleston pastor Richard Furman insisted that special days of observance were imperative for the American people due to the "striking similarity" between "the origin of the Jewish theocracy, and the rise, independence, and establishment of these United States."[44] Leland believed that such American exceptionalism was dangerous because it "supposed that Christian nations have a just right to dispossess the heathen of their lands and make slaves of their persons, as Israel served the Canaanites and Jebusites," a right which, coincidentally, Furman defended with Scripture in his *Exposition of The Views of the Baptists, Relative to the Coloured Population in the United States in Communication to the Governor of South Carolina* (1822).[45] The Lelandian school of religious liberty, in its rigid separation of church and state, was not always representative of Baptist politics as a whole in the early republic.[46] Simply put, most white Baptists preferred a bit of religion with their government. As Aaron Menikoff has shown, at least to a degree, Baptists believed that America was a Christian nation, and since religion should not be established, it was

---

congregation but submitted written "communications" to the church which her husband read aloud.

42. Susan Juster offers a more candid conclusion, "This was not a real trial, in which accuser and accused confronted each other in the presence of their peers, but a carefully staged reaffirmation of the church's confidence in their elder" (Juster, *Disorderly Women*, 1).

43. Menikoff, *Politics and Piety*, 106, 117–19; Greene, "Further Sketches," 56.

44. Furman, *America's Deliverance and Duty*, 393.

45. Leland, "Yankee Spy," 217.

46. Even Eric C. Smith has argued, "It is unhelpful to call Leland a 'strict separationist' if that term implies the creation of a totally secular public square" (Smith, *John Leland*, 94). Likewise, Thomas S. Kidd has contended that Thomas Jefferson "did little to manifest what today we would call a 'strict separationist' approach to church-state relations" (Kidd, *Thomas Jefferson*, 68).

certainly to be encouraged.[47] Rather than holding that religion has nothing to do with government, most Baptists would have agreed more with Savannah pastor Henry Holcombe in 1802 when he wrote in Georgia's *Analytical Repository*, "I need not prove, for it is evident, that without religion there can be no virtue; and it is equally incontestable, that without virtue, there can be no liberty."[48]

Religious liberty was therefore a prize that both Jefferson and Baptists sought for themselves in their new nation, albeit for different reasons. As a result, the Jeffersonianism of Baptists has been well attested by historians such as William McLoughlin, who concluded,

> It is not so strange, perhaps, that Baptist pietists should have been the great bulwark of the party of the deistic Thomas Jefferson. Lacking our knowledge of how deistic and anti-Calvinist Jefferson was, the Baptists saw him as the champion of religion voluntarism against an established-church system and of decentralized democracy against an oligarchic, stratified political system. Calvinistic Baptists and deistic Jeffersonians agreed that at the moment the most important issue for the new republic was its commitment to an individualistic rather than a corporate pursuit of happiness.[49]

By 1785, Jefferson and his Baptist bedfellows had accomplished in Virginia what Massachusetts would not claim until 1833: the abolition of tax-supported religion. Rejecting "a general assessment for the support of religion" advocated by Patrick Henry, the people had adopted a religious freedom bill drafted by Jefferson, sponsored by Madison, and supported "in a considerable degree" by Baptists.[50] Besides writing the Declaration of Independence and founding the University of Virginia, Jefferson wanted the Virginia Statute for Religious Freedom to define his legacy.[51] In terms of its secularism, the bill was truly revolutionary for its time, stating "that no man shall be compelled to frequent or support any religious worship, place, or ministry whatsoever, nor shall be enforced restrained, molested, or

---

47. Menikoff, *Politics and Piety*, 47–49.
48. Holcombe, "Address to the Friends of Religion," 230.
49. McLoughlin, "Editor's Introduction," 429.
50. Semple, *History of the Rise and Progress of the Baptists in Virginia*, 72.
51. Nevertheless, Esbeck and Den Hartog have called Virginia "an oddity among state disestablishments" for its apparent bias against churches (Esbeck and Den Hartog, "Introduction," 11).

burthened in his body or goods, nor shall otherwise suffer on account of his religious opinions or belief."[52]

As history would have it, and as scholars have demonstrated, the Jefferson-Baptist alliance in Virginia laid the groundwork for the First Amendment to the Constitution (1791).[53] Drawing from the momentum in Virginia, Baptists from New England to the deeper South campaigned for disestablishment in their respective states. In 1799, an attempt was made in the Vermont legislature "for a general assessment for the support of preachers, similar to what had been attempted in Virginia." However, "the powerful appeals to the public in defense of religious liberty" made by Baptist Asaph Fletcher silenced the bill's advocate and the general assessment was abandoned.[54] In 1798, Jesse Mercer even wrote the article in the Georgia constitution guaranteeing religious liberty for all. Indeed, it would be no exaggeration to suggest that behind every article for religious liberty in the national and state constitutions in the early republic, there were Baptists.[55] Methodists, on the other hand, with their strong ties to Britain, did not understand or accept the Baptist notion of freedom. In 1784, when Francis Asbury read *Tyranny Exposed* by Jesse Mercer's father Silas, he scoffed, "His is republicanism run mad. Why [be] afraid of religious establishments in these days of enlightened liberty?"[56] Baptists were not always supported by fellow evangelicals in their quest for religious liberty.

However, what has not been as well documented is the complexity and conflict with which black and white Baptists carried out their Jeffersonian project. Lott Carey was the son of a black Baptist preacher who amassed enough money working in a Virginia tobacco warehouse that in 1813 he was able to purchase his own freedom and that of his two children for $850 (his first wife passed away). While preaching in the surrounding counties, Carey was also drawn to the Jeffersonian ideal of self-improvement, earning

---

52. Article II, Virginia Statute for Religious Freedom. The bill began simply as Bill No. 82, "A Bill for establishing religious freedom."

53. Speaking of the Bill for Establishing Religious Freedom, Thomas Kidd notes, "This was a key precedent to the First Amendment to the Constitution and its prohibition of a national established church" (Kidd, *American History*, 102). Still, Carl H. Esbeck and J. Den Hartog have posited that "it cannot be said that the disestablishment story in any one state was more important than that of others" (Esbeck and Den Hartog, "Introduction," 10).

54. Crocker, *History of the Baptists in Vermont*, 262.

55. E. C. Dargan stated matter of factly in 1914: "It is well known that the first amendment of the Federal Constitution, guaranteeing religious freedom, was chiefly the result of Baptist activity" (Dargan, "Richard Furman and His Place in American Baptist History," 37).

56. In Noll, *America's God*, 338.

his own personal wealth by selling parcels of tobacco and reading works like Adam Smith's *Wealth of Nations*. On the other hand, when a minister friend inquired why a free black would leave such relative comfort to move to Africa, he replied assuredly, "I am an African, and in this country, however meritorious my conduct, and respectable my character, I cannot receive the credit due to either. I wish to go to a country where I shall be estimated by my merits, not by my complexion; and I feel bound to labor for my suffering race."[57] By leaving the United States for the shores of Africa, Carey was seeking his *own* freedom as well as the freedom of the African.

For many white Baptists, Jefferson's ideas posed another kind of threat. Contrary to McLoughlin, there were many Baptists who were fully aware of just how antithetical Jefferson's religion was to their own, and like so many Baptists before and after, they were vocal with their opinions.[58] Jonathan Maxcy, whose father Levi had testified in the famous Balkcom case in Attleborough, Massachusetts that had given Baptists their first significant (although short-lived) political victory in the state, was apparently so vocal about his disdain for Republicans in a Fourth of July sermon in Providence, Rhode Island that it nearly prevented him from being elected president of Union College three years later.[59] Maxcy, who succeeded James Manning as president of the College of Rhode Island, was judged by some to be a "violent politician" whose "sarcasms against the Anti-Federalists" were viewed as incompatible with a man of his office.[60] The year before "the revolution of 1800," Maxcy had warned his audience of "foreign foes and domestic traitors" in America who were "continually advancing opinions and doctrines

---

57. Taylor, *Biography of Elder Lott Carey*, 16.

58. In his recent spiritual biography of the third president, Thomas S. Kidd calls Jefferson's religion "a rationalist, ethics-focused version of Christianity" (Kidd, *Thomas Jefferson*, 167).

59. McLoughlin, *Soul Liberty*, 234. The Balkcom case was a test case under the recently adopted Massachusetts constitution of 1780. In December of that year, when the east precinct of Attleborough voted to raise money to repair the Congregational meetinghouse, a small number of Baptists in the parish were taxed for this purpose. After they refused to either file certificates of exemption or to pay the tax, the tax collector took cows from five of them for sale at auction. Since Elijah Balkcom did not have a cow, he was jailed. Balkcom then filed a lawsuit against the tax assessors of the east precinct of Attleborough, claiming the old certificate law had lapsed and the General Assembly had not enacted a new one under the constitution. Therefore, he argued, Article 3 did not permit the taxing of Baptists or any other dissenters. After the local judge ruled against the claim, Balkcom appealed, and the justices in the County Court ruled in Balkcom's favor. However, *Cutter v. Frost* (1785) essentially undermined the Balkcom verdict.

60. Guild, *Life, Times, and Correspondence of James Manning*, 402.

which tend to its subversion."⁶¹ Despite his circumlocution, Maxcy left no doubt of the true object of his wrath when he acknowledged "the existence of a set of men in our country, who have derived their political principles from foreign influence and foreign intrigue; who exert their utmost efforts to ruin our government, and to prostrate all permanent establishments."⁶² Ironically, at the root of Maxcy's contempt for the Francophile Jefferson was the danger he posed to religious liberty, the very thing most Baptists believed Jefferson to be defending. He reasoned,

> No government, except absolute despotism, can support itself over a people destitute of religion; because such a people possesses no principles on which governmental motives can operate to secure obedience. The most salutary laws can have no effect against general corruption of sentiments and morals. The American people, therefore, have no way to secure their liberty, but by securing their religion; for there is no medium between an entire destitution of religion and the most deplorable servitude. No nation, however ignorant and barbarous, except one, has ever attempted to support a government without some respect to a Supreme Being.⁶³

For Maxcy, without religion, and that of the Bible, religious liberty was no liberty at all. While Maxcy was outspoken in his criticism of Deists and Republicans, he was by no means the only Baptist with serious concerns about Jefferson's beliefs and motives. In 1795, Federalist Samuel Stillman, the pastor of First Baptist Church of Boston, cautioned his listeners, "Though a republican form of government . . . is the best calculated to promote the freedom and happiness of the people, there always will be found men of boundless ambition, who become heads of parties, and spare no pains to get into place."⁶⁴ With his friendship to John Adams, Stillman's tongue-in-cheek allusion to "heads of parties" was almost certainly a thinly veiled reference to Jefferson. Other Baptists had already become disillusioned by the entire party system in America. For years Jesse Mercer did not exercise his right to vote, "for he said all parties had aberrated so far from the constitution, that he could not conscientiously vote for the candidates."⁶⁵

61. Maxcy, "Oration," 381, 384.
62. Maxcy, "Oration," 383.
63. Maxcy, "Oration," 392–93.
64. Stillman, *Thoughts on the French Revolution*, 10.
65. Mallary, *Memoirs of Elder Jesse Mercer*, 100–101. Antipartisanship was a growing sentiment across the republic and across denominations. In Massachusetts, Governor Caleb Strong (a Congregationalist) called the "party spirit" an "evil." As Jonathan J.

With the rise of political parties, white Baptists were caught between a rock and a theological hard place, forced to align themselves either with establishmentarians who shared their belief in the value of religion or with Deists who shared their commitment to liberty. They often did both. As one Baptist remarked a generation later, "The most pious of the Baptists of that day found themselves often making common cause, in behalf of religious freedom, with errorists and infidels."[66] In turn, Deism became a theological and political wedge by which Baptist partisanship was forged. The way in which a Baptist responded to the specter of Deism, or, rather, where they located its source, was a consistent indicator of how they identified themselves politically. For Republicans, Deism was largely the product of state religion. In John Leland's view, establishment "tends to make Deists, and support infidelity, more than any one cause."[67] In other words, by falsifying true religion and corrupting the kingdom of God with the kingdom of men, establishments provoked unbelief of the worst sort. Sylvanus Haynes of Middletown, Vermont represented the popular Baptist thinking when he explained, "to prop up religious institutions with legal establishments, and to represent that religion cannot stand without human legislative authority, is a reproach to its divine Author, a scandal to religion, and a grand occasion of infidelity." In Haynes's mind, state religion provided "the most powerful temptation to infidelity of any thing that has ever appeared in our world."[68] Therefore, as most Republicans argued, religious liberty was not simply the best means to promote religion; it also served as a bulwark against heresy.

Federalists, on the other hand, generally had a much different take on the cause of Deism. For men like Henry Holcombe, the true culprit of infidelity was a place, not a polity. In his 1800 eulogy of "the American sage" George Washington, Holcombe condemned "the heathens and deists" who would seek to "infest the United States," from "the smoke and flame in which they have involved miserable Europe."[69] Behind every Deist conspiracy or infidel plot to subvert religion lay France, whose revolution represented in the Federalist mind the anarchy and godlessness of a country without any semblance of religious liberty. Coupled with a strong anti-Catholic prejudice

---

Den Hartog has shown, antipartisans believed that "Partisanship disrupted the public order, threatened the unity necessary for the survival of the republic, and caused legislators to lose sight of the public interest" (Hartog, *Patriotism and Piety*, 84).

66. Wayland and Wayland, *Memoir of the Life and Labors of Francis Wayland*, 1:14n1.

67. Leland, "Blow at the Root," 252.

68. Haynes, *Bible Method of Supporting the Gospel Ministry*, 17, 5.

69. Holcombe, *Sermon, Occasioned by the Death of Lieutenant-General George Washington*, 2:400, 1410.

in Baptist life, Francophobia was a common phenomenon amongst Baptist Federalists and their associates, particularly in the South.[70] In a funeral sermon for Alexander Hamilton in 1804, Richard Furman argued that, despite the regrettable circumstances of his death, Hamilton was to be honored for his defense of liberty against those who would "desire to copy after the principles and measures of France, which he foresaw would end in military despotism and royalty."[71] Deism, the so-called "religion of the Enlightenment," was abhorred by Baptists of all theological stripes, but the way in which a Baptist repudiated this philosophical religion was often a reflection of their political leanings, and more importantly, their approach to nation-building.

Although Furman's brand of genteel politics was hardly representative of the majority of his Baptist brethren, most shared his conviction that America was "originally designed as an asylum for religion and liberty, and a theatre, on which the power and excellency of both were to be exhibited to the greatest advantage."[72] According to Bernard Bailyn, this was part of an "ancient idea, deeply embedded in the colonists' awareness, that America had from the start been destined to play a special role in history."[73] Baptists believed that special role was to bestow religious liberty upon the world. Furman later charged his congregation to "justly venerate the virtues, and honor the names of Washington, Adams, Jefferson, Franklin, Laurens, Rutledge, Green, and other eminent characters."[74] Not surprisingly, Jefferson was the only Republican in Furman's Federalist hall of fame.[75] But even for Furman, who counted Federalist Presidential candidate Charles Cotesworth Pinckney among his best friends, no list of patriots would have been complete without Thomas Jefferson, "the defender of the rights of man and the rights of conscience."[76] Baptist Jeffersonianism was a complex political

70. This will be discussed further in chapter 4.

71. Furman, *Death's Dominion Over Man Considered*, 242.

72. Furman, *America's Deliverance and Duty*, 399–400. Furman, however, was not born into high society, or in Charleston. Within less than a year after his birth in New York in 1755, his "family moved to a frontier settlement in South Carolina" (Rogers, *Richard Furman*, 3).

73. Bailyn, *Ideological Origins of the American Revolution*, 140.

74. Furman, *America's Deliverance and Duty*, 402.

75. Even the sometimes militantly Federalist Jonathan Maxcy included Jefferson in his list of patriots. Perhaps with the passage of time, Maxcy's view of Jefferson had softened a bit. In 1819, he exclaimed, "Whom do I behold! An Hancock, a Jefferson, an Adams, a Henry, a Lee, a Rutledge!—Glory to these illustrious spirits!" (Maxcy, "Discourse, Delivered in the Chapel of South Carolina College, July 4th, 1819, at the Request of the Inhabitants of Columbia," 282).

76. Pinckney was a Federalist Presidential candidate in both 1804 and 1808. Cook, "Biography of Richard Furman," 135; Leland, "Blow at the Root," 225.

organism that took many forms, but at its core was a fierce pursuit of religious liberty rivaled only by Jefferson himself, who found common cause with a marginalized and disregarded people.[77]

"We Are the Poor of the World"

In order to comprehend how Baptists viewed their new nation, one must first understand how their new nation viewed Baptists. From state to state, perception of Baptists differed, but a common thread of social dislocation was found in almost all. In New England, over a century and a half after Roger Williams was banished from Massachusetts Bay Colony, Baptists were still viewed as instigators, disturbers of the peace, and the "madmen of Munster."[78] Even though the Constitution decreed that "Congress shall make no law respecting an establishment of religion; or prohibiting the free exercise thereof," it did not proscribe individual states from doing so. Despite the fact that most of the thirteen states quickly adopted the Baptist position of disestablishment, complete disestablishment was not achieved in Vermont until 1807, in Connecticut until 1818, in New Hampshire until 1819, or in Massachusetts until 1833. Therefore, Baptists endured no small amount of persecution for their dogged belief in the separateness of the regenerate church from the state.[79] In a Thanksgiving sermon in 1815, the former Congregationalist Daniel Merrill condemned "these anti-christian Babylonish persecutions, for which New England has been famous," noting that "many were imprisoned, more were fined, and a still greater number were arrested, and in many ways vexed by the civil power."[80] In Massachusetts, where Baptists had been outlawed altogether in 1645, the opposition was especially intense. After the Ashfield "persecutions" in 1770, when local tax collectors auctioned off Baptists' land for refusing to pay religious taxes,

---

77. In his classic work on Southern religion, Donald G. Mathews remarks, "To men anxious about social ranking, power, and stability, Baptists seemed troublesome at best and dangerous at worst" (Mathews, *Religion in the Old South*, 27).

78. Backus, *Appeal to the Public for Religious Liberty*, 337. The reference to Munster pertains to the violent rebellion in Munster, Germany which occurred in 1534 by Anabaptists. The city was besieged, and leaders were captured, imprisoned, and in many cases murdered. The result was that the Anabaptist movement (and by association Baptists) for centuries evoked images of of anarchy and political revolt.

79. Baptists were drawn mostly from the unlearned and lower classes of society. E. Brooks Holifield explains that the early Baptist movement "took hold mainly among the uneducated, and many saw little need for educated theologians to guide them." However, Holifield also acknowledges that this populist impulse was not uniform across Baptist life in the early republic (Holifield, *Theology in America*, 273).

80. Merrill, *Balaam Disappointed*, 7.

Baptists had actually appealed to King George III for relief, an action that resulted in the charge of loyalism that followed Baptists during the war.[81]

However, the persecution of New England Baptists persisted even in the land of the free. In fact, Baptists like Merrill believed that, in some ways, it actually *increased* after 1776: "When the Constitutions of the different States were framed, the Clergy wished for more religious shackles to be incorporated in some, or in all of those instruments, than were obtained, and they obtained the insertion of more than were compatible with equal religious liberty; and have made a more extensively oppressive use of what they did obtain, than was hoped for by the friends of liberty at the time."[82] The political (and often physical) fight for religious liberty only escalated in the northern parts of the new republic. In 1778, for example, an angry mob chased Baptists out of Pepperrell, Massachusetts because such an "irregular, disorderly people" would have prevented them from calling a "gentlemen of worth."[83] The leader of the mob threatened to whip the itinerant preacher from Chelmsford, Mr. Samuel Fletcher. In New England, Baptists were not only seen as subversive to the public order; their very presence in society was perceived as a financial and even spiritual liability. They were, as McLoughlin has called them, "social pariahs" and "outcasts" of New England society.[84] In the words of Thomas Kidd and Barry Hankins, they were "the ultimate religious outsiders."[85] When the Baptists of Pepperrell resisted their aggressors, members of the horde "took a Dog into the Water and Plunged him in Imitation of Baptism," threatening, "Hold your Tongue or I will Beat your Teeth Down your throat."[86] In 1782, a large mob at Hingham, armed with clubs and planks, drove out a Baptist minister named Richard Lee and his friends.[87] After mocking their recitation of the Scriptures, "one of them cast soft cow dung in Mr. Lee's face."[88]

Such instances of religious hate and bigotry had prompted the Warren Association in 1767 to form its Grievance Committee to document

---

81. Lieutenant Governor Thomas Hutchinson had personally urged the Baptists to appeal to the king (McLoughlin, *Soul Liberty*, 185, 205).

82. Merrill, *Balaam Disappointed*, 8.

83. In McLoughlin, *Soul Liberty*, 207.

84. McLoughlin, *Soul Liberty*, 206.

85. Kidd and Hankins assert, "In America, the Baptists were once the ultimate religious outsiders" (Kidd and Hankins, "Preface," xi).

86. "Daniel Davis and Simeon Shattuck, Pepperell, September ye 5th, 1778," in McLoughlin, *Soul Liberty*, 211.

87. Backus, *Door Opened for Christian Liberty*, 434.

88. Abijah Brown, Jaccheus Lambort, Betty Brown, Molly Loring, Rith Simmons, Lucy Loring, "The Hingham Riot," in McLoughlin, *Soul Liberty*, 224.

complaints of persecution and to advocate for victimized Baptists in court and in the legislature. After John Davis resigned, Isaac Backus succeeded him as chairman in 1773. When Backus visited Pepperell to take affidavits from the Baptists a few months after they had been driven from town, Colonel Henry A. Woods threatened that if Backus ever showed up again, "I'll wring his nose and kick his arse."[89] Certainly, if any Baptist had reason to suspect that Federalism was the party of religious tyrants, it was the Congregationalist-turned-Separate-turned-Separate Baptist Isaac Backus, who consistently petitioned and testified against the abuses of the Standing Order.[90] Suppression of Baptists also had a non-violent side, and outside of the urban and intellectual centers, it had a tendency of producing steady Republicans. In 1781, for instance, when a young Thomas Baldwin told his old pastor in Norwich, Connecticut about his conversion to Baptist theology, he was called a reprobate if he ever got re-baptized. Baldwin records, "I was much shocked at the remark, and after a moment's silence, replied, 'I hope, Sir, I shall be directed to do what is right.' Thus we parted, perhaps with mutual dissatisfaction."[91]

Baptist persecution was not isolated to New England. In Virginia, before Jefferson and Madison introduced their religious liberty bill, Baptists faced opposition in the earliest years of the republic. When John Leland came to preach in York County in 1781, a Colonel Harwood stormed the house in which Leland was preaching and declared, "Sir . . . I am come to stop you from preaching here to-day." On this particular occasion, the son of a city official inquired, "Col. Harwood, you are a representative in the General Assembly, and the Assembly has just made a law to secure the religious rights of all, and now you come to prevent them. What does that look like?" Ultimately, Harwood's protest was to no avail and Leland continued preaching.[92] Interruptions like these were quite common in the 1770s in the Upper South, and could even turn violent.[93] Stories of Virginian Baptists being grabbed by the neck and lashed twenty times, like in Caroline County in 1771, were fewer as time passed.[94] By the time of the Revolution, laws were no longer enforced that made persistent absence from Anglican

---

89. Backus, *Independent Chronicle*, October 15, 1778, in McLoughlin, *Soul Liberty*, 207.

90. The "Standing Order" is the name given to the alliance between local and state governments and the Congregationalist clergy in New England.

91. Baldwin, *Memoir of Rev. Thomas Baldwin*, 27.

92. Leland, "Events in the Life of John Leland," 21.

93. Najar, *Evangelizing the South*, 30.

94. Isaac, "Evangelical Revolt," 347.

services punishable.[95] In fact, after 1776, petitions from Baptist districts "swamped the Virginia Assembly" calling for the disestablishment of the official Anglican church.[96] Although Virginia Baptists in the early republic did not encounter the level of persecution they did in New England, their denomination was still composed mostly of small farming families and members of the lower-class, such that, according to Rhys Isaac, the Baptist movement in Virginia "must be understood as a revolt against the traditional system."[97]

Baptists farther south did not face anything close to the hegemony of New England or, for a lesser time, Virginia. However, on the whole, they did not enjoy the toleration of the Middle Atlantic states. The original Constitution of South Carolina in 1776 retained the privileged place of the Church of England and the 1778 Constitution expanded privileges only to certain Protestant groups, but Anglican dominance rarely approached what might be called "persecution." In fact, South Carolina Baptists sometimes imitated Anglicans. In Charleston, Baptist ministers Richard Furman and Oliver Hart wore robes that mirrored the formality of Anglican worship.[98] By 1790, the Constitution began to strike down ecclesiastical privileges altogether, declaring that "free exercise and enjoyment of religious profession and worship, without discrimination or preference, shall forever hereafter be allowed within this State to all mankind."[99] Signaled by Furman's opening sermon and prayer at the convention, disestablishment in South Carolina was more dramatic along social than political lines. While the Church of England retained much of its power for decades in the form of glebes (land owned by the church) and wealth, the liberty of 1776 removed the stigma placed upon Baptists by the British government.[100] The establishment became "more a legal fiction than a reality and more nuisance than an obstacle."[101] Baptists in the state enjoyed a much better reputation than anywhere else in the South, cooperating closely with other dissenting groups during the Revolution and

---

95. Isaac, "Evangelical Revolt," 349.

96. Wilentz, *Rise of American Democracy*, 17.

97. Isaac, "Evangelical Revolt," 358. This is consistent with minister William Fristoe's assertion in 1808 that those who joined the early Baptists in Virginia were "of the mediocrity or poorer sort of people . . . and we have been encouraged to believe that it gave clearer proof of the genuine quality of religion among us" (Fristoe, *Concise History of the Ketocton Baptist Association*, 148).

98. Woodson, *Giant in the Land*, 5.

99. The Constitution of South Carolina, 1790, Article VIII, Section 2, in Poore, *Federal and State Constitutions*, 2:1633.

100. Smith, "South Carolina," 188.

101. Mathews, *Religion in the Old South*, 55.

swiftly becoming the most numerous in South Carolina. Nevertheless, the vestiges of Anglican privilege in the early years of the republic were still reminders that religious establishment had not been completely removed. According to E. C. Dargan, "In South Carolina it never amounted to much in the way of persecution, but was an unfair thing in itself and was in many ways an annoyance and hindrance in the way of religious liberty."[102] In the early years of the American Revolution, a young Richard Furman encountered the "wealth and power" of the Church of England when he was barred from preaching in the Camden Court House because he was not Anglican.[103] In 1776, after the temporary constitution upheld the establishment of the Episcopal church in South Carolina, Furman and Oliver Hart convened a meeting of dissenters of all denominations at the Church of High Hills in the Carolina upcountry to discuss how to disestablish religion in the state. Two years later, thanks in large part to a "Dissenters' Petition" that "came up before the House," and to Furman and Hart's amicable relationship with men such as Henry Laurens and Charles C. Pinckney, the constitution of 1778 secured "an equality in religious privileges which were afterwards carried into operation."[104]

In Georgia, a neighboring state with a weaker Anglican establishment similar to North Carolina, Baptists faced political subservience and poverty though not as much in the way of real persecution. Even after the Church of England became the state church in 1758, "relations between religious groups were relatively harmonious."[105] However, despite the prominent role of dissenters in public life, many white Baptist congregations still struggled to support their pastors and the heavy hand of the religious establishment could occasionally be felt by Baptist preachers.[106] In 1770, for example, Daniel Marshall was arrested by a local constable for preaching in the Parish of St. Paul (Augusta) contrary to the rites of the Anglican Church.[107] After 1776, these kinds of accounts largely ceased. By the 1790s, not only had the British lost their authority in Georgia, but Baptists had become the largest denomination in the state, protesting hotly against a 1785 general establishment of religion bill that was hardly enforced. In Savannah, former slave Andrew Bryan pastored First African Baptist Church, one of the largest

---

102. Dargan, "Richard Furman and His Place in American Baptist History," 51.

103. Cook, "Biography of Richard Furman," 82–83, 130.

104. Cook, "Biography of Richard Furman," 130–31; Dargan, "Richard Furman and His Place in American Baptist History," 51–52.

105. Nichols, "Georgia: The Thirteenth Colony," 225.

106. Harris, *Georgia's First Continuing Baptist Church*, 235.

107. Campbell, *Georgia Baptists*, 16–17.

Baptist churches in the nation. After suffering persecution early on, Bryan reported that the growing congregation enjoyed the "rights of conscience to a valuable extent," indicating that even black Baptists desired to worship "without molestation" from earthly authorities.[108] In 1798, a "measurable Baptist presence" behind the religious freedom section of the 1798 Constitution testified to the new political power of the denomination.[109] Baptists still stood apart socially from the Episcopalians, but their status was rising in Georgia life. When Abraham Marshall, whose father Daniel had been arrested for his patriotism during the war, visited Yorktown in 1786, he wrote in his journal, "This is the place where the 'God of war' wrought salvation for his American Israel." He asked, "Shall we ever trifle with our lives and our civil and religious liberty, when blood—blood is the price of both?" Yet Marshall's disdain for the Episcopalians remained. Upon passing through Maryland and Delaware, he wrote, "Oh Lord! How long shall the superstitious ignorance make the people cry out, 'Great is Diana of the' Episcopalians."[110]

One might say that Baptist politics, regardless of one's social predilections or degree of persecution, was driven by an inveterate underdog mentalité, forged by decades and even centuries of dissent.[111] To begin, white Baptists like Richard Furman believed that the War of Independence could not be blessed by God and would not end in victory unless Americans acknowledged their own religious hypocrisy. Emphasizing "the unnatural union of civil authority with the power of the church," he exclaimed, "Oh! That a great nation, long borne with gigantic force, against the combined force of its enemies, and emerging to a new and important state of empire, may learn to make this distinction, between the truth of our holy religion and its perversion."[112] Although not a Regular Baptist like Furman, Isaac Backus's patriotism was very similar. In the same year that Furman was calling for "Unity and Peace," Backus published *An Appeal to the Public* (1773), a treatise that McLoughlin has called "the Declaration of Independence for

108. Bryan, "Letter from the Negro Baptist Church in Savannah," 50; Kidd and Hankins, *Baptists in America*, 105.

109. Nichols, "Georgia: The Thirteenth Colony," 239.

110. In Ray, *Daniel and Abraham Marshall*, 24, 96, 103.

111. Many American Baptists were aware of their own history. Isaac Backus cited the "uncivil treatment" of those who opposed infant baptism in the 1640s and accused the New England fathers of "acts of imposition and persecution as have left a great blemish upon their character" (Backus, *Appeal to the Public for Religious Liberty*, 342.) Even in South Carolina, Richard Furman was alarmed at those who "pursued them with persecuting rage: of which not only the history of the old world, but even the early part of the American, furnishes melancholy proof" (Furman, *Unity and Peace*, 310).

112. Furman, *Unity and Peace*, 310–11.

the Separate Baptists against the tyranny of the Standing Order."[113] Backus asked, "how can any reasonably expect that He who has the hearts of kings in his hand will turn the heart of our earthly sovereign to hear the pleas for liberty of those who will not hear the cries of their fellow subjects under their oppressions?"[114] In other words, by what logic could Americans deny Baptists liberty of conscience while fighting a war for the very same freedom? Baptists were not afraid to personally confront their oppressors with their hypocrisy. As he recorded to Isaac Backus, when Joshua Austin challenged the mob at Pepperrell, he "told them we ought to be Extreamly Causious how we made Enemies at this all important Crysus, when the Liberties of America were Evaded by a powerful enemy. And told them Liberty of Conchance was allow'd them By the King of Briton from whom we had Justly revolted." After his accusers replied that "it was no matter whose side" Baptists took in the war, Austin shouted, "Good God! Is this the Liberties our Country affords?"[115] With such a second-class consciousness among Baptists in New England, it is little wonder how even a patrician Baptist like James Manning could confess to an English Baptist in 1783, "the Baptists here are the poor of this world."[116] Even in Mid-Atlantic states like Delaware, where a common British ancestry and a culture of education and toleration prevailed, Baptists were reminded of their lack of wealth and status, going without church buildings or even houses for many years while Independents and Presbyterians enjoyed both.[117]

However, after the Revolution, this underdog mentalité was also the bond that seemed to unite white Baptists despite their manifold divisions. Baptists were a fissiparous people, but they were not generally a balkanized people. Although partisanship existed in the Baptist denomination as much as and perhaps more than any other religious group in the nation, religious liberty was a rallying cry among Baptists that seemed to transcend nearly every other ideological and political difference. The night before the first session of the Triennial Convention in Philadelphia in 1814, John Leland, who was critical of both Baptist formal education and missions societies, preached at the church of William Staughton, one of the most pro-education and pro-missions Baptists in the early republic. He preached from Isaiah 10:27 ("and the yoke shall be destroyed, because of the anointing"), a text

---

113. McLoughlin, "Editor's Introduction," in *Isaac Backus on Church, State, and Calvinism*, 305.

114. Backus, *Appeal to the Public*, 338.

115. Austin, "Statement of Joshua Austin," 217–18.

116. "James Manning to Samuel Stennett, Providence, Nov. 8th, 1783," in Guild, *Life, Times, and Correspondence of James Manning*, 315.

117. Cook, *Early and Later Delaware Baptists*, 32, 34, 37.

he naturally applied to religious liberty, warning his audience of the "kings who confederated" against the people of God.[118] During Hezekiah Smith's absence from his church in Haverhill, Massachusetts to serve as chaplain for the Continental Army, both Federalists and Republicans filled his pulpit, including James Manning, Samuel Stillman, John Gano, and Isaac Backus.[119] Jonathan Maxcy's ordination service in 1791 likewise included both Federalists and Republicans.[120] Even when politics injected itself into the pulpit, as was so often the case in Baptist life, it did not seem to splinter the Baptist churches themselves. Thomas Armitage describes the warm relationship between Samuel Stillman and Thomas Baldwin at First and Second Baptist Churches of Boston:

> Dr. Stillman and [Baldwin] were fast friends and true yoke-fellows in every good work. As politicians, Stillman was a firm Federalist and Baldwin as firm a Jeffersonian Democrat, and generally on Fast Day and Thanksgiving-day they preached on the points in dispute here, because, as patriots, they held them essential to the well-being of the Republic, especially, in the exciting conflicts of 1800–01; yet, there never was a moment of ill-feeling between them. On these days, the Federalists of both their congregations went to hear Dr. Stillman and the Democrats went to Baldwin's place, but on other days they remained at home, like Christian gentlemen, and honored their pastors as men of that stamp.[121]

In Boston, where the Standing Order united Trinitarians and Unitarians alike against Dissenters, Baptists of all kinds were "yoked" together by a common foe and a political raison d'etre: religious liberty. Beginning in 1778, for example, Baptists engaged in a two-year newspaper war in the Boston press with Congregationalists over the separation of church and state. Using the pseudonym "Milton," Samuel Stillman, a Federalist, wrote four letters. Isaac Backus, a Republican, wrote five.[122]

---

118. Hatch, *Democratization of American Christianity*, 96.

119. Broome, *Life, Ministry, and Journals of Hezekiah Smith*, 140.

120. Jonathan Maxcy's ordination service in 1791 is recorded as follows: "Rev. Samuel Stillman, D.D., of Boston, Mass. preached the ordination sermon, Rev. Hezekiah Smith, D.D., of Haverhill, Mass. gave the charge, Rev. Isaac Backus, of Middleborough, Mass. presented the right hand of fellowship, Rev. Benjamin Foster, D.D., of New York, made the introductory prayer, and the consecrating prayer was made by Rev. William Van Horn, of Scotch Plains, N.J." (Elton, "Memoir," 12–13).

121. Armitage, *History of the Baptists*, 2:852–53.

122. McLoughlin, "Editor's Introduction," 368.

Of course, this is not to suggest that Baptists did not suffer serious divisions in their ranks due to the political issues of their day. When Backus devised a bold plan in 1773 for Baptists in the Warren Association to engage in nonviolent civil disobedience in order to protest religious taxes, Stillman was its primary opponent.[123] After James Manning discovered that his friend Noah Alden, one of the leaders of the Friends of Religious Liberty (and the man who baptized John Leland), had voted against the ratification of the Massachusetts constitution at the convention in 1788, he was "mortified."[124] Revolutionary politics often exacted a heavy toll on Baptist relationships. Nevertheless, due to their mutual political and social condition in the early republic, white Baptists always had more in common than they had differences. They were, after all, "the poor of the world."[125] Even during the Revolution, a spirit of brotherhood existed between many American and English Baptists who were convinced that their churches were not in conflict even if their countries were waging war.[126] Calls for bipartisan unity were very common among Baptists in the early republic, like when Sylvanus Haynes declared, "We find, and sincerely bewail that discontent, discord, party spirit and faction have been so prevalent in our land. These are awful omens of approaching judgment."[127] In 1812, Baptist William Parkinson acknowledged the political divisions among them, but called for peace. He insisted,

> for although our citizens have been, unhappily, long divided and distinguished by the appellations of *Federalist and Republican*, I have always thought, and now think, that there are men of equal integrity, abilities and patriotism on both sides. And indeed the distinction itself is as unfounded as it is impolitic; for, under our government, no man can be a Federalist without being a Republican, nor a Republican, without being a Federalist; the one having respect to the confederacy of the states, the other to the sovereignty of the people; and both being comprehended in our excellent constitution.[128]

123. McLoughlin, *Soul Liberty*, 172.

124. "James Manning to the Rev. Dr. Smith, Providence, Feb. 11, 1788," in Guild, *Life, Times, and Correspondence of James Manning*, 406.

125. "James Manning to John Rippon, Providence, Aug. 3, 1784," in Guild, *Life, Times, and Correspondence of James Manning*, 328.

126. "James Manning to Rev. Benjamin Wallin, Nov. 12, 1776," in Guild, *Life, Times, and Correspondence of James Manning*, 245.

127. Haynes, *Sermon, Delivered Before His Excellency the Governor*, 19.

128. Parkinson, *Sermon, Delivered in the Meeting House of the First Baptist Church, in the City of New York*, 19.

Baptists demonstrated time and again that their common cause for religious liberty and their shared plight as social interlopers was a magnetic force that could draw them together for the sake of the gospel. By 1814, the same year that the ill-fated Hartford Convention sounded the death knell for the Federalist party, Baptists had finally established their first national convention, symbolizing not only their ability to mobilize for the sake of missions and education, but their arrival as a legitimate religious body in the new American marketplace.[129] According to Harvey T. Cook, after observing God's favor upon their newly constituted nation, "it was only a matter of time when the Baptist people in all the states would feel the same promptings to come together in a general union by representatives of all the states. Whatever stirs the body politic affects in the same way to a less or greater extent all its patriotic parts."[130] The early republic was a coming of age for the Baptist people in terms of denominational life. But while the scale was much larger, the goal was always the same: the salvation of souls.

Revolution as Reformation

For Baptists, the relationship between church and state was a two-way street. Just as religion influenced civil government, civil government inevitably shaped religion. Therefore, Baptists regularly argued that religious freedom wasn't simply about civil liberty; it was essential to biblical Christianity. When Caesar kept his hand out of the church, the Lord's hand remained upon it. When this happened, the outcome was revival. Baptists everywhere recognized an outpouring of the Holy Spirit in the early republic. In 1809, Sylvanus Haynes celebrated the "glorious revivals of religion in our land," emphasizing that "that this blessed work has not been promoted by civil coercion."[131] Many believed that God had begun to bring revival upon the Baptist church in 1776. Acknowledging the political and spiritual challenges in New England, James Manning nevertheless conceded the "glorious time of revival in our church when the war first commenced."[132] Baptists had reason to believe in God's blessing. Along with the Methodists, the Baptist church was the fastest growing in the infant nation in terms of sheer numbers.[133]

---

129. Dargan, "Richard Furman and His Place in American Baptist History," 52.

130. Cook, "Biography of Richard Furman," 171.

131. Haynes, *Sermon, Delivered Before His Excellency the Governor*, 9.

132. "James Manning to Samuel Stennett, Providence, Nov. 8, 1783," in Guild, *Life, Times, and Correspondence of James Manning*, 313.

133. Mark Noll posits, "The invisibility in high political culture during the late

However, unlike the Methodists, Baptists believed that their exponential growth during the Second Great Awakening was directly linked to the political developments in America. In some sense, in the Baptist mind, revolution begat revival. As the "Angel of Liberty" descended upon the new nation, and the gospel was less adulterated by the carnal institutions of men, the Spirit of God had begun to introduce pure and undefiled religion into the land.[134] Even the hard separationist John Leland identified religious liberty as a catalyst for the outpourings of the Spirit, contending that the Southern states had experienced the most revival because they enjoyed the most religious freedom. After noting "the late marvelous work of God in Kentucky," Leland inquired, "But what shall we say to these things? Kentucky was settled at first upon the plan of religious liberty."[135] As a result, Leland celebrated that "the extent and population of the western section of the United States, will soon outweigh the Atlantic states."[136] Baptists' emphasis on revival was linked to their indomitable sense of manifest destiny, and the logic went something as follows: as America pushed west, religion would be less entangled with civil authorities and the traditions of the old world; and with less state religion, the Baptist church would flourish as Christ originally intended before the "gross error" of Constantine.[137] For Leland, revival was also politically auspicious. He entreated, "Can there be an instance given where there has been a like display of God's power is any state in the Union, which has left the people as generally federalists?"[138] In other words, revivalism didn't just produce converts; it bred Republicans. Nevertheless, in a republic that valued their long-held ideals of liberty and conscience, white Baptists believed that the stars had aligned in their favor. Due in large part to the influence of the theological tradition of Puritan Jonathan Edwards, Baptists subscribed to an optimistic end-times theology that affirmed a golden age of the church, "when all the mists and fogs of civil and religious tyranny that becloud mankind shall be dispelled like

---

1780s of the evangelicals who would soon spearhead a national revival is suggested by the scarcity of Methodists and Baptists at the Constitutional Convention . . . Although Baptists accounted for about 15% of colonial churches in 1776, and probably close to 20% by 1790, not a single one of the fifty-five members of the Convention was a Baptist" (Noll, *America's God*, 164).

134. Maxcy, "Oration," 367.

135. Leland, *Rights of Conscience Inalienable*, 192; Maxcy, "Oration," 264.

136. Leland, "Short Sayings," 577.

137. Leland, "Address at the Dedication of the Baptist Meeting-House in Lanesborough, February 16, 1829," 553.

138. Leland, "Oration," 264.

the glooms of evening before the rising sun."[139] In New York, a young John Mason Peck recorded in his journal in 1815, "When I reflect that but a few years since all this country was one vast wilderness—properly missionary ground—I must exclaim: What hath God wrought!"[140]

More than any other denomination in America, Baptists believed that the Revolution in America would give way to an actual reformation of the church, a refining of any traces of civil authority from the kingdom of God. State religion, at least in their mind, had "kindled" the very war which birthed the United States.[141] James Manning spoke confidently of a "glorious reformation" that was taking place during the war.[142] Isaac Backus predicted "a much greater reformation" than any the world had ever seen.[143] Baptists, after all, had always had an uneasy relationship with the Protestant Reformation. Calvinists like Manning and Backus admired the Reformers like Martin Luther and John Calvin for liberating the church from "popery" and recovering the doctrines of grace in the church. However, in the true spirit of reformation, they believed that the so-called "Magisterial Reformers" had not gone far enough in purging the church from the "unnatural" union of church and state.[144] In their view, "Roger Williams began the reformation from hierarchy" in the 1630s, and they sought to complete that work in the new nation.[145] Therefore, by contending that only Jesus Christ had authority over his church, and not a civil magistrate, Baptists believed themselves to be reforming the Protestant church just as Luther and Calvin had reformed Roman Catholicism. They were following a tradition that dated back to the very first English Baptists, when Thomas Helwys campaigned for religious

---

139. Haynes, *Sermon, Delivered Before His Excellency the Governor*, 23; Leland, *Rights of Conscience Inalienable*, 192; Maxcy, "Discourse," 294, Maxcy, "Oration," 377. This optimistic end-times theology, or eschatology, is known as postmillennialism. According to this view, the kingdom of God will advance through the gospel and introduce a Golden Age of peace, progress, and knowledge (a millennium), after which time the resurrected and ascendant Christ will return in bodily form.

140. In Babcock, *Forty Years of Pioneer Life*, 45.

141. According to Isaac Backus, "it is well known that contests about that matter kindled this bloody war. So that the scheme of religious establishments by human laws, is stained with the guilt of all this blood" (Backus, *Government and Liberty Described*, 356).

142. "James Manning to Rev. Benjamin Wallin, New Jersey, May 23, 1783," in Guild, *Life, Times, and Correspondence of James Manning*, 294; Also see "James Manning to the Rev. John Ryland, Providence, Nov. 8, 1783," in Guild, *Life, Times, and Correspondence of James Manning*, 308–9.

143. Isaac Backus, in McLoughlin, "Editor's Introduction," 429.

144. Furman, *Unity and Peace*, 310.

145. Leland, "Mosaic Dispensation," 666.

liberty in *A Short Declaration of the Mystery of Iniquity* (1611). "In our country," Daniel Merrill averred,

> both the civil and ecclesiastical powers strove excessively to strangle religious liberty in her infancy, but prevailed not. Like Moses in the ark of bulrushes, she was preserved, and has been so nourished and instructed, that she bids fair to lead the true Israel out of Egypt's iron bondage of Ecclesiastical tyranny. But it will be attended with more tremendous plagues on Babylon, than were poured upon Egypt of old. As religious liberty has prevailed, so has the church of Christ increased in our land.[146]

Baptists viewed such opposition as further validation of their sacred quest to liberate the world of religious tyranny. Merrill even went so far as to argue that the Congregationalist church was apostate, insisting "that the church comprising New England clergy, is as different from the church of Christ, as was the Jewish high priest from Paul."[147] He held "that the Church, in which the New England Clergy are leaders, is not the Church of Christ, they themselves being judges. Otherwise, why their cry, Alas! Alas! The Church is in danger! When nothing appears to threaten them, save the prevalence of religious liberty."[148]

While Merrill's anathematizing of Congregationalism was not necessarily shared by all Baptists, it demonstrates the bitterness caused by religious and civil hegemony as well as the importance placed on religious liberty by Baptists to reveal the true people of God. So deep-seated was this resentment that, among Baptists before and after 1776, religious establishment was either identified as the Antichrist or closely associated with his nefarious work.[149] Religious liberty was more than a Baptist cause; it was spiritual warfare.

Protestant Pluralism

If Baptists agreed on one thing, it was the evil of state-sponsored religion. Removing it from America was "a polar star" of Baptist politics.[150] Never at a lack for words, John Leland had a host of interesting names for religious

---

146. Merrill, *Balaam Disappointed*, 17.
147. Merrill, *Balaam Disappointed*, 22.
148. Merrill, *Balaam Disappointed*, 21.
149. Backus, *Government and Liberty Described*, 355; Parkinson, *Sermon, Delivered in the Meeting House of the First Baptist Church*, 22.
150. Leland, "Speech Delivered in the House of Representatives of Massachusetts, on the Subject of Religious Freedom, 1811," 354.

establishment. He called it "spiritual tyranny," "a shocking monster," "a creature of state," "the worst hag above hell," "the greatest engine of tyranny in the world," "anti-Christocracy," and "that rotten nest-egg, which is always hatching vipers."[151] At stake in this war of words and worship was the freedom of conscience, the most inalienable and sacrosanct of human rights. In a sermon before the governor and legislature of Vermont, Sylvanus Haynes expressed, "of all the freedoms that men possess, that of conscience is the sweetest."[152] Isaac Backus called it "the dearest of all rights," and its protection, "the Golden Rule."[153] When the mob attacked the Baptists of Pepperrell, Isaiah Parker "reminded them of that Liberty of Conscience in manner of worship had Ever been allowed. by all Protestant Rulers, Even by the King of Britain, and Coated [quoted] many Texts of Scripture to Prove his Proceeding."[154] In a world of kings and kingdoms, Baptists believed that the primary duty of the American government was to defend the "empire of conscience."[155]

However, if Baptists disagreed on one thing, it was the nature of this "court of judicature, erected in every breast," and to what extent it should be respected in those outside the Protestant faith.[156] Baptists were the first to recognize this liberty for themselves, but they were not always so quick to defend it for others. For instance, although John Leland argued that "religious liberty is a right and not a favor," his fellow Republican Isaac Backus branded those who insisted upon natural rights as deists and infidels.[157] For Backus, who struggled to balance Locke with Calvin, religious liberty was more of a gift from God than something owed to every sinner. Jonathan Maxcy, another Baptist Edwardsean, had a similar suspicion of natural rights. Like Backus, his argument was grounded in religious liberty:

> Government is by no means founded on what are called natural rights, but on conventional agreement. Every man in the uncivil

---

151. Leland, "Oration," 267, Leland, "Short Essays on Government, and the Proposed Revision of the Constitution of Government for the Commonwealth of Massachusetts," 476, Leland, "Virginia Chronicle," 107, Leland, "Which Has Done the Most Mischief in the World, The Kings-Evil or Priest-Craft?," 493, Leland, "Address to the Association of the Sons of Liberty, Cheshire, March 4, 1813," 375, Leland, "Government of Christ a Christocracy," 281, Leland, "Blow at the Root," 241.

152. Haynes, *Sermon before His Excellency*, 5.

153. Isaac Backus, in McLoughlin, "Introduction," 338.

154. Parker, "Pepperell Riot," 210.

155. Leland, "Virginia Chronicle," 123.

156. Leland, "Transportation of the Mail," 565.

157. Leland, *Rights of Conscience Inalienable*, 188; McLoughlin, "Editor's Introduction," 305.

state claims a right to every thing. Of consequence, every man sets himself up for a tyrant. War and bloodshed ensue, till the strong arm determines whose right is best founded. Every man in the uncivil state claims a right to be the judge of his own cause, and the avenger of his own wrongs. He relinquishes both these rights when he enters into society. He now has a claim to assistance and protection from the aggregate wisdom and force of the community. Every right which he now possesses, rests on the social compact.[158]

Maxcy and Backus and others were hesitant to assert with Locke that a sinner must somehow "give up" their freedom in order to join civilized society. In their Calvinistic minds, a so-called "state of nature," or a pre-civilized human condition, was simply a carnal nature held in bondage to sin. Instead, they argued, Christian society is where one discovers true freedom.[159]

For most Baptists, even religious liberty had its limits. Like Isaac Backus, who supported the test oath in the Massachusetts Constitution which discriminated against Roman Catholics, the majority of Baptists believed that a person's religion (or irreligion) could disqualify them from holding public office. Speaking to the legislature in Vermont in 1792, Caleb Blood tried to reconcile his belief in the separation of church and state with his support for religious laws and leaders. "I am far from wishing," he confessed, "to have America involved in the great error of blending the government of church and state together. But I heartily wish that all her rulers may be truly virtuous, and such as shall rule in the fear of God." Attempting to draw a line between freedom of conscience and the authority of religion in society, Blood explained, "As religion at all times, is a matter between God and individuals, your honors will never think it within the limits of your legislation, to dictate the consciences of a single individual. The unchangeable law of righteousness, forbids us to delegate such a power to any man, or body of men, either in church or state." Nevertheless, he did not believe that this "prohibits the civil magistrate from enacting those laws that shall enforce the observance of those precepts in the christian religion . . . And among others, that of observing the Sabbath, should be enforced by the civil

---

158. Maxcy, "Oration," 390–91. For an example of Maxcy's Edwardsean theology, see Maxcy, "Discourse Designed to Explain the Doctrine of the Atonement," 87–110.

159. In his introduction to *An Appeal to the Public*, Isaac Backus warns, "What a dangerous error, yea, what a root of all evil then must it be, for men to imagine that there is anything in the nature of true government that interferes with true and full liberty! A grand cause of this evil is ignorance of what we are and where we are" (Backus, *Appeal to the Public*, 309).

power."[160] Baptists were not as individualistic as many today have often assumed, either theologically or politically. In fact, some like Jonathan Maxcy decried the "pernicious system of equality" advocated by those who pleaded for natural rights.[161] According to Maxcy, society admitted of certain racial, social, and moral distinctions that should be maintained for the good of all.

Still, others criticized the use of religious tests for public office. For William Parkinson, test oaths simply returned a free people back to the religious tyranny from which they had been liberated. He contended,

> But is it not awfully to be feared that the greater part of those who make such an outcry against statesmen whom they deem irreligious, are themselves strangers to experimental religion; and that their ideas of religious men, extend no further than to men who by education or otherwise are connected with some religious sect, attend public worship and approach the Lord's table. But who does not discover that all this may be true of all men, strangers to a work of grace upon the heart, and even of Deists? . . . to make a profession of religion, especially a partaking at the Lord's table, a test of qualification for civil office is to hold out a strong—if not the strongest inducement to *hypocrisy* and *impiety*.[162]

For Parkinson, religious liberty meant religious liberty *for all*. If Baptists had claimed their freedom from the Congregationalist and Episcopal churches, certainly they would not recapitulate such an establishment by denying the same liberties to other denominations. Among Baptists, John Leland was remarkably ahead of his time when he insisted, "Government should be so fixed, that Pagans, Turks, Jews and Christians, should be equally protected in their rights."[163] Leland was somewhat of a political realist. In his view, religious liberty was the best way to ensure that the gospel remained unhindered in every state and in other parts of the world. He reasoned, "If Christian legislatures have a right to regulate religion of individuals, Mahomedan and Pagan legislatures have the same."[164] Religious liberty wasn't just good policy; it was good for evangelism. At the root of Leland's radical opposition to any vestiges of religious establishment was his confidence in

---

160. Blood, *Sermon Preached Before the Honorable Legislature of the State of Vermont*, 27, 34–35.

161. Maxcy, "Oration," 388.

162. Parkinson, *Sermon, Delivered in the Meeting House of the First Baptist Church*, 17.

163. Leland, "Speech Delivered in the House of Representatives of Massachusetts," 358.

164. Leland, "Transportation of the Mail," 564.

the kingdom of God and the power of the gospel message to go forward without the aid of human government. Christians were to "render to Caesar the things that are Caesar's, and to God the things that are God's." (Mark 12:17) Daniel Merrill captured this same confidence when he asserted, "The church of Christ never sought a union with Caesar, or the civil sword to be drawn in support of the christian religion. She never asked for such a thing. She never wished it. She never needed it."[165] Politically speaking, Baptists were contending for a level playing field in their new republic.

Although Republicans often campaigned against religious tests on the grounds of separation of church and state, Baptists found ways to qualify this separation in their respective state constitutions. For example, at the South Carolina constitutional convention in 1790, Richard Furman

> opposed that article of the new constitution which excludes ministers from a seat in the legislature; not from a belief that in ordinary cases they should be chosen, or should be willing to serve; but thinking it their right, as being equally bound with their fellow-citizens to contribute to their support and defense of the State, and better qualified than the majority of those who are eligible; also that on certain occasions it would be highly proper for them to use the privilege.[166]

Although the article passed which prohibited clergy from holding public office, Furman's vision of America included the possibility of pastor-legislators. (Furman himself had been selected "among other leading men of the State" to frame the South Carolina Constitution.[167]) After all, if virtue was the most important criteria for leadership in a republic, and virtue itself was found principally in the Christian religion, who better to lead the body politic than ministers of the church? And if religious liberty was inclusive of Muslim magistrates, so Baptist Federalists argued, certainly it would not exclude Christian ones, regardless of their vocation. Even John Leland ran successfully for public office in Massachusetts in 1811, arguing that just as clergy should not be privileged by the civil authority, neither should they be completely barred from political service.[168] Baptists were the most ardent defenders of disestablishment, but they often distinguished between state religion and a religious state, between state clergymen and clerical statesmen. In 1798, at the Georgia constitutional convention, Jesse Mercer encountered

---

165. Merrill, *Balaam Disappointed*, 22.
166. Cook, *Biography of Richard Furman*, 94.
167. Cook, *Biography of Richard Furman*, 216.
168. Smith, *John Leland*, 90.

similar opposition to clergymen in the state government. However, Mercer had his own unique way of responding to his fellow delegates:

> It was moved, during the session of the convention, by one of the members who, it seems was a lawyer, that *ministers* be ineligible to the office of legislator, and the motion was warmly urged by both *lawyers* and *doctors*. Mr. Mercer moved so to amend the resolution, as that *lawyers* and *doctors* should be included. During an adjournment which ensued before the matter was adjusted, Mr. Mercer was visited by some of the members of the body, and urged to drop his amendment, as the projectors of the original motion had agreed to yield their ground. To this he assented.[169]

Whereas some Baptists believed that clergymen had a dangerous "desire for religious domination" immediately following the Revolution, others believed that they were "better qualified" than anyone to secure the laws and liberties of the new nation.[170] Either way, Baptist leaders would play a significant role in the shaping of America, and as they believed, the entire world.

Politics of Optimism

Like so many in the Revolutionary generation, Baptists were a Janus-faced people, looking forward and backward in the same political moment. Harking back to the War of Independence, Thomas Baldwin called 1776 "a new epoch in the history of the world."[171] Indeed, God was doing something new before their eyes. John Leland declared, "The revolution of American has been an event which . . . has promised more for the cause of humanity, and the rights of man, than any revolution that can be named." On the other hand, for Leland and the Baptists, the Revolution was also a recovery of something from ages past, and "may be justly esteemed the returning dawn of long lost liberty, and the world's best hope."[172] Baptists believed that, millennia ago, religious liberty had once allowed the gospel to flourish and to reach the farthest corners of the earth. Now, with the advent of Jeffersonianism into the world, "America's God" was once again preserving freedom of conscience and performing a mighty work in the world. Like Thomas Jefferson, Baptists in the early republic were convinced of the power of progress.

---

169. Mallary, *Memoirs of Elder Jesse Mercer*, 100.
170. Merrill, *Balaam Disappointed*, 8.
171. Baldwin, *Sermon, Delivered February 19, 1795*, 14.
172. Leland, "Oration," 259.

If any religious group shared Jefferson's view for an "empire of liberty" that would serve as a light of freedom to the nations, it was the Baptists, who saw themselves and the United States as "the light of the world and the pillar and ground of the truth."[173] Even in the face of flint-hearted bigotry, Baptist politics was ultimately an optimistic enterprise, devoted to the idea that religious liberty should not be relegated to one people, one state, or even one nation. When Isaac Backus articulated the Baptists' continued opposition to the infamous Article Three of the Massachusetts Constitution which upheld religious establishment, his treatise was entitled *Truth is Great and Will Prevail* (Boston, 1781).[174] Baptists from New England to Georgia believed that God and history were on their side. Speaking of Baptists in Vermont at the turn of the century, Nicholas P. Miller explains, "As their numbers grew, so did their political muscle—and their willingness to flex it through petitions for freedom from the religious tax system."[175] John Leland actually marveled at the progress of the Baptist denomination in the far Northeast. "In the state of Vermont," he reported, "the Governor and Lieutenant-Governor are both Baptist preachers—Ezra Butler and Aaron Leland. This is a new thing in the world."[176] By the end of the early national period, Baptists had established themselves as those who would help determine the liberties of others, rather than simply "religious outsiders" vying for their own basic rights and freedoms. As active participants in the new American marketplace and as zealous defenders of the freedom of conscience, Baptists embodied in some sense the future of America in the public square. William McLoughlin was thus correct when he suggested, "It is not too much to say that the Baptists (especially in the south and west) embodied the basic outlook of the American people for most of the nineteenth century."[177] Forged by centuries of marginalization and sustained by an optimistic political outlook, Baptists believed they were chosen by God to usher religious liberty to the world and "render the glory to America's God."[178]

173. "Empire of Liberty" is an expression utilized by Thomas Jefferson to describe the role of the United States in spreading freedom to the rest of the world. For instance, in 1809, Jefferson wrote to James Madison, "we should then have only to include the North in our confederacy, which would be of course in the first war, and we should have such an empire for liberty as she has never surveyed since the creation: & I am persuaded no constitution was ever before so well calculated as ours for extensive empire & self-government" (Thomas Jefferson to James Madison, April 27, 1809, in Looney, *Papers of Thomas Jefferson*, 1:160. Backus, *Address to the Inhabitants of New England*, 443).

174. Backus, *Truth Is Great and Will Prevail*, 397–425.

175. Miller, *Religious Roots of the First Amendment*, 111.

176. Leland, "Events in the Life of John Leland," 36.

177. McLoughlin, *Soul Liberty*, 2.

178. Leland, "Oration," 261.

Chapter 2

Baptism Patriotism

AT THE DAWN OF the Revolution, Baptists were somewhat of a political wild card. Due to their intense dissatisfaction with the hierarchical social and religious system that had developed in most colonies, the War of Independence seemed to Baptists like a war on two fronts: against the British for civil liberty and against establishmentarians for religious liberty.[1] In some sense, Baptists were waging an internecine and international struggle simultaneously. Although white male Baptists were no longer prohibited from voting or holding public office as they were in some colonies in the seventeenth century, they were not content to remain second-class citizens in a first-class society, and their quest to disestablish religion brought many to question their patriotism.[2] In New England, the epicenter of patriotic fervor, Baptists were often perceived as nettlesome fanatics who undermined and even opposed the Revolution itself. In the maelstrom of 1773, just months before the Boston Tea Party, Isaac Backus issued his call for nonviolent civil disobedience, a rather bold strategy aimed at civil leaders just as inter-colonial unity and hostility to Britain were reaching their climax. In Virginia, James Madison wrote to William Bradford in the spring of 1774 that petitions would be filed with the colonial assembly on behalf

---

1. McBeth, *Baptist Heritage*, 260.

2. Gordon S. Wood contends, "the social conditions that generally are supposed to lie behind all revolutions—poverty and economic deprivation—were not present in colonial America. There should no longer be any doubt about it: the white American colonists were not an oppressed people; they had no crushing imperial chains to throw off. In fact, the colonists knew they were freer, more equal, more prosperous, and less burdened with cumbersome feudal and monarchial restraints than any other part of mankind in the eighteenth century" (Wood, *Radicalism of the American Revolution*, 5).

of the "persecuted Baptists." Madison was skeptical of success, noting that in the previous session of the assembly efforts to help the Baptists had been stonewalled after supporters of the "ecclesiastical establishment" had told "incredible and extravagant" stories about the "monstrous effects" of religious "enthusiasm" among dissenters.[3]

Isaac Backus even turned the cry of "no taxation without representation" against his fellow Americans. He charged, "I need not inform you that all America are in arms against being taxed where they are not represented. But it is not more certain that we are not represented in the British Parliament than it is, that our *civil* rulers are not our representatives in *religious* affairs. Yet ministers have long prevailed with them to impose religious taxes entirely out of their jurisdiction."[4] Religious establishment was inconsistent with the cause of freedom, Separate Baptists argued. The Standing Order were zealous to claim liberty for themselves, but they refused to extend that very liberty to others in their own land. They call themselves "*Sons* of LIBERTY," Backus poked, "but they treat me like *sons* of VIOLENCE."[5] While Congregationalist patriots like Samuel Hopkins and Lemuel Haynes used the Revolution to spotlight the hypocrisy of slaveholding, Backus exploited the political moment to denounce the Pharisaism of state religion.[6]

Baptist patriotism could therefore be described as a kind of patriotism-under-protest. As a whole, Baptists supported the Revolutionary cause without conditions, but not without complaints. Eventually, the spirit of 76 filled Baptists no less than Congregationalists, but it was mediated through their own political and religious experience.[7] While this protestant patriotism grabbed the attention of their fellow patriots, it did not offer the most immediate formula for success. On one hand, when Revolutionary Baptists fought alongside the very groups who persecuted them, they forfeited their political leverage, and their Baptist identity was sometimes overshadowed by their Protestantism.[8] In a sermon after the Battle of Lexington (1775), Isaac Backus sounded like the ministers of the Standing Order when he

---

3. Feldman, *Three Lives of James Madison*, 13.

4. Backus, *Government and Liberty Described*, 357.

5. Backus, *Letter to a Gentleman in the Massachusetts General Assembly, Concerning Taxes to Support Religious Worship*, 18.

6. Hopkins, *Dialogue Concerning the Slavery of the Africans*; Lemuel Haynes, "Liberty Further Extended," 17–23.

7. According to McLoughlin, "Spirit of '76 got into them just as the Holy Spirit got into them in revival meetings" (McLoughlin, *Soul Liberty*, 190).

8. McLoughlin argues that the Warren Association's patriotism actually "weakened" the effect of Backus's *Government and Liberty Described* (1778). (McLoughlin, "Introduction," 347).

insisted that "the doctrine of passive obedience and non-resistance to kings" had brought America "upon the brink of popery and slavery."[9] For Backus, the only force on earth that rivaled the evil of religious establishment was Roman Catholicism. The Quebec Act, which guaranteed free exercise of the Catholic faith in the Canadian province, was enough to disqualify King George III from his throne and to unite all Americans against English tyranny. Other Baptists heartily agreed. In August 1774, William Henry Drayton, a Baptist layman from Charleston who served in the Continental Congress in 1778 and 1779, wrote to the First Continental Congress, warning of a plan to "establish the Romish religion, in a very considerable part of the British Empire."[10] Patriotism and Protestantism were difficult to separate for many colonists, including Baptists.

On the other hand, when Baptists dared to list their grievances in the public square, many New Englanders doubted their motives. For instance, Boston Congregationalist minister Andrew Eliot wrote to Thomas Hollis in 1771, "Our Baptist brethren all at once complain of grievous persecutions in the Massachusetts! These complaints were never heard of till we saw them in the public prints. It was a great surprise when we saw them, as we had not heard that the laws in force were not satisfactory."[11] While conceding that religious taxes were not ideal in a free nation, the incredulous Eliot did not understand why a certificate excusing Baptists from such taxes and submitted by a minister of their own denomination was an infringement upon their religious liberty. As the Revolution intensified, Congregationalists responded to Baptist appeals for religious liberty with even greater suspicion and scorn. By 1778, the Warren Association reported that Baptists had "been accused repeatedly of acting the part of enemies to our country only for being in earnest to have that liberty established."[12] In the eyes of many, Baptists were more than a pell-mell group of extremists; they were unpatriotic.

9. In McLoughlin, *Soul Liberty*, 190.

10. Drayton, "Letter from Freeman of South Carolina, to the Deputies of North America," 11.

11. Andrew Eliot to Thomas Hollis, Boston, January 29, 1771, *Collections of the Massachusetts Historical Society*, 4th ser., IV, 455–57, in Bailyn, *Ideological Origins of the American Revolution*, 263–64.

12. In Backus, *Government and Liberty Described*, 360.

Patriotism Questioned

Amongst a people of destiny, New England Baptists proved to be the proverbial fly in the ointment. In 1774, when Isaac Backus took his case of disestablishment to the Continental Congress, he encountered a "cool reception" from Massachusetts delegates John Adams and Samuel Adams, both of whom seemed agitated by Backus's request.[13] When Backus contended for "the liberty of worshipping God according to our consciences, not being obliged to support a ministry we cannot attend," the sons of Puritans replied that the establishment in Massachusetts was "a very slender one, hardly to be called an establishment." Both founders had no shortage of words for their Baptist counterparts. After each Adams "made a long speech," the Baptist delegation "brought up facts, which they tried to explain away, but could not." Following some polite back and forth on the duty of the General Court to hear complaints of religious liberty, Backus then apologized for any appearance of hostility to the government. The agents from the Warren Association were sensitive to public perception and eager to avoid any potential accusations of loyalism. Nevertheless, Backus stood his ground "that facts proved the contrary to their plea; and gave a short account of our Legislature's treatment of Ashfield, which was very puzzling to them." In 1771, the Baptists of Ashfield had sent a petition for redress to the king, who revoked the local law forcing Baptists to submit taxes to support the Congregationalist minister.[14] The ordeal had left Baptists with a loyalist stigma, and Backus was undoubtedly aware of this when he gave an account of the Ashfield persecutions to the men in Philadelphia. However, to the Adamses, Backus was nothing more than a religious radical:

> In their plea, S. Adams tried to represent that *regular* Baptists were quite easy among us; and more than once insinuated that these complaints came from enthusiasts who made it a merit to suffer persecution; and also that enemies had a hand therein . . . In answer, I told them they might call it enthusiasm or what they pleased; but I freely own, before all these gentlemen, that it is absolutely a point of conscience with me; for I cannot give in the certificates they require without implicitly acknowledging that power in man which I believe belongs only to God.[15]

---

13. Kidd, *God of Liberty*, 171.
14. McLoughlin, *Soul Liberty*, 134.
15. Backus, *History of New England*, 2:201–2. See John Adam's account of this scene in Adams, *Works of John Adams, the Second President of the United States*, 2:397–99.

In the Adams' view, calls for disestablishment were nothing more than "enthusiasm" and not necessarily representative of most Baptists. In other words, Backus was just a fanatic. At times, Backus did exhibit a degree of radicalism unmatched by other Baptists. Just one year before, a fellow Baptist had contended in the *Boston Evening Post* that the burden of the Episcopalian establishment was "comparatively light" to that of the "Presbyterians of New England" and that their taxes were therefore to be accepted. Calling him a "pretended Baptist," Backus wrote to Mr. Draper of the Boston paper and retorted, "And is not the hand of Joab in all this? For my part, I am not able to get a pair of scales sufficient to weigh those two great bodies in, the Episcopal hierarchy and the New England Presbyterians, so as to find out exactly which is heaviest. But if this pretended brother had felt what father Obadiah Holmes once felt in Boston from our opponents, he would not have been so easy as he now seems to be."[16]

While Separate Baptists were certainly more vehement and vocal in terms of their opposition to the Standing Order (and this undoubtedly affected their politics), men like John and Samuel Adams greatly misunderstood the Baptist principle of conscience and how it overlapped with Baptist patriotism. Most Baptists could not dissociate civil and religious taxation as if they were two separate issues. The very beliefs that compelled them to fight the British were often the same that brought them to confront their fellow Americans who likewise trampled their inalienable rights. Consequently, as James P. Byrd notes, "No Americans were more patriotic than the Baptists, in Backus's view, because Baptists embraced complete patriotism, along with both civil and religious liberty."[17] At such a critical moment in America's founding, Baptists were beckoning their fellow patriots to broaden their concept of liberty, but the Unitarian John Adams and Calvinist Samuel Adams (who were second cousins) were far too interested in preserving New England's social and religious order. Although New England had come a very long way since 1637, when America's first heretic Anne Hutchinson was banished to Rhode Island, the political and religious fabrics of Massachusetts were still so tightly intertwined that its inhabitants still perceived ecclesiastical change in anarchical terms. A shock to the religious system was a threat to political order. Therefore, even in 1774, Baptists were not simply requesting religious freedom; they were proposing a new fundamental reality. This is no doubt why John Adams then scoffed at Backus that "we

---

16. Backus to Draper, October 14, 1773, in Backus, *History of New England*, 2:179.
17. Byrd, *Sacred Scripture, Sacred War*, 135.

might as well expect a change in the solar system, as to expect they would give up their establishment."[18]

Established clergy were more severe than the Adamses. Some, like the acerbic Ezra Stiles, openly accused Baptists of loyalism. The foremost Congregationalist minister in Rhode Island and eventual president of Yale reserved his most scathing rebuke for James Manning, who had come to blows with Stiles years earlier when the College of Rhode Island had asked Stiles to draft the charter of the school. Perhaps not surprisingly, Stiles's vision for Brown University was a bit too ecumenical for the trustees, nineteen of thirty-five of whom were Baptists.[19] When the Governor of Rhode Island, a Baptist, discovered Stiles's intention to hand more authority to the Fellows (eight out of twelve of which were Congregationalists), the plan was scrapped. Years later, the seeds of resentment apparently remained. Just twelve days after the nation's independence, Rev. Stiles wrote from Newport,

> Mr. Manning, the President of the Baptist College [in Rhode Island] is a Tory affecting Neutrality. He never prayed for the Congress or [for] Success to our Army till Gen. Washington, returning from Boston last Spring, being at Providence on Lordsday, he went to Mr. Manning's meeting [at the First Baptist Church]—then, for the first time, he prayed for the Congress and Army. But he and most of the Heads of the Baptists, especially Ministers, thro' the Continent are cool in this Cause, if not rather wishing the King's side Victory . . . [Mr. Manning lately made] some sneering reflexions on the public affairs— he suggested that this was a Presbyterian [Congregational] War—the Congregationalists to the Northward had prevailed upon the [Anglican] Churchmen to the Southward [in Virginia] to join them—and that it was worth considering [whether] the Baptists could be crushed between them both if they overcome [the king]. This is the heart of the bigotted Baptist Politicians.[20]

Among Congregationalist pastors, few were more patriotic than Ezra Stiles, whose sermon *The United States Elevated to Glory and Honor* (1783) embodied one of the clearest examples of American exceptionalism in the new republic.[21] In his Revolutionary zeal, however, Stiles failed to understand how "bigoted" Baptists could view the war in such a different way.

---

18. Backus, *History of New England*, 2:202.
19. Guild, "Portrait of James Manning, D. D.," 47–50.
20. Stiles, *Literary Diary of Ezra Stiles*, 23.
21. Stiles, *United States Elevated to Glory and Honor*.

From Ezra Stiles's point of view, all Americans stood to gain from the liberty of 1776. But through Baptist eyes, even the liberty of Revolutionary America did not necessarily guarantee freedom for all. The Congregationalist establishment was a corrupt regime, they argued, designed to place fallible men in the judgment seat of God and to uphold the same tyranny the patriots had fought to abolish. "That churches remain voluntaristic is essential to their health, it was believed, for too close an embrace by the state would only detract from and even corrupt the church."[22] By foisting their taxes upon Baptists in order to support their own state church, Congregationalists were repeating the very despotism from which Americans were seeking to free themselves in their conflict with Britain. In short, religious establishment undermined the Revolution itself.

Although Stiles only suspected loyalism (and falsely) on the part of Manning, other Baptists were indeed outspoken loyalists. Morgan Edwards, one of the leading Baptists in Philadelphia and Delaware, publicly proclaimed his loyalty to King George III in 1774. Of Welsh origin, Edwards had preached in Ireland and England before arriving in the colonies. Therefore, his allegiance to the crown was less surprising. He "was justly ranked with the Tories; although his Toryism seemed rather a matter of principle than of action."[23] One of Edwards's sons, however, put his loyalty into action when he became an officer in the British military. In Georgia, Baptist Matthew Moore of Big Buckhead Church was also a staunch supporter of British authorities. Baptized at his church was the first black Baptist missionary, Georgie Liele. In 1791, Liele recorded, "the Rev. Matthew Moore, baptized me, and I continued in this church about four years, till the vacuation" of Savannah by the British.[24] As white Americans were seeking their freedom by fighting the British, blacks like Liele was seeking their own by *leaving with* the British. Henry Sharp, Liele's owner who had eventually freed him, was a deacon at the Baptist church near Savannah and was killed during the Revolutionary War fighting for the crown. Despite the fact that white Baptists were some of the most ardent patriots in the new nation, such examples of Baptist loyalism only confirmed the suspicions of their enemies. Throughout Massachusetts and the Northeast, the "odious name of Tory" was cast upon Baptists as the worst of epithets.[25] Rev. James Chandler, a Standing Order minister in Rowley, reported an alleged tory plot by the Baptists in

22. Esbeck and Hartog, "Introduction," 11.

23. Guild, "Portrait of James Manning, D. D.," 45. Also see Edwards, *Materials Towards a History of the Baptists in Delaware State*, 3:46.

24. Liele, "Account of Several Baptist Churches," 46.

25. Backus, *Government and Liberty Described*, 363.

retaliation for the 1780 Massachusetts Constitution which upheld its establishment of the Congregationalist church. According to Chandler, the Baptists "had voted at a convention that if Article Three were not eliminated 'they would help no more in the war.'"[26] Isaac Backus denied the charge and traced the rumor back to a disaffected Baptist in Chelmsford. In *Truth Is Great and Will Prevail* (1781), Backus refuted Chandler and insisted, "Some would have us look to Britain for help against these oppressors, but we have no idea of any such thing."[27]

Although only a fraction of Baptists were in fact guilty of loyalism, and while some of the leading patriots in the Revolution even threatened to harm local Baptists, neither of these prevented the majority of Baptists from throwing their full support behind the Revolutionary cause. Of the Baptists who did initially side with Britain, some eventually reversed course. At Dutchman's Creek Baptist Church in North Carolina, minister William Cook and five other members signed a document called "The Protest" along with almost 200 other denizens of Rowan and Surry counties in defiance of the Revolution. However, on July 18, 1775, after "much dissatisfaction" was expressed by the local inhabitants, Cook offered an apology to the Committee of Safety of Rowan County, "professing his sorrow for signing the Protest against the cause of liberty, which lately circulated in the Forks of Yadkin."[28] By all accounts, Cook kept his position at the church. Baptists were quick to forgive those who turned from their loyalist sin. In his research in *God Against the Revolution: The Loyalist Clergy's Case Against the American Revolution*, Gregg L. Frazier located only two Baptists who remained outspoken loyalists during the Revolution.[29]

Joining the Cause

In New England, where "Baptists were accused of 'not being hearty' in the American cause," Isaac Backus and others were determined to show that Revolutionary and Baptist interests were one and the same.[30] Leaning on the freedom of conscience and the "right of private judgment," a good Baptist was a good patriot. After all, more than anyone else, Baptists celebrated personal liberty and eschewed civil and religious oppression. They were,

---

26. Backus, *Truth is Great and Will Prevail*, 398.
27. Backus, *Truth is Great and Will Prevail*, 423.
28. Paschal, *History of North Carolina Baptists*, 2:122.
29. Frazier, *God Against the Revolution*, 28.
30. Nelson, *American Tory*, 90.

as historians have called them, "spiritual republicans."[31] Noting that most Americans could not by conscience submit themselves to a tyrant, Backus questioned, "You tell us you cannot because you are taxed where you are not represented. And is it not really so with us? You do not deny the right of the British Parliament to impose taxes within their own realm; only complain that she extends her taxing power beyond her proper limits. And have we not as good right to say you do the same thing?"[32] These kinds of arguments in favor of religious liberty were not political ultimatums, as many like Rev. Chandler suspected. Instead, Backus's rhetoric was designed to demonstrate the inconsistency of patriotism and religious establishment. Baptists believed that they were indeed *true* patriots, willing to extend Revolutionary principles like freedom, rights, and conscience to their purest form. In fact, Baptists like John Leland argued that if an American possessed "any patriotism" at all, he would resist the establishment of religion.[33] Patriotism, at least undefiled patriotism, demanded religious liberty and the protection of the right of conscience. Anything less was a kind of popish despotism masquerading as republicanism, a seed of tyranny buried in the soil of freedom. In Leland's illustrative words, even the most well-meaning American has "a pope in his belly," but "true patriotism will rope the pope, and cause the patriot to seek the good of his country (of all the world) and not his own aggrandizement."[34]

Baptists even influenced the events leading to the Revolution, contributing to the Whig ideology that fomented in the colonies. The Baptist pastor John Allen, whom scholars have called "New England's Tom Paine," wrote one of the best-selling pamphlets of the pre-Revolutionary crisis in the aftermath of the Gaspee affair entitled *An Oration, Upon the Beauties of Liberty, Or the Essential Rights of the Americans* (1772).[35] Like Tom Paine, Allen had fallen into debt, losing his pastorate in London in 1767. After being tried and acquitted for forgery, Allen immigrated, like Paine, to the colonies in the 1770s. "My Lord," Allen asked the Earl of Dartmouth, "are not the Liberties of the Americans as dear to them as those of Britons?" He continued, "How would your Lordship like to be fetter'd with irons, and drag'd three thousand miles, in a hell upon earth? No! But in a HELL upon

---

31. Heimert, *Religion and the American Mind*, 537.
32. Backus, *Appeal to the Public*, 339.
33. Leland, "Blow at the Root," 251.
34. Leland, "Oration, Delivered at Cheshire, July 5, 1802," 265.
35. Bumsted and Clark, "New England's Tom Paine," 561–70.

water, to take your trial? Is not this contrary to the spirit of the law, and the rights of an Englishmen?"[36]

Yet Baptists did not simply theorize about the Revolution; they also joined it. Pastors such as Rev. John Angel of Grassy Knob, North Carolina served virtually the entire war as soldiers.[37] In New York, Baptist preachers like Elnathan Phelps (who established churches in both New York and Vermont) defended the Champlain Valley and Fort Ticonderoga against British invasion.[38] Soon after the Declaration of Independence, a young Richard Furman took the oath of allegiance to the United States under General Richard Richardson. Marching down to Charleston with a volunteer company commanded by his brother Josiah, Furman was eager to guard his beloved South Carolina against invasion. However, Governor Rutledge advised him to return to his church and to serve his country in the pulpit. Furman became such a spirited supporter of the Revolution that Lord Cornwallis allegedly offered a thousand-pound bounty for "so notorious a rebel."[39] Years later, when Furman was introduced to Colonel James Monroe, then on President Madison's cabinet, Monroe recalled Furman as "the young patriot for whom Cornwallis had offered a reward, and of whom the British General is said to have remarked that 'he feared the prayers of the godly youth more than the armies of Sumter and Marion.'"[40] While the latter half of this account is almost certainly apocryphal, Furman's renown in the Charleston area as a patriot and leading religious voice for the Revolution was unquestionable. Furman insisted that "there is great reason to believe, the American revolution was effected by the special agency of God."[41] Preaching on "America's Deliverance and Duty," he believed that the clergy were as invaluable to the Revolutionary cause as the founders themselves. He reasoned,

> Days of solemn fasting and prayer were frequently set apart and observed, by voluntary association, among the different denominations of christians: and I hope, I may say, in modesty and truth, that while our patriot statesmen and soldiers, exerted and displayed their abilities, generosity, and heroism, in defence of our country and liberties, in a manner that has immortalized their names; the clergy though acting in an humbler sphere, did

36. Allen, *Oration*, 6–7.
37. Paschal, *History of the North Carolina Baptists*, 2:134.
38. Rowe, *God's Strange Work*, 4–5.
39. Cook, "Biography of Richard Furman," 84–85; Rogers, *Richard Furman*, 39; Yarnell, "Early American Political Theology," 71.
40. Dargan, "Richard Furman and His Place in American Baptist History," 47–48.
41. Furman, *America's Deliverance and Duty*, 393.

not render a less essential service to the national interests; by inculcating those sentiments, setting those examples, and taking that lead in religion, which inspired our citizens with zeal in the cause of liberty; formed their minds into a suitable temper for receiving the Divine blessing, and rendered them, in the expectation of it, courageous to meet the dangers they had to encounter.[42]

In Furman's view, the Revolution could not have been accomplished without patriotic pastors who spiritually prepared the American people for the toll of war and trained them in godliness as to be worthy of victory. Just as historians have emphasized that "New England's Congregational ministers played a leading role in fomenting sentiments of resistance and, after 1774, open rebellion," so Baptists like Richard Furman wielded the pulpit for a similar purpose.[43] Furman was so bold in his patriotism that he even took it upon himself to address a group of loyalists in the northwest corner of the state, explaining his views and entreating them to join the American cause.[44] Fellow Baptists Oliver Hart and William Henry Drayton, along with Presbyterian minister William Tennent, also spread the patriot gospel to backcountry farmers in the region. However, hailing from the Low country, their success did not match that of Furman, a native of High Hills of Santee.[45]

Almost all Baptist congregations were favorable toward military service, even in New England. For instance, when the Baptist church at Haverhill voted in 1776 to allow Hezekiah Smith to serve as chaplain, only a very small group led by Deacon Jonathan Shepard did not approve of the pastor leaving the flock in order to join the army (although when Smith arrived home on furlough in 1779, the church voiced its desire that Smith should stay home). By January 8, 1776, Hezekiah was one of only nine chaplains serving among twenty-seven American regiments.[46] Baptists served the Revolutionary cause where and when they were needed most. During his service, Smith even exchanged worship services with other Baptist chaplains like William Van Horne (and with Congregationalists like Enos Hitchcock).[47] David Jones, who served in both the Revolutionary War

42. Furman, *America's Deliverance and Duty*, 396–97.
43. Stout, *New England Soul*, 291.
44. Cook, "Biography of Richard Furman," 83–84.
45. Smith, "South Carolina," 188. Furman was in fact born in New York, but his family moved to South Carolina when he was a young boy. For some years, Furman lived on the coast. However, he returned to pastor the Baptist church at Hill Hills of Santee for thirteen years before accepting the pastorate at First Baptist Church of Charleston.
46. Smith, *Life, Ministry, and Journals of Hezekiah Smith*, 129–30, 140.
47. Smith, *Life, Ministry, and Journals of Hezekiah Smith*, 132.

and the War of 1812, was a seasoned veteran, earning him the nickname "The Old War Horse."[48] The following anecdote reveals Jones's well-known love of country:

> Howard Malcolm was walking with Dr. Staughton and Rev. Jesse Mercer D.D. of Georgia and saw David Jones approaching. Staughton said to Mercer "There comes an old brother who could not stay home if we had another war." On meeting Jones, Staughton repeated this: 'Brother Jones I was telling Brother Mercer that if we had another war with England you would be ready in a week to go out with the troops.' Mr. Jones lifted his cane and bringing it down with force upon a wheelbarrow that stood nearby, replied with earnestness, "Today Sir."[49]

Baptists were certainly no strangers to the costs of war. Barely a decade old, the College of Rhode Island shut down during the Revolution (1776-1782).[50] During the conflict, the college building in Providence became a barracks for soldiers.[51] Although President Manning had resumed academic affairs by 1780, he was apparently told after preaching one Sunday morning at First Baptist Church of Providence that the college would be turned into a French hospital.[52] The college served this function until 1782. Nevertheless, a year later Manning could write to an English Baptist, "I cannot say in what light you view the American Revolution, but to serious people here it appears to be of God."[53]

According to William G. McLoughlin, Baptists "became patriots after 1775 because they finally saw in the rise of imperial control a potential hindrance or obstruction to the free flow of God's grace, even a greater hindrance than that of the Standing Order in New England."[54] In some sense, the American Revolution was to Baptists the lesser of two evils. By 1779, Isaac Backus could proudly boast, "we have joined as heartily in the general defense of our country as any denomination therein, and I have a better opinion of my countrymen than to think the majority of them will

---

48. Jones, *Life, Journal and Works of David Jones*, 175.
49. Jones, *Life, Journal and Works of David Jones*, 120–21.
50. Manning, *Life, Times, and Correspondence of James Manning*, 243, 289.
51. The College of Rhode Island was not the only institution to be captured and used by the British. When the Redcoats occupied Princeton from December 7, 1776 to January 3, 1777, they used Nassau Hall as a barracks and stable, leaving the school in terrible condition (Noll, *Princeton and the Republic (1768–1822)*, 73).
52. McLoughlin, *Soul Liberty*, 272.
53. Manning, *Life, Times, and Correspondence of James Manning*, 317.
54. McLoughlin, *Soul Liberty*, 189.

now agree to deny us liberty of conscience."[55] Not only did Backus come to believe that the Baptist quest for religious liberty would be aided by Revolution, but he also thought that Baptist patriotism would ameliorate relations with other denominations, curtailing the popular prejudices against Baptists that had long plagued American society.[56] Perhaps, with time, complete disestablishment of religion would be among those "blessings that were bought with blood."[57]

American Exceptionalism

Scholars like William G. McLoughlin, Thomas S. Kidd, and Barry Hankins have examined the nature of Baptist patriotism during the Revolution, but very few have treated this subject as it developed *after* the war. Did Baptist patriotism evolve over time? How did issues of religious liberty in the early republic impact Baptists' love of country? And in what way did Baptists embrace a kind of early nationalism?[58] The relationship between America and Britain, and particularly between American and British Baptists, is germane to the issue of Baptist patriotism because it demonstrates how Baptists viewed their new nation in comparison with the old. Although very few white Baptists would have denied the fact that their denomination faced significant obstacles of religious liberty in their new republic, the way in which they interacted with their brethren overseas indicates that the Revolution had become for them a sign of God's favor not only upon their country, but upon their denomination. Writing to John Rippon in London in 1794, David Jones bragged, "I am now appointed Chaplain to the army and am the only one in America; by this you may learn that our Society [the Baptists] appears in a different point of view to your's in England where you are bound with the odious character of a dissenter."[59] Even though Baptists would be

---

55. Backus, *Policy As Well As Honesty*, 383.

56. Baptists often enjoyed a degree of authority in local and state governments in the earliest days of the republic, albeit subordinately to the Standing Order. For instance, Noah Alden of Bellingham was chosen by the Massachusetts Constitutional Convention (1779–1780) to serve as chairman of the committee tasked to draft the clauses on ecclesiastical law and practice. The majority of the committee, however, opposed his views on disestablishment (McLoughlin, *Isaac Backus and the American Pietistic Tradition*, 144).

57. Leland, "Oration," 261.

58. Daniel Walker Howe asserts, "The word 'nationalism' did not come into usage until the 1830s, but the attitude antedated the name for it." He also contends, "American 'nationalism' developed a variety of permutations" (Howe, *What Hath God Wrought*, 116, 124).

59. Jones, *Life, Journal and Works of David Jones*, 119.

persecuted in New England for decades to come, in most parts of the United States Baptists still believed that they were treated better in America than under England's religious establishment. After the war, former British soldiers joined Baptist churches, contributing to a sense of American spiritual victory. In Virginia, John Taylor celebrated that former British prisoners Duncan McLean, Garsham Robertson, and Donald Holmes were baptized by him at the Albemarle Barracks in 1783. Although McLean and Holmes eventually preached a universalist gospel, and McLean became a Deist along with Robertson, Holmes was later restored to fellowship and joined Clear Creek Church in Woodford County, Kentucky, becoming an abolitionist like Taylor.[60] John Ewing of Hopewell Baptist Church in New Jersey was actually a British Army deserter. Baptists had helped America defeat Britain in the War of Independence; now they were winning their souls to Christ.

The optimistic spirit that seized Baptists in America only increased after the war, and they believed that the fruits of victory would eventually be enjoyed by all Baptists. In a remarkable correspondence with James Manning in 1784, less than a year after the Treaty of Paris, John Rippon of London wrote,

> I believe all our Baptist ministers in town, except two, and most of our brethren in the country, were on the side of the Americans in the late dispute. But sorry, very sorry were we to hear that the college was a hospital, and the meeting-houses were forsaken and occupied for civil or martial purposes. We wept when the thirsty plains drank the blood of your departed heroes, and the shout of a king was amongst us when your well-fought battles were crowned with victory. And to this hour we believe that the independence of America will for a while secure the liberty of this country; but if the continent had been reduced, Britain would not long have been free.[61]

Indeed, even British Baptists celebrated American Independence as a victory for religious freedom and for religion itself. In his funeral sermon for George Washington, Richard Furman called the patriot cause "that cause which is intimately connected with the honor of God, and the interests of the Redeemer's kingdom."[62] The newly formed United States of America had been erected by nothing less than the power of God, and therefore Christianity and patriotism overlapped in the Baptist mind. In Massachusetts, on

---

60. Taylor, *Baptists on the American Frontier*, 111, 114.
61. Manning, *Life, Times, and Correspondence of James Manning*, 324.
62. Furman, *Humble Submission to Divine Sovereignty*, 382.

days of prayer or thanksgiving or fasting, "Hezekiah Smith seldom failed to preach two or three sermons on the day of the observance."[63]

For some, love of country *was* love of God. After Stephen Gano enlisted on a privateer and shipwrecked in 1781, his mother, Sarah, a Baptist pastor's wife, received the tragic news. The account of her response to the news of her son's death (although he would later be found to be alive), illustrates how many Baptists sanctified military service. "I do not believe that Stephen is dead," she calmly replied. "When I gave my son to my country, I gave him to my God. After his departure, I felt an assurance that God had accepted the gift for his own service. I believe that he will yet be an able, faithful, successful, and it may be, deeply-tried minister of the Gospel of Christ."[64] Indeed, his mother's prophecy would be fulfilled— on both counts.

By contributing to the War of Independence, Baptists had claimed their stake in the future of the American nation, believing they had earned a voice in the public forum and were now entitled to participate in the new religious marketplace. In August 1786, the Baptist General Committee petitioned the Virginia general assembly to repeal the recent *Incorporation Act*, which granted a corporate charter to the Protestant Episcopal Church. Emboldened from their victory over Britain, the Baptists began by reminding the assembly that they too had played a vital role in the Revolution.[65] By the providence of God, Baptists believed they had earned a seat at the political table. In 1811, Leland faced the Massachusetts House of Representatives and used Baptist patriotism to his advantage:

> These are peaceable subjects of state—ready to arm in defense of their country—freely contribute to support Protestant Christianity, but cannot pay a legal tax for religious services; this, sir, is one of the essentials which constitutes them a distinct sect: and what have these endured since the adoption of the constitution? Have they not been reduced to subordinationism?[66]

In New England as well as Virginia, Baptist patriotism did not diminish their pursuit of religious liberty. Instead, it became political leverage by

---

63. Broome, *Life, Ministry, and Journals of Hezekiah Smith*, 103.

64. Wolever, *Life and Ministry of John Gano*, 1:377.

65. Esbeck, "Disestablishment in Virginia, 1776–1802," 163. For an examination of Baptists and dissenters in late-eighteenth century Virginia, also see Spangler, *Virginians Reborn*.

66. Leland, "Speech Delivered in the House of Representatives of Massachusetts, on the Subject of Religious Freedom, 1811," 354.

which Baptists lobbied harder against the Standing Order and the Episcopal establishment.[67]

In order to move forward in their new republic, however, Baptists were forced to confront and sometimes revise the American past. By all accounts, America's future was promising, but its history was riddled with religious bigotry and crimes against Baptists. "From those seasons of the cruel opposition of our forefathers against religious liberty, even down to the glorious revolution, a degree of the same spirit of intolerance prevailed," Daniel Merrill lamented, citing Roger Williams as a victim of such intolerance.[68] Likewise citing Williams, who he identified as the true pioneer of religious liberty, Richard Furman grieved the "spirit of intolerance" and "persecuting rage" that had stained "the early part of the American" history.[69] Nevertheless, ever the patriot, Furman saw the history of America in a mostly positive, providentialist light:

> I lay it down as an evident fact, that a special, merciful providence has uniformly watched over the people of the United States, from their first migration to the continent, to the present day; and that this has appeared to design this part of the globe for a theatre of great and virtuous actions; where all the arts of civilization, and sound policy, the refinements of science, the exercise of moral virtue, and the genuine influence of religion are to be displayed in their most engaging forms.[70]

No religious group saw the paradox of American history more clearly than the Baptists. Though blackened with bigotry, the story of America carried seeds of liberty and virtue. Even Isaac Backus, who railed against the pernicious union of church and state, still admitted of his Puritan forbears, "We are far from trying to represent the fathers of New England as the worst of the colonies; we believe the contrary."[71] Baptists walked a fine line between persecution and patriotism, between manifest destiny and marginalization. In fact, Backus's argumentation against religious establishment was often predicated on retrieving the true spirit of American Puritanism, insisting

---

67. Baptists in the Revolutionary period were not the last religious group in the history of the United States to attempt to use combat to their political advantage. During the Civil War, Irish Catholics fought for the Union, and many "saw military service as an opportunity to prove their loyalty to the United States" (Byrd, *Holy Baptism of Fire and Blood*, 65).

68. Merrill, *Balaam Disappointed*, 7–8.

69. Furman, *Unity and Peace*, 310.

70. Furman, *Oration, Delivered at the Charleston Orphan-House*, 349–50.

71. Backus, *Appeal to the Public*, 342.

that measures like the Saybrook Platform (1708) and the ecclesiastical laws of New England were inconsistent with the original Cambridge Platform of 1648 which maintained the distinction between "congregational" and "national or provincial" polity.[72]

Other Baptists viewed American history through a more rose-colored lens. Thomas Baldwin envisioned his ancestors in a patriotic, even Baptist, light. In his sermon to the Massachusetts House of Representatives, Baldwin described the earliest Puritans as if they were proto-Jeffersonians, men and women "who cheerfully encountered the numerous perils of an inhospitable wilderness, in order to secure to themselves and their posterity, the unmolested enjoyment of civil and religious liberty."[73] Baldwin tended to overlook the religious intolerance of his spiritual forbears in order to locate those ideals which he believed they had in common with Baptists. He explained, "The right of private judgment, or what is commonly called liberty of conscience, is one of our dearest privileges. This right is inalienable in its nature. For the enjoyment of this, our forefathers left their friends and country, and sought an asylum in this then howling wilderness."[74] However, the pastor of Second Baptist Church of Boston may have been guilty of a bit of historical revisionism. Whatever Baldwin intended by "liberty of conscience," it was almost certainly not what William Bradford and the separatists at Plymouth Colony had in mind when they covenanted themselves together "into a civil body politic."[75] Nevertheless, American history was being Baptized for the sake of a new wave of evangelicals who sought to ground their faith in the greater American tradition.

Baptists were making America's history their own. In 1807, Baldwin preached to an artillery company that "every page of our history, from their landing at Plymouth, to the establishment of our national government, is marked with signal interpositions of divine providence."[76] For Baldwin, American history was "our history." With the birth of the United States, Baptists now saw themselves as an important, though often marginalized, part in *all* of the American story. As a result, from New England to the South, from the classroom to the church, Baptists would romanticize the War of Independence for years to come. In 1811, Brown University President Asa Messer challenged his students, "I would especially exhort you

72. McLoughlin, "Introduction," 38.

73. Baldwin, *Sermon, Delivered Before His Excellency Caleb Strong*, 7–8.

74. Baldwin, *Sermon, Delivered Before His Excellency Caleb Strong*, 25.

75. Bradford, *Of Plymouth Plantation*, 19.

76. Baldwin, *Discourse, Delivered Before the Ancient and Honourable Artillery Company*, 20.

ever to keep burning in your own breasts that patriotic fire which was ever burning in the breasts of the great pillars of the American liberty and Independence."[77] Similarly, in the aftermath of the Great Georgia Revival of 1827, Adiel Sherwood recalled "when the spirit of Revolution was leaping from one patriot bosom to another, when father and son were shouldering their muskets and rushing to the tented field to discomfit the common foe or die in the attempt."[78]

With such a sense of destiny, Baptists' patriotism was thus fueled by a spirit of American exceptionalism dating as far back as the Puritans, a belief that God had chosen the United States for enormous, unprecedented achievements.[79] In a discourse at Rhode Island College in 1799, then-professor Asa Messer reflected,

> Perhaps it lies beyond the wisdom of man to devise a government more rational in itself, or more beneficial in its effects, than that under which we live; and perhaps there never was a government on earth, which had the patronage of greater or better men, than our own. Let all the ancient, and all the modern nations in every part of the globe be thoroughly examined, you can find among none of them a government worthy to be compared with the American; nor can you find among any of them, more wise, experienced, faithful, patriotic, illustrious characters, than those who have ever filled our presidential chair.[80]

For Messer, all of these blessings were irrefutable proof of the existence of God, who had, in the words of John Leland, "a peculiar regard for the United States."[81] By virtue of being citizens in America, Baptists were participating in a divine plan to raise humanity to new cultural, scientific, moral, and religious heights. "Religion in America is, as it ought to be," Richard Furman stated matter-of-factly, "free and unconfined."[82] Among all the hard-fought blessings enjoyed in America, religious liberty was the most precious gem. As a city on a hill, the United States, "that land of

---

77. Messer, "Address, Delivered to the Graduates of Brown University, at the Commencement, September 4, 1811," 417.

78. Sherwood, *Strictures on the Sentiments of the Kehukee Association*, 5–6. Sherwood authored the treatise under the pseudonym "Nehemiah." See Burch, *Adiel Sherwood*, 70–75.

79. Bercovitch, *American Jeremiad*, 66.

80. Messer, "Discourse, Delivered in the Chapel of Rhode Island College," 430.

81. Leland, "Letter," 657.

82. Furman, *Oration, Delivered at the Charleston Orphan-House*, 350.

promise," had a duty to model this liberty to the world.[83] Jonathan Maxcy described this exceptionalist outlook when he prophesied in 1795, "The consequences of American independence will soon reach to the extremities of the world. The shining car of freedom will soon roll over the necks of kings, and bear off the oppressed to scenes of liberty and peace."[84] Very few Baptists, indeed very few Americans, would have differed substantially from Maxcy's worldview.

Not surprisingly, this patriotic spirit had a dramatic effect upon the way that Baptists interacted with governments foreign and domestic. For instance, in 1813, Baptists in Tennessee urged friendliness to the government as a condition of membership.[85] As America expanded westward, one's relationship to the Baptist church no longer hindered one's relationship to the state, as it had in certain colonies. Instead, the latter potentially hindered the former. That same year, John Leland addressed the Sons of Liberty in Cheshire, Massachusetts, rallying his fellow patriots against the British. According to Leland, Americans had "seven times the justification" for the War of 1812 as they did for the War of Independence![86] For Leland, the conflict was nothing less than a test of patriotism. In a matter of decades, many Baptists had evolved from protestant patriots to War Hawks.[87] Although Leland's partisanship almost certainly clouded his view of the conflict, his support for "Madison's War" was markedly different than Backus's in the War of 1776. One Baptist questioned the justice of a nation that went to war. The other questioned the justice of those who did *not* go to war.

Faith in the Founders

For a denomination that contributed so relatively little to the administration of the young nation, Baptists placed an extraordinary amount of faith in the men whom they believed that God had appointed to lead them. David Jones, for example, named his son after a Revolutionary War general. In fact, Horatio Gates Jones would eventually become ordained in 1800 as a Baptist minister. In the early republic, Baptists had no small amount of reverence for the founders. Even John Leland, who had originally expressed his dismay that the United States Constitution did not explicitly include an article on religious liberty, could speculate in 1829, "Perhaps an assembly of

83. Bailyn, *Voyagers to the West*, 36.
84. Maxcy, "Oration Delivered in the Baptist Meeting House in Providence," 377.
85. Menikoff, *Politics and Piety*, 68.
86. Leland, "Address to the Association of the Sons of Liberty, Cheshire," 374.
87. Cheathem, *Andrew Jackson and the Rise of the Democratic Party*, 19.

wiser patriots were never collected together, than at the convention in Philadelphia, in 1787."[88] No doubt the passage of the First Amendment (1791) had given Leland a more cheerful memory of the events of 1787. As the American project continued and greater advancements were made in the realm of religious liberty, the blemishes and shortcomings (and heresies) of the founders began to fade with time. At the First Continental Congress, Samuel Adams had dismissed the Baptist delegates as "enthusiasts" and denied the very existence of widespread Baptist persecution. However, just a few decades later, he was canonized as one of the greatest Americans who had ever lived. In 1828, Adiel Sherwood called Samuel Adams and John Hancock "as pure patriots as ever breathed the air of heaven." He continued, "For these very acts, the whole American people revere their memories, and will hold in grateful remembrance their patriotic virtues as long as this Republic has existence."[89] Baptists were no less nostalgic of the founders than any other patriots in the new republic.

In Virginia, the Baptist General Association had drawn up petitions and adopted a remonstrance against Patrick Henry's 1785 general assessment bill which essentially allowed for what scholars have called a "plural establishment" of religion.[90] Instead, they had sided with James Madison, who argued that religion was not within the "purview" of the civil authority, and who later convinced John Leland to support the Constitution.[91] Nevertheless, Baptists eventually chose to remember Henry less as the advocate for multiple tax-supported denominations and more as the hero of the Revolution. John Leland, who initially shared Henry's suspicion of government power under the Constitution, compared his famous "Give me Liberty, or Give me Death!" speech to the book of Job. "As Job was but *one* to *three*," Leland reflected, "it reminds us of Patrick Henry, in the Virginia legislature and convention, combatting the great Dons of that state."[92] So high was Leland's esteem for Henry that he concluded that the Virginia governor was the "foremost" of the "first orators that were ever on earth" to "plead the rights of the people."[93]

Aside from Washington, and although Deists like Madison and Jefferson vehemently supported the Baptist cause for religious freedom, no

---

88. Leland, "Address Delivered at Pittsfield, Jan. 8, 1829," 541.

89. Sherwood, *Strictures on the Sentiments of the Kehukee Association*, 18.

90. Esbeck, "Disestablishment in Virginia, 1776–1802," 157.

91. Esbeck, "Disestablishment in Virginia, 1776–1802," 150; Kidd, *God of Liberty*, 223.

92. Leland, "Book of Job," 707.

93. Leland, "Parts of a Speech, Delivered at Suffield, Connecticut, on the First Jubilee of the United States," 518.

founder garnered more respect from Baptists for his combination of virtue and defense of liberty than Patrick Henry. Calling Henry "the Virginia Demosthenes," Jonathan Maxcy declared in 1819,

> the mighty Henry! What dignity! What majesty! Every eye fastens upon him. Firm, erect, undaunted, he rolls on the mighty torrent of his eloquence. What a picture does he draw of the horrors of servitude and the charms of freedom? At once he gives the full rein to all his gigantic powers, and pours his own heroic spirit into the minds of his auditors; they become as one man; actuated by one soul—and the universal shout is 'Liberty or Death!' This single speech of this illustrious man gave an impulse, which probably decided the fate of America.[94]

The praises that many Baptists withheld from Jefferson and Madison due to their "infidelity" were not kept from Governor Henry, a friend of both liberty *and* religion. Baptists even had personal connections to Henry. After the capture of Charleston, Richard Furman and his family fled north to Virginia. Despite the ravage of war, Furman continued to preach inlocal churches, and Patrick Henry was among his regular hearers. Eventually, the two became such good friends that Henry even gifted Furman with volumes of John Ward's "Oratory," a well-known English work on rhetoric.[95] Likewise calling Henry "the Demosthenes of Virginia," Furman commended his "bold, unconquerable spirit" that "plead the equal rights of conscience" and which "held with integrity the reins of government in a powerful neighboring state."[96]

Of course, no star rose higher and more brightly in the Baptist mind than George Washington, the man Furman called a "*true* patriot" and "our beloved patriot."[97] Washington's legacy among Baptists was truly of biblical proportions. In fact, Richard Furman invoked seemingly every biblical parallel imaginable with which to compare the American president, likening him to everyone from "Samuel, the Prophet and Judge of Israel" to Elijah, "the chariot and horseman of our American Israel."[98] No single figure, it seemed, was sufficient to describe Washington's leadership and his role in delivering the American people. "It is sufficient for America that she had a Washington," Furman concluded in a funeral sermon in 1800. "Heaven has made him to us both a Moses and Joshua. His example will live, though his

---

94. Maxcy, "Discourse, Delivered in the Chapel of South Carolina College," 283.
95. Friend, "Biography of Richard Furman, Sr.," 25.
96. Furman, *Humble Submission to Divine Sovereignty*, 384.
97. Furman, *Humble Submission to Divine Sovereignty*, 372, 379.
98. Furman, *Humble Submission to Divine Sovereignty*, 373, 378.

body returns to its primeval dust."⁹⁹ Nothing less than God's own hand had placed just the right man at the helm of government at just the right time. Therefore, at his death, Furman could only point his listeners heavenward: "Washington was to American the valuable gift of God: he had a right to resume his own gift at his pleasure."¹⁰⁰

From the beginning of his presidency to his farewell address, Washington had exhibited a kindness to Baptists and a friendliness to religion. By 1789, the power of his presence was enough to attenuate Baptists' fears of oppression in the new republic. When the United Baptist Churches of Virginia wrote to Washington in 1789, congratulating him on being elected to the inaugural presidency, they confided that his signature upon the Constitution had convinced them of its validity. "The very name of Washington is music in our ears," they saluted.¹⁰¹ Washington replied with a word of gratitude. In the letter, Washington sought to allay the Baptists' fears of potential violations of the right of religious conscience under the new Constitution:

> If I could have entertained the slightest apprehension that the Constitution framed in the Convention, where I had the honor to preside, might possibly endanger the religious rights of any ecclesiastical Society, certainly I would never have placed my signature to it; and if I could now conceive that the general Government might ever be so administered as to render the liberty of conscience insecure, I beg you will be persuaded that no one would be more zealous than myself to establish effectual barriers against the horrors of spiritual tyranny, and every species of religious persecution—For you, doubtless, remember that I have often expressed my sentiment, that every man, conducting himself as a good citizen, and being accountable to God alone for his religious opinions, ought to be protected in worshipping the Deity according to the dictates of his own conscience.
>
> While I recollect with satisfaction that the religious Society of which you are Members, have been, throughout America, uniformly, and almost unanimously, the firm friends to civil liberty, and the persevering Promoters of our glorious revolution; I cannot hesitate to believe that they will be the faithful Supporters of a free, yet efficient general Government. Under this

---

99. Furman, *Humble Submission to Divine Sovereignty*, 379.

100. Furman, *Humble Submission to Divine Sovereignty*, 378.

101. "Address of the Committee of the United Baptist Churches of Virginia, assembled in the city of Richmond, 8th August, 1789, to the President of the United States of America," in Greene, *Writings of the Late Elder John Leland*, 53–54.

pleasing expectation I rejoice to assure them that they may rely on my best wishes and endeavors to advance their prosperity.[102]

By promising to protect "the liberty of conscience" from "the horrors of spiritual tyranny," Washington was identifying himself as a political friend, not a foe, of the Baptists. In Washington's letter, the Baptists of Virginia received the sweet reward for having fought for liberty in a nation that did not always fight for theirs: Presidential approval. Not only did Washington formally receive their congratulations, he replied with an approbation of Baptist past, present, and future: (1) Baptists had always been "firm friends of civil liberty," (2) they helped achieve "our glorious revolution," (3) and they would be "faithful Supporters" of the new American nation. In other words, Baptists were acknowledged patriots in the nascent republic.

The next year, accompanied by Thomas Jefferson, his Secretary of State, Washington visited the College of Rhode Island in Providence, escorted to the campus by the students and President Manning. After Manning paid homage to the "superintending Providence" that had called Washington to "establish, after having defended, our rights and liberties," President Washington returned thanks to the Baptists for their support in the Revolution: "In repeating thus publicly my sense of the zeal you displayed for the success of the cause of your country, I only add a single suffrage to the general testimony which all, who were acquainted with you in the most adverse and doubtful moments of our struggle for liberty and independence, have constantly borne in your favor."[103] In Providence, Washington once again attested to the patriotism of Baptists, recognizing not only their love of country but also their desire for education and nation-shaping in the early republic.

While both Washington and Jefferson believed that religion should be free of the state, Washington's vision of religious liberty in America at least appeared to align more closely with Baptists, as he nevertheless saw religion and government as inextricably linked. In his Farewell Address in 1796, Washington had emphasized religion as essential for civil society. "Of all the dispositions and habits which lead to political prosperity," he declared, "religion and morality are indispensable supports. In vain would that man claim the tribute of patriotism, who would labor to subvert these great pillars of human happiness, these firmest props of the duties of men and citizens. The mere politician, equally with the pious man, ought to respect and cherish

---

102. "From George Washington to the United Baptist Churches of Virginia, May 1789," https://founders.archives.gov/documents/Washington/05-02-02-0309.

103. George Washington, "To the Corporation of Rhode Island College," in Guild, *Life, Times, and Correspondence of James Manning*, 434–35.

them."[104] Despite his reticence to discuss his personal faith, Washington's public support of religion even further garnered the respect and the admiration of Baptists, who lauded Washington for his religious character. Thomas Baldwin confessed, "You cannot help, my brethren, observing a coincidence of character and circumstances, between the Jewish Lawgiver and American Patriot."[105] At least among Baptists, such a comparison would hardly ever have been made of Jefferson. Washington was not only the ideal republican; he gave Baptists hope that America would be a nation of both religion *and* religious freedom.

Nevertheless, with the death of Washington and the rise of America's first political parties, Baptists eventually favored those patriots who mirrored their own politics. Frontier missionary John Mason Peck named his youngest son after John Adams, revealing his allegiance to the Federalist party.[106] Just as John Leland extolled his "hero" Jefferson, the militantly Federalist Jonathan Maxcy favored his own heroes:

> No man stands so high in the esteem and veneration of all America as Washington; and yet perhaps, it may with truth be asserted, that the services rendered Adams and Franklin; though less splendid, as from their nature they must be, are nevertheless not less meritorious; not less important, than those performed by Washington. Had it not been for those services, perhaps Washington himself, with all his greatness could not have achieved what he did.[107]

Richard Furman was even more complimentary of his fellow Federalist Alexander Hamilton. In a funeral sermon after Hamilton's tragic death from a now-infamous duel with Aaron Burr, Furman attempted to defend the founder's legacy. Reminding his audience of Hamilton's authorship of *The Federalist*, Furman preached, "His learned comments on [the Constitution] afterwards, and masterly reasoning in its support, are known to have contributed more towards its adoption, than the labors of any other man." After praising Hamilton's endeavors in the department of treasury, Furman paid homage to "a man of transcendent genius; a refined scholar; an accomplished gentleman; an eloquent, powerful orator; a profound civilian; a

---

104. "Washington's Farewell Address," *The Papers of George Washington*, September 19, 1796, http://gwpapers.virginia.edu/documents/washingtons-farewell-address/.

105. Baldwin, *Sermon, delivered to the Second Baptist Society in Boston, on Lord's Day, December 29, 1799*, 23.

106. Peck, *Forty Years of Pioneer Life*, 215. Peck got the chance to meet President Adams while on a visit to Washington, DC in 1826.

107. Maxcy, "Discourse, Delivered in the Chapel of South Carolina College," 287.

heroic soldier; a great statesman; and, I hope I may add, without exaggeration, or offence to any, a sincere patriot."[108]

Baptists may have been "the most consistent, the most numerous, and the most effective" dissenters in the fight for a separation of church and state, but the American Revolution reoriented the way that Americans viewed Baptists, and, in turn, the way Baptists viewed their new nation.[109] Although Baptists in New England had been suspected of loyalism during the war due to their protests against religious persecution, and while full disestablishment of religion was a slow, grinding process even in the most liberal of states, Baptists' ardent patriotism in the War of Independence helped soften the prejudices that had long been carried against them by their countrymen and emboldened their pursuit of religious liberty. In some ways, the Revolution also changed the way that many Baptists viewed themselves, as the national identity helped ameliorate relations between rival Baptists. In 1787, the same year that Virginia ratified the Constitution, Regular and Separate Baptists officially united in a reformed Kehukee Association (VA). One year later, in language that reflected the spirit of the new nation, the Association recorded their motion that "those *bars* which heretofore subsisted between the baptists amongst us . . . be taken down; . . . and that the names *Regular* and *Separate* be buried in oblivion, and that we should be henceforth known to the world by the name of the *United Baptist*."[110] National unity bolstered denominational unity. America was indeed a home for Baptists, they believed. With the imprimatur of the founders and a solid service record from the war, Baptists wielded their patriotism as political leverage in order to engage their fellow citizens in the nation they had helped create.[111] As a result, the future of the denomination seemed, at least to Baptists, tied to the fate of the American nation itself.

---

108. Furman, *Death's Dominion Over Man Considered*, 240–41.

109. McLoughlin, *Soul Liberty*, 20.

110. Burkitt and Read, *Concise History of the Kehukee Baptist Association from its Original Rise Down*, 98.

111. Baptists even sought the wisdom of the founders on non-political matters. In March 1813, from Georgetown, South Carolina, Baptist John Waldo wrote a letter to Thomas Jefferson, asking the aging founder to examine an English grammar he had recently written. Originally from the North, Waldo had temporarily pastored the Baptist church in Georgetown. However, he eventually became an educator, running a boys' academy (where he taught William B. Johnson, the inaugural president of the Southern Baptist Convention in 1845) and writing a number of English and Latin grammar textbooks. Jefferson responded with lengthy notes on the English language (John Waldo to Thomas Jefferson, March 27, 1813 https://founders.archives.gov/documents/Jefferson/03-06-02-0036).

Chapter 3

Baptist Republicans

BAPTISTS COULD BE THE most ardent of patriots and the most zealous of partisans. After Washington's presidency, the "party spirit" that gripped the nation also seized Baptists, and Sunday mornings were not always insulated from the politics of the age. When Francis Wayland, the president of Brown University (1827–1855), reflected back to his childhood in the early days of the republic, he recalled that certain pastoral candidates were judged not by their piety, but according to their politics:

> You would hear a congregation of immortal beings, nay, you would hear pious men, asking concerning a minister of the gospel, not, Is he devout, but, What are his politics? The very *sine qua non* of his acceptableness, as his supporting of their candidate, and approving their measures; and it was not serious disqualification if he were prepared, when the occasion presented, to anathematize their opponents.[1]

Wayland was by no means the only Baptist to observe an alarming partisan divide. John Leland called the rise of parties a "kind of revolution" in America.[2] Some pastors warned that such division could sunder the union itself. "I am sure many well-informed persons have been seriously alarmed at the progress of party disaffection," Thomas Baldwin warned his audience in 1802, "and have feared lest some untoward circumstance should provoke the mad attempt to divide our hitherto happy Republic. Should we once begin the work of separation, God knows where it may end, and what

---

1. Wayland, *Death of Ex-Presidents in Occasional Discourses*, 93.
2. Leland, "Oration," 262.

the consequences may be."[3] Baldwin was an outspoken Republican in a state not known for its friendliness to Baptists, but as chaplain of the General Court of Massachusetts, he was often conciliatory to the Standing Order.[4] Nevertheless, Baldwin and Baptists across America did not like what they saw in the infant republic. In 1801, the Georgia Baptist Association reported that "amongst many of you, a friendly, uniting and endearing spirit is too little cultivated."[5] In 1807, the Elkhorn Association in Kentucky announced, "It is with deep distress we view our society as convulsed and mutilated by intestine broils and contentions, which appears to us to be more the wrath of man than the righteousness of God. These things ought not to be. You have not so learned in the school of Christ."[6]

This "party disaffection" took root as deeply in the Baptist denomination as in any other religious group in the new nation. As a result, Baptists went to great lengths to condemn it. Some Baptists even exhibited partisanship while condemning partisanship. Before his close friend Charles Cotesworth Pinckney opposed James Madison in the Presidential election of 1808 (Pinckney lost in both 1804 and 1808), Richard Furman wrote an op-ed in the Charleston newspaper and Federalist organ *The Courier*. After painting Pinckney as a man of character and an "influential advocate of religious as well as civil liberty," Furman concluded,

> The State of South Carolina gave the casting vote in a former election and it is probable, will have it in her power to do so at the next ensuing. A laudable self-love calls for her attention to her distinguished citizen, who by the voice of the northern states is invited to the Presidential chair. Gratitude for important services requires it of her. Mr. Madison may be a good and great man; we know that Gen. Pinckney is so. Let not our citizens then under the influence of party spirit again do violence to their friendship and their feelings as well as justice and propriety, by withholding their votes from a man, most worthy of them, and by bestowing them on one who has no claim to their confidence and regard.[7]

---

3. Baldwin, *Sermon, Delivered Before His Excellency Caleb Strong*, 28.

4. Chessman, *Memoir of Rev. Thomas Baldwin, D.D.*, 63.

5. Georgia Baptist Association, "The Present State of Religion Amongst Our Churches," in Mercer, *History of the Georgia Baptist Association*, 100.

6. Elkhorn Baptist Association, Circular Letter, 1807, from Elkhorn Baptist Association Minutes (1807), 4.

7. Foster, *Life and Works of Dr. Richard Furman, D.D.*, 136–37.

Furman's censure of a "party spirit" was a Federalist hallmark. Nevertheless, Federalist Baptists were not the only ones to show their political colors underneath a banner of non-partisanship. In an 1814 issue of *The Massachusetts Baptist Missionary Magazine*, of which Thomas Baldwin was the sole editor from 1803 to 1817, an anonymous woman wrote a letter to the editor, stating, "I long for *peace*—not to gratify the avarice or pride of this or that political party;—but, that the peaceable kingdom of Jesus might be made universally known; and especially, that it might be made known to the original proprietors of our soil—the now ferocious allies of Britain."[8] Even those Baptists who decried the evils of partisanship could sometimes not help but belie their true political leanings.

Not surprisingly, the War of 1812 only widened the political gap. In Maine, where the war was generally unpopular, the Cumberland Association issued a circular letter rebuking "the unreasonable jealousy, acrimony and illiberality manifested by political partisans," the "illicit and unwarrantable measures, resorted to to carry their point, to increase a party, or to gain a place of trust, honor or emolument," and "the divisions and party spirit now predominant among all classes of our citizens, which have wrecked that happy union once so prominent among the only free people on earth."[9] If Baptists captured the *zeitgeist* of the early republic by tapping into its spirit of liberty and optimism, they also adopted its tendency for dissension.[10]

The Party of Jefferson

The Baptist support for the Republican party during this tumultuous chapter of American history has been well documented by historians.[11] Baptists spoke openly and often about their Republican convictions. Decades after the first party system, Francis Wayland recalled, "In the church to which my father belonged, I have frequently heard it mentioned that there was but one member who was not a Republican; and the wonder among his brethren was, how so good a man could, in so important a matter, err so

---

8. "Extract of a Letter to the Editor, dated March, 1814," 3:136.

9. Burrage, *History of the Baptists in Maine*, 151.

10. One group that did not represent Baptist optimism were the Primitive Baptists, who believed they were living in a new dark age. *History of the Church of God* (1886), written by long-serving Primitive Baptist elders Cushing Biggs Hassell and Sylvester Hassell, has been regarded by many as the definitive history of Primitive Baptists.

11. Kidd, *God of Liberty*, 38, 52, 177, 223, 230, 238–40, 243; Hatch, *Democratization of American Christianity*, 9, 10, 21, 34, 42–43; Driesbach, *Thomas Jefferson and the Wall of Separation Between Church and State*, 1, 3, 6, 17, 20, 23–24, 52–53, 82, 95–97, 105, 120, 130.

grievously."[12] This kind of Republican majority was commonplace among white male Baptists in cities and towns across the union. In Poultney, Vermont, Congregationalists were Federalists "with one exception," and Baptists were Republicans "with one exception, also."[13]

More than any other issue, religious freedom drove Baptists to yoke themselves politically with Enlightenment liberals who cared little for their evangelical faith but who nonetheless shared their desire to untether the civil from the ecclesiastical. For both Deists and Baptists, the conscience was sacrosanct, even if these groups decided to exercise their consciences very differently, and even if Baptists judged Deists to be heretics. In the public forum and even in the pulpit, theological enemies often became political allies. For example, in a sermon on 2 Kings 6:6 ("The Iron Did Swim"), Georgia pastor Abraham Marshall boasted in "our holy religion" before commending "the glorious Jefferson, deep read in the laws of nations, replete in the policy of the past and present ages—able to fabricate constitutions and laws equal to the glories of our rising realm."[14] Noticeably absent was any mention of Jefferson's faith. Baptist Republicans offered up Jefferson as an example of Christian ideals, even if he wasn't a Christian himself. Marshall even wrote a piece of poetry praising the local teachers and students by likening them to the two men who occupied the highest place of honor in Marshall's mind:

> One high encomium, as a bounty,
> I'll pass upon Columbia County.
> Her schools and scholars, sure, will rate
> Higher than any in the State.
> They're eloquent upon the stage,
> Equal to any of the age:
> No doubt they'll shine in time to come,
> Like Jefferson or Washington.[15]

Amazingly, anti-slavery or "emancipation" Baptists could even cite Jefferson, a slaveholder, against the institution of slavery. In a sermon in Versailles, Kentucky in 1806, Baptist preacher Carter Tarrant condemned "the political evil" of slavery by quoting liberally from Jefferson's *Notes on the State of Virginia* and from one of Jefferson's speeches on the close of the international slave trade.[16]

12. Wayland and Wayland, *Memoir of the Life and Labors of Francis Wayland*, 14.
13. Joslin et al., *History of the Town of Poultney*, 74.
14. Marshall, "Sermon, on II Kings VI. 6," 202.
15. Marshall, "Lazy Student's Apology," 204–5.
16. Najar, *Evangelizing the South*, 158.

The "Mammoth Priest" John Leland, a self-professed "dyed in the skin" Republican, has become for most scholars the *par excellence* of Baptist Republicanism.[17] According to L. H. Butterfield, Leland was a "Jeffersonian Itinerant" and "as courageous and resourceful a champion of the rights of conscience as America has produced."[18] In his recent biography of Leland, Eric C. Smith has called him a "thoroughgoing Jeffersonian."[19] For others, Leland was a picture of Jeffersonian politics more than Jefferson himself. Padraig Riley has argued that Leland was "far more representative of the new class of men Jeffersonian politics brought into power, relative unknowns who rose to prominence in the midst of a democratizing, anti-deferential political culture."[20] As Amanda Porterfield has attested, Leland hailed from hotbeds of Republicanism:

> Baptist demands for the right to worship without impediment enabled the success of Jeffersonian politics. In Virginia, harassment of Baptists by the established Anglican Church since colonial days contributed to popular support for the Virginia Statute of Religious Freedom drafted by Jefferson in 1779 and passed into law in 1786. In Massachusetts and the District of Maine, where Baptists had long been subjected to legal discrimination, Republicans drew heaviest support from towns with strong Baptist churches. Republican political activists counted on Baptists as a base of support in New England and Baptists came through; in John Leland's hometown of Cheshire, Massachusetts, Federalists never drew more than 7 out of 241 votes in the years between 1800 and 1812.[21]

Just as "the very name of Washington" had been elevated to near-Messianic status, so Leland exalted Jefferson and described him in redemptive terms.[22] In Leland's pantheon of legends, the "great names of Alexander, Caesar, Washington, or Jefferson" came to mind.[23] However, instead of Washington delivering America from the despotism of Britain, Jefferson rescued his people from the tyranny of Federalists. Like Jesus Christ who bruised the head of the Serpent (Gen. 3:15), Leland envisioned the "Apostle

---

17. Greene, "Further Sketches," 32; Leland, "Letter to Hon. R. M. Johnson, June 9, 1834," 648.
18. Butterfield, "Elder John Leland, Jeffersonian Itinerant," 157.
19. Smith, *John Leland*, 5.
20. Riley, *Slavery and the Democratic Conscience*, 22.
21. Porterfield, *Conceived in Doubt*, 152–53.
22. Greene, "Further Sketches," 54.
23. Leland, "Government of Christ a Christocracy," 277.

of Liberty" as striking an initial severe blow to the Standing Order. "At the appointment of Mr. Jefferson," Leland bragged, "the Federalists received a deadly wound, which has never healed, although the beast struggled for life, and kicked at every measure of the administration of government until it died."[24] At times, Baptist partisanship was as biblically rooted and reasoned as Baptist patriotism.

More than most, Baptists imagined "the revolution of 1800" and the election of Thomas Jefferson to the presidency as its own form of independence. John Leland considered 1800 "as radical in its tendency, as that which took place in 1776."[25] Even Baptists on the other side of the political aisle could not ignore the social unrest and political upheaval that pierced through the American landscape with a shrill cry of liberty. When the Philadelphia Association proposed a general conference in 1800, the Federalist-laden Charleston Association cautiously replied that there "appears to be some danger of abuse arising."[26] But Baptist Republicans only mocked this kind of Federalist fearmongering. In their view, Jefferson had not come to bring tyranny or anarchy but freedom, something that many Baptists had not received in full under the yoke of the Standing Order or the Episcopalian regime. According to Daniel Merrill, the only reason for the alarm at Jefferson's presidency was a deep-seeded opposition to liberty itself:

> When it was contemplated to elect Thomas Jefferson into the Presidential chair, there was, as many of us perfectly remember, and hue and cry through New England, Religion is in danger, our meeting houses will become stables for horses, and our Bibles burnt, should Jefferson be President. Why was all this noise, this bustle, this fear excited? Why every excitement used to inflame the passions of the people, and every prejudice and superstition enlisted against Jefferson's election? For this simple reason, he was known to be hostile to superstition and religious tyranny; those twin furies which have been, for a long time, drunken with the blood of the saints.[27]

Merrill's Republicanism was not founded so much on the orthodoxy or sainthood of Jefferson, but against the perceived injustices and hypocrisy of Federalists. The very people who warned in 1800 that religion was in danger, Merrill argued, were those who posed the greatest threat to true religion.

---

24. Leland, "Part of a Speech, Delivered at Suffield, Connecticut, on the First Jubilee of the United States," 520.

25. Leland, "Oration," 263.

26. In Cook, *Biography of Richard Furman*, 173.

27. Merrill, *Balaam Disappointed*, 9.

Therefore, most Baptists supported Jefferson not because he brought true religion to the Gentiles, but because He spoke prophetically against the irreligion of America's Jerusalem. One Primitive Baptist newspaper quoted Jefferson in his belief that the "Eastern States will be the last to come over" to religious liberty "on account of the dominion of the Clergy, who had got a smell of union between Church and State."[28] In 1834, a year after the disestablishment of America's last state church in Massachusetts, John Leland thought back to the election of Jefferson in 1800 and remembered how "the pulpits rang with alarms, and the presses groaned with predictions, that the Bibles would all be burned; meeting-houses destroyed; marriage bonds dissolved, and anarchy infidelity and licentiousness would fill the land." He scoffed, "These clerical warnings and editorial prophecies all failed."[29] The disestablishment process in America combined with the meteoric rise of the Baptist denomination during the Second Great Awakening validated the divine appointment of Jefferson and the Republican party in the eyes of most white Baptists.[30]

The sun was indeed rising for the Baptists in America. In a circular letter in 1804, the Georgia Baptist Association noted that "Civil and religious liberty have spread with astonishing rapidity," boasting, "What grand events have taken place in half a century past? And we believe still more great, more good, more glorious things are just at the door."[31] In terms of its impact on religious liberty, 1800 was a revolution of sorts for Baptists, a people who aligned themselves with anti-Trinitarians in order to seek refuge from the persecution from their fellow evangelicals. Although Federalists like Jonathan Maxcy and Samuel Stillman aligned themselves with the "splendid" John Adams and were suspicious of Jefferson's beliefs, the extent to which Baptist Republicans were aware of Jefferson's theology is not exactly certain.[32] Nevertheless, the lack of moral or spiritual commentary on Jefferson from Baptists suggests that they were far more interested in

---

28. "Church and State," 64.

29. Leland, "Address at a Democratic Meeting Held at Cheshire, August 28, 1834," 652.

30. Baptists were not the only group to celebrate the new-found religious liberty in the land. New Divinity Presbyterian Lyman Beecher hailed disestablishment as "the best thing that ever happened to the State of Connecticut." He acknowledged that it "cut the churches loose from dependence on state support" and that it "threw them wholly on their own resources and on God" (Hirrel, *Children of Wrath*, 81). Also see Koester, *Harriet Beecher Stowe*, 26.

31. Ray, *Daniel and Abraham Marshall*, 230.

32. Maxcy, "Discourse, Delivered in the Chapel of Rhode Island College," 430.

what the President was doing for their religion than in what their religion was doing for the President.

For this reason, Baptist Republicanism did not subside under President Madison, another Deist from Virginia who had once claimed that "Religion flourishes in greater purity without than with the aid of Government."[33] As recent scholarship has shown, "Madison cultivated a more visceral commitment to religious freedom" than Jefferson after "he observed persecution against Virginia dissenters in the 1760s and '70s."[34] And at least at the state level, Madison had as much if not more influence upon the arduous process of full disestablishment as did Jefferson. For example, "in 1776 Madison stood virtually alone in Virginia's assembly in support of anything resembling disestablishment of the Church of England." Furthermore, his *Memorial and Remonstrance* against Patrick Henry's general assessment bill in 1785 had "proven the more timeless American document on the subject of religious freedom."[35] According to Carl H. Esbeck and Jonathan J. Den Hartog, "Even in Virginia, it was the writings and actions of James Madison, in both theory and practice, that played the leading role in disestablishment. Jefferson's *A Bill for Establishing Religious Freedom* . . . was widely admired by free thinkers. But it was replicated only in Rhode Island, and even there only after first excising the bill's phrases discounting theism."[36] Ultimately, the religion clauses of the First Amendment were a team effort by Baptists and Madison to realize their shared vision of religious liberty in America.[37]

Before Virginia's Constitutional Convention, John Leland originally opposed ratification as a threat to religious freedom. "What is clearest of all—Religious liberty, is not sufficiently secured," he wrote to the Antifederalist candidate.[38] But in 1788, Leland and the Baptists of Virginia changed their mind about the Constitution. The reason was James Madison. Madison was not only an architect of the Constitution, but in 1788 he was running as a delegate from Orange County to Virginia's ratifying convention. Leland, who was also from Orange County, had actually led the opposition to Madison. In Leland's view, the Federal Constitution lacked a bill of rights which protected the fundamental freedoms of Americans. However, Madison, another non-evangelical founder, struck a deal with the well-known evangelical preacher: in return for the entire Baptist voting bloc and support

---

33. Madison, "To Edward Livingston, July 10, 1822," 275–76.
34. Kidd, *Thomas Jefferson*, 62.
35. Esbeck, "Disestablishment in Virginia, 1776–1802," 143, 157.
36. Esbeck and Hartog, "Introduction," 16–17.
37. Kidd and Hankins, *Baptists in America*, 74.
38. In Smith, *John Leland*, 76.

for ratification, Madison would include a bill of rights in the Constitution. As Eric C. Smith has shown in his recent biography of the Baptist, "Leland had attained such prominence in the Baptist movement that James Madison himself had come to him, hat in hand, to seek his blessing among Virginia's Baptists."[39] Leland, the itinerant revivalist, was also a savvy negotiator (and eventual party whip). The result was the First Amendment. Madison would deliver on his promise in Congress. And Leland would continue campaigning against religious tyranny and extolling Jefferson, whose 1779 Bill for Establishing Religious Freedom finally passed into Virginia law in 1786 largely through Madison's efforts.

With this proven track record in favor of religious liberty for dissenters, President Madison was a friend of Baptists and Baptists of Madison—even in war. (James Madison Pendleton, the Landmarkist Baptist, was even named after the fourth president.)[40] After William Parkinson defended the War of 1812 at First Baptist Church of New York City from Psalm 46:9 ("He makes wars cease to the end of the earth"), the congregation sang a hymn at the end of the service as a prayer for the nation. Before interceding for Congress and political leaders, they sang their requests on behalf of President Madison, most likely revealing the political sympathies of the congregation:

> Our President with wisdom crown,
> His soul with thy rich grace adorn;
> Resolve his heart, 'midst all his foes,
> "To launch the stream which duty shows."[41]

Not far from Parkinson, when David Jones returned to the chaplaincy for the third time in 1813, he rode from New Brunswick to New York in a stage coach to join the Army of the North. Inside the coach, the subject of politics emerged:

> Among them was a young lawyer, who was criticizing, in no measured terms, the policy and spirit of President Madison. A "weak administration—a miserably weak administration," was the epithet which he applied to the powers that then were. Mr. Jones had sat quietly, taking but little part in the animated discussion. But now he woke up—"Yes Sir," said he, "it is a weak administration,—a miserably weak administration—if President Madison were half the man he ought to be," looking full in the eye of the young lawyer,—"he would have hung, long ago,

---

39. Smith, *John Leland*, 125.
40. Pendleton, *Reminiscences of a Long Life*, 8.
41. Parkinson, *Sermon, Delivered in the Meeting-House of the First Baptist Church*, 27.

scores of such confounded Tories as you!" "Sir," said the lawyer, with a great deal of warmth,—"if you were not an old man, you would not say that to me." "Yes, yes Sir"—replied Mr. Jones, shaking his head energetically toward the angry youth—"and if I were not an old man, you would not dare to say that to *me*."[42]

Some Baptists were quite literally willing to fight for their country *and* for the Republican party. "Madison's War" only exacerbated the partisan divide.

Although achievements like the Louisiana Purchase and the diminution of the national debt promised to "keep in memory the presidency of Mr. Jefferson," Madison's administration was perhaps best remembered by Baptist Republicans not just for the second conflict with Britain but for what it ultimately achieved at home: the death of the Federalist party.[43] When New England Federalists convened from December 15, 1814 to January 5, 1815 in Hartford, Connecticut to discuss their political and economic interests endangered from the war, the report that ensued did not explicitly advocate secession, but its strong stance on states' rights appeared to Republicans as treasonous during wartime, and especially as the conflict was coming to a close at the Treaty of Ghent (December 24, 1814). Just two days before the three representatives from the Hartford Convention left for Washington to meet with President Madison about their demands, the news of the British defeat at New Orleans made it to Boston. Just a day before they arrived, the treaty reached the nation's capital. Madison refused an official meeting with the Hartford commissioners. "What Federalists intended as their moment of triumph turned into the beginning of their end as a viable national party. In light of the news of Jackson's victory at New Orleans and the signing of the peace treaty, Federalists now appeared as traitors in the public mind."[44] The Hartford Convention was such a black mark upon Federalists that it sounded the death knell for the party itself.[45]

---

42. Rogers, *Life, Journal and Works of David Jones*, 120.

43. Leland, "Part of a Speech, Delivered at Suffield, Connecticut, on the First Jubilee of the United States," 520.

44. Cheathem, *Andrew Jackson and the Rise of the Democratic Party*, 23.

45. J. M. Pendleton had a somewhat ambivalent view of the conclusion to the war, perhaps revealing how Baptists came to view the conflict itself over time: "Men are, in some respects, very much like children . . . England claimed 'the right of search;' we denied it, and the issue was joined. After two years' fighting peace was agreed upon, but the question which brought on the war was ignored in the treaty of peace. England did not relinquish the right she claimed, and the United States did not insist that she should. This was like children's play" (Pendleton, *Reminiscences of a Long Life*, 9).

Baptist Republicans were unrelenting in their ridicule for the Convention. Daniel Merrill jeered, "Witness their Hartford Convention and their mission to Washington; the latter of which has met with its deserved contempt: The members of the other will be of lasting ill-fame." He continued, "Now Britain, the scourge of the world, was ready to give us peace upon terms honorable to America; but the displeasure of the Lord was not, as yet, sufficiently manifested. New Orleans was the place He chose, to complete their disgrace."[46] John Leland's disdain for the Hartford Convention was so severe that he wrote an anonymous satirical letter as a Federalist! Designated only as "Broken-Leg," Leland mocked everything from their love for high taxes to their contempt for Napoleon Bonaparte. He then took aim at the Hartford Convention:

> The late treaty of peace is an unkind affair to me. I once said that the government could not be kicked into war, and did all in my power to prevent, not the aggression of Great Britain, but the declaration of war, to fulfill my prediction; but I failed—war was declared. I then said that Great Britain would never make peace while Madison presided; and used to tell my neighbors, at election terms, that the democrats had plunged them into a ruinous war; but, if they placed the Federalists in power, peace would immediately follow; but peace is made while Madison presides, without the aid of Federalists, or the Hartford Convention. But even here, I find some food to cheer me. Great Britain has not agreed to desist from a single thing that the war was declared for; the democrats, therefore, I say, have lavished blood and treasure for nothing.[47]

For Leland, who was not known for his subtlety, the terms of Jay's Treaty in the aftermath of the American Revolution had begun in earnest the era of political parties. The subject of war debts and the value of slaves "confirmed the hostility of the Federalists and Republicans, which had been rising for some time, so strongly, that for twenty years the pulpits rang and the presses groaned with anathemas against each other."[48] Conversely, in the view of Leland and most Republicans, it was the Treaty of Ghent two decades later, and more specifically Jackson's victory at New Orleans, that cemented the informal end of the nation's first party system. Partisanship had arisen from the denouement of one war with Britain only to be terminated—or

---

46. Merrill, *Balaam Disappointed*, 13.
47. Leland, "Broken-Leg," 448–49.
48. Leland, "Part of a Speech, Delivered at Suffield, Connecticut, on the First Jubilee of the United States," 520.

translated—by the conclusion of another. Thereafter, Leland would continue to align himself with those candidates who he believed would defend religious liberty against the tyranny of "the self-named peace party, who are always at war with their own government."[49] For this reason, according to L. F. Greene, "In his attachment to the administrations of Jefferson, Madison, Jackson and Van Buren, he [Leland] felt that he was contending for the same principles of democracy that nerved the arms and strengthened the hearts of the whigs of '76."[50] Foremost among those democratic principles was the sanctity of the human conscience.

God and the Individual

When John Leland refused to administer the Lord's Supper to his congregation due to its inefficiency in saving souls, he did so as a matter of conscience.[51] According to Leland, who, surprisingly enough, enjoyed the support of his own church for his controversial decision, no external structure or tradition had the authority to determine where and how and to whom a person practiced their religion.[52] His most popular treatise, published in 1791, was entitled *The Rights of Conscience Inalienable, And, Therefore, Religious Opinions Not Cognizable by Law; Or, The High-Flying Churchman, Stripped of His Legal Robe, Appears a Yaho*. The colorful title was also consistent with Leland's overarching project: to keep the conscience holy by keeping it free. "If government can answer for individuals at the day of judgment," Leland declared, "let men be controlled by it in religious matters; otherwise let men be free."[53] In his mind, the only way to sanctify the conscience was to keep anyone or anything from forcefully imposing their will upon it.

49. Leland, "Address to the Association of the Sons of Liberty, Cheshire, March 4, 1813," 373.

50. Greene, "Further Sketches," 51.

51. Nathan O. Hatch explains it thus: "Leland was too iconoclastic to permit a religious structure to form around him; even his relationship with his own congregation was troubled over his refusal, as a matter of conscience, to administer the Lord's Supper. Leland defended his position by saying that in thirty years of practical experience he had never seen the ordinance move a single sinner to conversion" (Hatch, *Democratization of American Christianity*, 100).

52. For an examination of the Lord's Supper controversy at Third Baptist Cheshire, see Smith, *John Leland*, 111–18. Sydney E. Ahlstrom posits that "probably most of the preachers shared the feelings of John Leland" in his "blending of revivalistic and 'orthodox' tendencies" that emphasized both the providence of God and the freedom of the human will. Representative of the age, Leland's theological individualism was mirrored by his political individualism (Ahlstrom, *Religious History of the American People*, 322).

53. Leland, *Rights of Conscience Inalienable*, 181.

Therefore, consistent with most Baptist Republicans, Leland was prone to describe religion less in corporate terms and even less in structural terms and more as a relationship between God and the sinner. He stated, "let it be observed, that religion is a matter entirely between God and individuals."[54] In *The Rights of Conscience Inalienable*, Leland repeatedly emphasized this point: "religion is a matter between God and individuals: the religious opinions of men not being the objects of civil government, nor in any way under its control."[55] Although more communitarian in his religion, Isaac Backus held much to the same Republican mantra. In *A Door Opened for Christian Liberty* (1783), he asked, "since religion is ever a matter between God and individuals, how can any man become a member of a religious society without his own consent? And how can a man who believes it to be impossible practically say that it is possible without contracting guilt to his conscience? This is the exact state of our controversy about religious liberty."[56] The Danbury Baptists agreed. In their letter to President Jefferson, they began by stating, "Our sentiments are uniformly on the side of religious liberty—that religion is at all times and places a matter between God and individuals."[57] If all Baptists advocated for freedom of religion, Baptist Republicans affirmed and re-affirmed the individuality of that religion.

Since virtually every Baptist was principally concerned with protecting their liberty of conscience, it might be said that Baptist Republicans and Federalists quarreled over the best way to procure and protect this most sacred freedom. In general, Baptist Republicans emphasized the *restraint* of government and the importance of individual rights while Baptist Federalists stressed the *responsibility* of government and the importance of public virtue. These differences were not so much in principle, but in degree. While each party contained elements of the other, Baptists in the party of Jefferson were more prone to believe that civil government was merely the best alternative in a sinful world and that the public good was achieved when religion was privatized. Abraham Marshall called democratic government a "necessary evil" and John Leland a "choice among evils."[58] On the other hand, their Federalist counterparts typically accentuated the "energy" of government and the obligation for service in the public forum. One conceived the ideal government as protecting men from false religion; the other conceived of true religion as sustaining the ideal government. In short, Baptist Federalists

---

54. Leland, "Virginia Chronicle," 108.
55. Leland, *Rights of Conscience Inalienable*, 181.
56. Backus, "Door Opened for Christian Liberty," 432–33.
57. Danbury Baptist Association, "From the Danbury Baptist Association," 408.
58. Marshall, *Daniel and Abraham Marshall*, 180; Leland, "Blow at the Root," 238.

did not trust a godless government to protect their religious freedom and Baptist Republicans did not trust a religious government to keep its hands out of their free religion.

For this reason, Baptist Republicans frequently employed the Jeffersonian language of "rights" to convey their individualist vision of the church-state relationship. For John Leland, this was the heart of the issue in a nutshell. "Gentlemen, you have taken notice that some men are always contending for the energy of government, while others are pleading for the rights of the people." Predictably, he then added, "I would as soon give my vote to a wolf to be a shepherd, as to a man, who is always contending for the energy of government, to be a ruler."[59] In this sense, the difference between Republicans and Federalists, at least at Leland saw it, was found in the level of inherent virtue and goodness that each ascribed to government. Leland hypothesized,

> if the rights of the citizens clash with the energies of government or the letter of the law, the rights of the citizens should always have the pre-eminence; for natural right is anterior to all law. These rights are the gifts of God; constitutions and laws are the creatures of men. This is a glass in which we may see the faces of the two parties in the United States, let them be called by what names soever. In the construction or interpretation of those things that are necessarily obscure, or not expressly provided for, one has the honor of government, and his own honor and importance, for his land-mark; the other, the rights of the people for his polar star. One gratifies his own will, at the expense of being burnt in effigy by an indignant people; the other executes the known will of his constituents, to the sacrificing of his own opinion.[60]

Since the rights of the people were their "polar star," Baptist Republicans understood the freedom of conscience as the most basic right that a human being could possess. Leland echoed the language of the Declaration of Independence when he asserted, "religion is a matter between individuals and their God—a right inalienable—an article not within the cognizance of civil government, nor any way under its control."[61] Leland also absorbed this Republican grammar through James Madison who spoke to Leland in

---

59. Leland, "Oration," 266.

60. Leland, "Address Delivered at Pittsfield, Jan. 8, 1829," 542.

61. Leland, "Speech Delivered in the House of Representatives of Massachusetts, on the Subject of Religious Freedom, 1811," 353.

1788 about "a certain quantity of their rights."[62] As a result, Leland became so convinced of "the empire of natural individual rights" in America that he questioned the necessity of a bill of rights in a truly republican government.[63] After all, wasn't republicanism itself but a defense of individual rights?

Checks on Power

Of the 355 delegates to the Massachusetts ratifying convention who registered their vote in February 1788, over twenty were Baptists and five were Baptist ministers. "Virtually all of them came with instructions from their towns to vote against ratification."[64] Among the five ministers was the illustrious Isaac Backus, who shared the sentiment of most of his fellow Republicans that too much governmental power posed a deep threat to individual liberty.[65] Therefore, after Backus changed his mind and voted to ratify, he returned to his Middleborough constituents who were not pleased with his reversal. Backus records in his diary, "Elder Alden of Bellingham, Elder Rathbun of Pittsfield, Elder Tingley of Waterborough... all voted against it and so did two-thirds of the baptist members of the Convention, of which there were above twenty. Elder Stillman and I, with twelve Congregational ministers, voted for it, though doubtless with very different reasons."[66] Backus had found the prohibition of any religious tests for federal officeholders to be a sufficient step toward religious liberty in America. Although Backus was a Republican and Stillman a Federalist, they both believed that national unity was imperative for freedom of religion to thrive. One might say that Backus was thinking like a Federalist: every freedom needed a framework, every liberty needed leadership. No doubt the former Puritan in Backus had been more inclined to listen to the arguments in favor of ratification in 1788. Nevertheless, most Baptist Republicans did not adopt this mindset.

The Virginia Baptists laid out perhaps the clearest rationale for the Baptist hesitance to ratify the Constitution when they wrote plainly to President Washington in 1789, "When the Constitution first made its appearance in

---

62. Leland, "Letter to Hon. R. M. Johnson, June 9, 1834," 649.

63. Leland, "Extracts from a Letter to Hon. R. M. Johnson, March 29, 1830," 568; Leland, *Yankee Spy*, 220.

64. McLoughlin, *Soul Liberty*, 193.

65. Although Anti-Federalism was a diverse movement, Saul Cornell has identified 9 primary issues that appeared in Anti-Federalist writings. They include consolidation, aristocracy, representation, separation of powers, judicial tyranny, the absence of a Bill of Rights, taxes, a standing army, and extensive powers given to the executive branch. (Cornell, *Other Founders*, 30).

66. McLoughlin, *Soul Liberty*, 193.

Virginia, we, as a society had unusual strugglings of mind, fearing that the liberty of conscience, dearer to us than property or life, was not sufficiently secured. Perhaps our jealousies were heightened by the usage we received in Virginia, under the regal government, when mobs, fines, bonds and prisons were our frequent repast." Memories of persecution were still fresh in the Baptist mind. Therefore, quite naturally, they were hesitant to allot more authority to a government administered by those who had once violated their freedoms. Once again, Baptists found themselves between a rock and a political hard place: either secure liberty and flirt with anarchy or promote unity for freedom's sake and sign off on despotism: "Convinced, on the one hand, that without an effective National Government, the States would fall into disunion and all the consequent evils; and, on the other hand, fearing that we should be accessory to some religious oppression, should any one society in the Union preponderate over the rest."[67] The letter to Washington, authored by a committee chaired by John Leland, expressed the Baptist Republican plight in a way that very few other documents ever did.[68] Washington and other Virginia leaders heard them loud and clear. Calling the First Amendment a Baptist "triumph," Thomas S. Kidd and Barry Hankins explain, "In the Constitution, Baptist pressure pushed Madison further than he originally sought to go."[69] Once-skeptical Baptists like Sylvanus Haynes now believed that the U.S. Constitution was "the nearest to perfection of any we have ever seen" and that a "good constitution" was that "which secures the equal rights of every citizen."[70]

Especially in the midst of a "Great Revival" that reinforced the personal nature of faith, Baptists believed that no person could believe for another and no church could determine the proceedings of another. In this sense, Baptists could be both epistemological and ecclesiastical individualists. As a result, Baptist Republicans were often apprehensive to subject themselves to governing bodies outside their local congregation. For instance, in Cheshire, Massachusetts, Elder Peter Werden reasoned that his church could not join an association because he did not believe "the rights and liberties of particular churches are sufficiently secured by what is said in your plan."[71] When the Scipio General Conference met in Aurelius, New York in September 1801 for the purpose of forming an association, a "diversity of opinions prevailed in the churches" and were expressed either by delegate or

---

67. Greene, "Further Sketches," 53.
68. Howell, *Early Baptists of Virginia*, 226.
69. Kidd and Hankins, *Baptists in America*, 74.
70. Haynes, *Sermon, Delivered Before His Excellency the Governor*, 4.
71. McLoughlin, *Soul liberty*, 8.

in letter form. "Many, ever watchful against any infringement of individual rights, and ever vigilant in their defense of Baptist views of unrestricted liberty of conscience, and church independence, expressed their fears" about forming such a body.[72] Even Isaac Backus was originally cautious of Baptist associations. The latter did not function like presbyteries or consociations in determining clergy hiring or membership, however, Baptists often believed they still possessed far too much authority over the local church. Many of the same arguments that Baptists wielded against ecclesiastical power they also used against civil powers.[73] In the Baptist mind, local church autonomy and religious liberty were both linked to the freedom of conscience. For this reason, especially in New England and in Virginia where Baptist Republicanism was strongest, Baptists were wary of a Constitution which seemed to limit their freedoms, a viewpoint held most strongly in the rural regions of the country.[74]

According to John Leland, who was, unlike many Federalists, happy that the Constitution did *not* mention God, the "genuine meaning of republicanism is self-government."[75] For most Baptist Republicans, the power of the vote was the greatest single weapon in defense of liberty. Leland called it the "stronghold of republicanism."[76] For Thomas Baldwin, free suffrage (for adult males) was "the very *primum mobile* in the republican system."[77] Neither Baptist Federalists nor Republicans could deny the existence of corruption in government. But whereas Federalists leaned heavily on public virtue as the cure for bad government, Republicans instead emphasized the temporary nature of office-holding. If an official failed to properly serve the American people, he could simply be replaced and a better candidate elected. In a republic, leaders worked for the people, not vice versa. Baldwin called this "right of electing our own civil rulers" the "distinguishing

---

72. Belden, *History of Cayuga Baptist Association*, 8.

73. As James A. Patterson has shown, Backus's "local church protectionism" was a forerunner to the Landmarkism of James Robinson Graves, who was also from New England (Patterson, *James Robinson Graves*, 6–7).

74. McLoughlin, *Soul Liberty*, 192.

75. Leland, "Miscellaneous Essays, in Prose and Verse," 428; Leland, "Oration," 267. Daniel Merrill also celebrated the fact that the Constitution included no mention of God. He asked, "Amongst all the Constitutions or governments of the European nations, is there one which does not assume the oversight and control of the church of Christ? But, happy America, the framers of thy Constitution thought it enough to frame laws to govern men, and to leave it with Christ, to give laws for the government of his own kingdom" (Merrill, *Balaam Disappointed*, 20).

76. Leland, "Address Delivered at Dalton, Massachusetts, January 8, 1831," 607.

77. Baldwin, *Discourse, Delivered Before the Ancient and Honourable Artillery Company*, 22–23.

criterion of a free government."[78] He thus warned, "If our elections are biased and corrupted, our government will be corrupt, and, consequently, our liberty will be endangered."[79] Consequently, both Leland and Baldwin campaigned against the idea (suggested by Federalists like Adams and Hamilton) that legislative or executive offices should be held for life. Leland would not brook those who wished to "make offices permanent," even going so far as to contend for an elective judiciary.[80] Thomas Baldwin insisted, "One great security against the abuse of power, is the short tenure by which it is held. No offices are made hereditary, and for this reason I conceive, that talents and virtue, which are essential qualifications, are not hereditary."[81] The non-genetic nature of virtue touched at the heart of republicanism and the American sense of honor.[82] Therefore, the idea that Americans would appoint life-long offices smelled to Republicans like monarchy, the very web of tyranny from which they had just freed themselves in 1776.

Baptist Republicans were also interested in checking the economic power of the American government. When Daniel Shays led his Rebellion in Western Massachusetts in 1786 against the high taxes forced through the legislature by wealthy eastern bankers and merchants, many rural Baptists sided with the Rebellion.[83] (A Separate Baptist Church in Coventry, Rhode Island even split over conflicts stemming from the Rebellion.[84]) Due to the grassroots and working-class identity of Baptists, taxes were scorned and viewed as an oppressive tendril of big government. This kind of political unrest was not relegated to the North. In John Leland's Virginia, a tax to reduce the debt from the war had compelled a group of farmers in 1787 in Greenbrier County to revolt.[85] In addition to the Alien and Sedition Acts and the insistence on a Standing Army, John Leland called Adams's direct tax one of "the most obnoxious" of the Federalist administration.[86] In the Baptist Republican mind, less taxes meant less spending. Only fiscal responsibility could erase a national debt which ultimately harmed the lower and middle classes. Baptists returned fire with Scripture. Citing Deuteronomy

78. Baldwin, *Sermon, Delivered Before His Excellency Caleb Strong*, 12.
79. Baldwin, *Sermon, Delivered Before His Excellency Caleb Strong*, 26.
80. Leland, "Elective Judiciary," 288–89.
81. Baldwin, *Sermon, Delivered Before His Excellency Caleb Strong*, 12.
82. See Smith, *American Honor*.
83. McLoughlin, *Soul Liberty*, 192.
84. Jones, *Economic and Social Transformation of Rural Rhode Island*, 192n73.
85. See Holton, *Unruly Americans and the Origins of the Constitution*, 10–13.
86. Leland, "Part of a Speech, Delivered at Suffield, Connecticut, on the First Jubilee of the United States," 520.

28:43–44, Sylvanus Haynes preached that "a national debt is considered as a national judgment, and Jehovah threatens it as a punishment for national sins."[87] With texts like Luke 19:14 and Isaiah 66:1–5, Isaac Backus opposed the use of paper currency because of how difficult it became to pay back debts.[88] For John Leland, the taxes imposed by Federalists did nothing to actually diminish the national debt. "Notwithstanding the immense sums collected by external and internal taxes," he reasoned, "yet the debt increased. An army and navy were raised, when there was no more prospect of war, than there is at the present moment."[89]

Ultimately, due to the prohibition of religious tests and the guarantee of religious liberty in 1791, the Constitution was accepted and even celebrated by the majority of Baptist Republicans despite their complaints about its loose interpretation by Federalists. After having been convinced by James Madison to support it, John Leland eventually concluded, "one of the great excellencies of the Constitution is, that no religious test is ever to be required to qualify any officer in any part of the government. To say that the Constitution is perfect, would be too high an encomium upon the fallibility of the framers of it; yet this may be said, that it is the best national machine that is now in existence."[90] Leland also strongly approved of the two-thirds vote to amend the Constitution, calling it "a signal of a patriotic people."[91] Any measure that placed authority in the hands of the people was cheered by Baptists, who believed in the "constitutional voice of sovereign people."[92] Due to their overarching commitment to separate church from state, Baptist Republicans welcomed the omission of God or religion from the language of the Constitution. Baptists like Daniel Merrill even mocked the Standing Order jeremiads after the ratification of the Constitution, as New England clergy decried the absence of God in the document and warned Americans of the godlessness to come.[93] Humorously distinguishing between a constitution and a catechism, Leland brought the issue back to God and the individual:

> To say that the government of the United States is perfect, would be arrogant; but I have no hesitancy in saying, that the Constitution has left religion *infallibly* where it should be left in all

---

87. Haynes, *Sermon Delivered Before His Excellency the Governor*, 15.
88. Backus, "Address to the Inhabitants of New England," 444.
89. Leland, "Oration," 262.
90. Leland, *Yankee Spy*, 220.
91. Leland, *Yankee Spy*, 229.
92. Leland, "Delivered at North Adams, on the 4th of March, 1831," 614.
93. Merrill, *Balaam Disappointed*, 9

government, viz.: in the hands of its author, as a matter between God and individuals; leaving an open door for Pagans, Turks, Jews or Christians, to fill any office in the government, without any religious test, to make them hypocrites.[94]

Although he did not approve of the lifetime appointments in the "judiciary despotism," Leland voted in favor of ratification and almost always endorsed the Constitution as a sublime legal document due to its protection of the freedom of conscience.[95] At stake for Baptist Republicans was their rights. Showing his Republican colors, Baldwin called the Constitution "the great charter of our rights and privileges" and "the foundation of our national civil policy."[96]

Still, political parties are never monolithic, and neither were Baptists. Therefore, for instance, even though John Leland and Isaac Backus were firm Republicans, they did not always align on matters of governmental authority and even the nature of democracy itself. As Nathan Hatch notes, "The greatest difference between Backus and Leland was their contrasting views of the social order."[97] On one hand, Leland rejected any hint of a Protestant establishment and even defended religious liberty for Muslims and Jews.[98] On the other hand, Backus supported religious tests for public offices and had actually been a leading proponent of the controversial Article 3 in the 1780 Massachusetts Constitution, which required every citizen to pay religious taxes to support their own churches. Leland would not countenance military chaplaincy because it bridged, albeit innocuously, church and state. David Jones, another staunch Republican, served as military chaplain for almost sixteen years![99] Republican Thomas Baldwin, who was repeatedly chosen chaplain of the General Court of Massachusetts, delivered the election day sermon in 1802, just as Federalist Samuel Stillman had in 1779.[100]

Even though Isaac Backus referred to the inclusive Rhode Island as an "irreligious colony" and a poor example of separation of church and state, Leland viewed it much more approvingly.[101] As expected, the Puri-

94. Leland, "Miscellaneous Essays, in Prose and Verse," 428.

95. Leland, "Extract of a Letter from J. L. to His Inquisitive Friend," 497; Leland, "At a Democratic Meeting Held at Cheshire, August 28, 1834," 652.

96. Baldwin, *Sermon, Delivered Before His Excellency Caleb Strong*, 12.

97. Hatch, *Democratization of American Christianity*, 99.

98. Leland, "Speech Delivered in the House of Representatives of Massachusetts, on the Subject of Religious Freedom, 1811," 358.

99. Rogers, *Life, Journal and Works of David Jones, 1736–1820*, 117.

100. Chessman, *Memoir of Rev. Thomas Baldwin, D.D.*, 63; Torbet, *Social History of the Philadelphia Baptist Association: 1707—1940*, 47.

101. McLoughlin, *Soul Liberty*, 258.

tanical Backus was not quite as Lockean as his fellow Republican. While Leland taught that government "costs individuals some of their natural rights," Backus dismissed the notion, contending that "it is so far from being necessary for any man to give up any part of his real liberty in order to submit to government that all nations have found it necessary to submit to some government in order to enjoy any liberty and security at all."[102] Leland clearly subscribed to a kind of social contract theory that Backus did not, proving that Baptist Republicanism was a complex of different political philosophies. Leland argued that compact is "the basis of civil government," even claiming that the government established in Genesis 3 and 4 was formed by "mutual agreement."[103] Thomas Baldwin stated similarly that "All legitimate governments are, or ought to be founded in compact," yet Isaac Backus thought this was a potentially sinful error. "What a dangerous error, yea, what a root of all evil then must it be, for men to imagine that there is anything in the nature of true government that interferes with true and full liberty!"[104] In short, while Backus shared a common aversion to the "Federal folly," he did not necessarily believe that Baptist Republicans were without their own misunderstandings.[105] Despite the fact that Leland and Backus were superior Baptist thinkers, one should not assume that they theologized in a vacuum or that their systems of thought were crafted seamlessly. Sometimes they could be prone to seeming contradiction. For example, on one occasion Leland submitted that government should have "reverence for the precepts and spirt of religion" yet on another occasion he insisted that Christianity was *not* "essential to good government."[106] Just as Backus's thinking exhibited a tension between Calvin and Locke, Leland often failed to articulate exactly how Christianity helped to protect freedom of conscience in the public square. What Leland and other Baptist Republicans *did* make clear is that religion flourishes best when government influence upon it is least. Leland summed up his opinion in these terms:

> The federalists and Deists agree in one point, viz: they both believe that if Christianity is not protected by law, it will fall to the ground. But then they disagree in their wishes: the federalists

---

102. Leland, "Letter," 658; Backus, *Appeal to the Public for Religious Liberty*, 312.

103. Leland, *Rights of Conscience Inalienable*, 179; Leland, "On Sabbatical Laws," 441.

104. Baldwin, *Sermon, Delivered Before His Excellency Caleb Strong*, 7; Backus, *Appeal to the Public for Religious Liberty*, 309.

105. Leland, "Oration," 268.

106. Leland, "Address Delivered at Pittsfield, Jan. 8, 1829," 545; Leland, "Which Has Done the Most Mischief in the World, The Kings-Evil or Priest-Craft?," 497; Leland, "At a Democratic Meeting Held at Cheshire, August 28, 1834," 489.

wish that what they call Christianity, may stand, but the Deists wish it might fall. The republicans and Deists agree in the counterpart, viz., that it would be delivering the world from one of its greatest curses, to have all legal establishments of religion abolished: but their conclusions are diametrically opposed to each other. Republicans believe that pure Christianity would gain much by such a dissolution, but the Deists suppose it would utterly fall.[107]

Baptist Republicanism was a defense of the individuality of religion, the freedom of conscience as a fundamental human right, and the separateness of the church from the civil authority in a fallen world. In order to protect these ideals, Baptists aligned themselves with the party of Jefferson. However, Leland was somewhat mistaken in his generalization of Federalists. There were indeed many of the latter who also believed strongly in the separation of church and state. They were Baptists.

---

107. Leland, "Oration," 264.

Chapter 4

Baptist Federalists

IN HIS CANONIZED LETTER to the Danbury Baptists in 1802, President Thomas Jefferson famously described the relationship between the church and civil government in the First Amendment as a "wall of separation." According to Jefferson, who that same New Year's Day welcomed Elder John Leland and his "mammoth" Cheshire cheese to the White House, he and his Baptist bedfellows shared a common cause in religious liberty. He assured them,

> Believing with you that religion is a matter which lies solely between Man & his God, that he owes account to none other for his faith or his worship, that the legitimate powers of government reach actions only, & not opinions, I contemplate with sovereign reverence that act of the whole American people which declared that *their* legislature should "make no law respecting an establishment of religion, or prohibiting the free exercise thereof," thus building a wall of separation between Church & State.[1]

In Connecticut, and indeed in all of America, Thomas Jefferson was received by Baptists as a welcome ally in the quest for disestablishment. For this reason, historians and theologians have traditionally painted Baptists in the early republic as decidedly pro-Jefferson, emphasizing figures such as the "cheesemonger" John Leland, Isaac Backus, and other Baptist Republicans who labored to maintain religious freedom for their brethren who continued to endure persecution in states with established churches.[2] In

---

1. "Letter from Thomas Jefferson to Messrs. Nehemiah Dodge, Ephraim Robbins, and Stephen S. Nelson."

2. Letter from Manasseh Cutler to Dr. Joseph Torrey, January 4, 1802, in Cutler

rightly framing Jefferson as the champion of Baptists, scholars from Nathan O. Hatch to Daniel L. Dreisbach to Thomas S. Kidd have tended to frame Baptists as Jeffersonians due to their mutual defense of the First Amendment.[3] However, this telling of Baptist and American history is incomplete, as it neglects the overwhelming historical evidence that America's Baptist leadership, though aligning with Jefferson on the issue of religious liberty, were in fact predominantly and distinctly Federalist.

While Baptists since Roger Williams had been some of the first Americans to advocate for a church-state separation, and although a multitude were ardent Republicans, there were indeed a significant number of Baptists who were not convinced that "religion is a matter which lies solely between Man & his God."[4] (Philip Hamburger has even cast doubt upon the assumption that the Danbury Baptists gave Jefferson's letter their approbation.)[5] Instead, consistent with their republican principles, they believed that religion was a very public affair. As Jonathan J. Den Hartog has demonstrated, "Federalists offered both a cultural and religious vision" of America, one that provided for a "public role for religion."[6] Baptist leaders such as Hezekiah Smith, Samuel Stillman, Oliver Hart, Morgan Edwards, James Manning, and a host of others were not as Jeffersonian as many have assumed, and they were certainly not interested in erecting a bilateral "wall" between church and state.[7] For the sake of the public virtue and stability necessary to protect

---

and Cutler, *Life, Journals and Correspondence of Rev. Manessah Cutler, LL.D.*, 2:66–67.

3. Hatch, *Democratization of American Christianity*, 34–36; Dreisbach, *Thomas Jefferson and the Wall of Separation Between Church and State*, 10–27; Kidd, *God of Liberty*, 6, 24, 41, 47–48. To be clear, none of these scholars have identified Baptists in the early republic as uniformly Republican nor have they contended that Baptists were in lockstep with Jefferson's overall view of the separation of church and state. However, without accounting for the significance of Baptist Federalism, their respective portraits of Baptist life do not present the relationship between Jefferson and Baptists in its proper context.

4. See Gaustad, *Roger Williams*.
5. Hamburger, *Separation of Church and State*, 163–65.
6. Hartog, *Patriotism and Piety*), 17.

7. Even Dreisbach notes, "Although the Baptists and the fellow dissenters undoubtedly approved of Jefferson's use of the narrow institutional term 'church,' rather than the more encompassing First Amendment term 'religion,' they may have been discomfited by the wall imagery. A wall of separation between church and state, given the bilateral nature of the barrier, imposes restraints on both the civil state and religion" (Dreisbach, *Thomas Jefferson and the Wall of Separation Between Church and State*, 52). Similarly, Kidd has emphasized their mutual opposition to establishment rather than an identical view of church-state separation: "Although the personal religious sentiments of the Baptists and Jefferson could hardly have been more different, their views of religious establishments were very similar" (Kidd, *God of Liberty*, 177).

freedom of religion, many of the most influential Baptist leaders in America aligned themselves with the party of establishmentarians, not because they believed that religion should be wedded to the state, but because they feared the tyranny of a state completely divorced from religion.

Baptist Federalists were found in the North and the South, on the coast and on the frontier, behind the pulpit and in the pew. Some like Richard Furman summoned fellow Federalists across the Mason-Dixon line and even across the Atlantic Ocean. With an abiding fear of the "infidelity" of the French Revolution, a wariness of non-British foreigners, a belief in the divinity of the Constitution, and a spirit of cooperation with all Protestant denominations, Baptist Federalism was animated by the idea that social and political stability and a reputable, virtuous, ecumenical class of Baptists were necessary in order to build "civil trust" and to preserve the hard-earned spoils of religious liberty.[8] Therefore, in their support for the First Amendment to the Constitution, Baptist Federalists were distinct from other varieties of Federalism in the new republic. For instance, like Timothy Dwight at Yale, whom John R. Fitzmier has called "New England's moral legislator" and "the architect of godly Federalism," Baptist Federalists sought to curtail the democratization and atomization of American society; however, unlike Dwight, they strongly opposed state establishments of religion as a means of doing so.[9] The Federalism of Baptists extended only as far as Dwight and other establishmentarians could help them to forge a republic secure enough and virtuous enough for religious liberty to flourish. As a result, ironically enough, many Baptists voted for John Adams for the very reason they aligned with Jefferson on the First Amendment: to procure, prioritize, and protect religious liberty.[10] By positioning themselves at the forefront of Baptist education, constructing new Baptist institutions, and promoting disestablished religion in the public square, these Baptists contributed to what Den Hartog has called the "Federalization of American Christianity" in the early republic.[11] Baptists and Federalists, two groups not typically yoked together in American historical studies, forged a seemingly unlikely

---

8. Furman, "To Rev. Mr. Pierce," 116.

9. Fitzmier, *New England's Moral Legislator*, 162.

10. Many Baptist Federalists did not openly support one candidate over another, however. For instance, John Boles writes of Henry Holcombe, "He had been a Federalist in 1788; he was a close friend of the former Federalist judge, the soon-to-be Baptist minister Joseph Clay; he had delivered a panegyric on Washington. Yet he supported a variety of reforms; he preached equal rights and the Christian duty to honor all men; he was no respecter of persons. Never did he advocate for one political figure in favor of another" (Boles, "Henry Holcombe," 391).

11. Hartog, *Patriotism and Piety*, 17.

partnership that lasted through the end of the War of 1812, and in many ways, well beyond.

"Infidelity" and the French Revolution

The traditional narrative that Baptists in New England embraced the party of Jefferson against the "Standing Order" is understandably predicated on the one thing that united all Baptists in the Revolutionary era: the First Amendment.[12] However, this commitment to a "separation" between church and state could not obviate partisanship even inside the Baptist ranks. A common cause for religious liberty did not translate into thoroughgoing Jeffersonianism. For instance, when Isaac Backus was sent by the Warren Association in Rhode Island to the Continental Congress in 1774 to plead their case for religious liberty, John Adams's dismissive comment that "we might as well expect a change in the solar system, to expect they would give up their establishment" was directed not only at Backus, but also to his fellow delegate James Manning—a future Federalist.[13] In fact, the Warren Association would eventually boast some of the most staunchly Federalist Baptists in the United States. Though not always pro-Adams, New England Baptists were not necessarily pro-Jefferson, and nothing evoked the Baptist ambivalence toward Jefferson more than his religion.

In the nation's first partisan elections between John Adams and Thomas Jefferson, the theological distinction between Adams's Unitarianism and Jefferson's Deism was critical in terms of the power of the press. While both rejected the historically fundamental doctrine of the Trinity, and although "Jefferson conceived of himself . . . as a rational Christian who believed that reason was the 'only oracle' provided by heaven," Unitarians nevertheless enjoyed, albeit unconventionally, the cultural epithet of "Christian."[14] Therefore, for Jefferson, who famously quipped that "it does me no injury for my neighbor to say there are twenty gods, or no gods," the opprobrious label of "infidel" stuck in a way that it did not for Adams, the son of a Congregationalist deacon.[15] Baptists were therefore in a somewhat precarious posi-

---

12. See Field, *Crisis of the Standing Order*.
13. Adams, "John Adams' Diary, October 14, 1774."
14. Holifield, *Gentlemen Theologians*, 62. In his movement-defining sermon entitled "Unitarian Christianity" delivered in Baltimore in 1819, the so-called father of American Unitarianism, William Ellery Channing argued, "Jesus Christ is the only master of Christians, and whatever he taught, either during his personal ministry, or by his inspired Apostles, we regard as of divine authority, and profess to make the rule of our lives" (Channing, "Unitarian Christianity," 72).
15. "Query XVII," in Jefferson, *Notes on the State of Virginia*, 166.

tion, enjoying the fruits of Jefferson's work on behalf of religious liberty yet believing that his ideas about God and religion could undermine the very fabric of society. As William G. McLoughlin has shown, even Isaac Backus himself often had more in common with Federalists than Republicans, endorsing Federalist petitions to request Congress to print Bibles and protesting Jefferson's opposition to national fast and thanksgiving days which sparked his letter to the Danbury Baptists. According to McLoughlin, "in certain respects Backus had more in common with the transformationists or theocrats than the separationists. Backus and the New England Baptists were Jeffersonians in politics primarily in reaction to the Standing Order's Federalism, but basically they shared the socially conservative heritage of their region, or at least their eastern spokesmen did."[16] But other conservative Baptist leaders could not so easily stomach Jefferson's "wall." Baptist Federalists rarely attacked Jefferson *ad hominem* as did so many of their Congregationalist countrymen; instead, their invectives against Republicans were launched primarily in the form of warnings against the atheism and irreligion of the French Revolution, an event they linked directly to Jefferson's Deism.

If the Danbury Baptists feared the tyranny of Congregationalism most in their new republic, other Baptists believed that the anarchy of France was a much more imminent threat to republican virtue and political stability. In his 1800 eulogy of "the American sage" George Washington, Southern Federalist Henry Holcombe condemned "the heathens and deists" who would seek to "infest the United States" but who remain "confined to the smoke and flame in which they have involved miserable Europe."[17] As James Broussard has shown, for all their differences, Southern Federalists were tied together by their mutual fear of France.[18] Still, even in Boston, where Baptists did not enjoy the same degree of religious tolerance as they did in Rhode Island or the deeper South, Baptist Federalists cautioned their churches against an unbridled love of liberty. Samuel Stillman (1737–1807), pastor of First Baptist Church of Boston for over forty years and one of the most influential Baptists in the new republic, applied Matthew 24:6–8 ("you shall hear of wars and rumors of wars") directly to the French Revolution itself.[19] In a 1794 Thanksgiving sermon entitled "Thoughts on the French

---

16. McLoughlin, "Introduction," 50–51.

17. Holcombe, *Sermon, Occasioned by the Death of Lieutenant-General George Washington*, 2:1400, 1410.

18. James H. Broussard explains, "The party drew its voting support from different groups of people in each state. There was, in fact, only one thing common to Federalists everywhere—the fear of France" (Broussard, *Southern Federalists*, 401).

19. Thomas Armitage describes the relationship between Stillman and Thomas

Revolution," Stillman equated the cataclysmic events in France with vain self-interest at the expense of the public good. The Bastille was simply the bloody conclusion to liberty without virtue. Exhorting his Baptist brethren to examine themselves, he warned, "Though a republican form of government . . . is the best calculated to promote the freedom and happiness of the people, there always will be found men of boundless ambition, who become heads of parties, and spare no pains to get into place."[20] With his friendship to John Adams, Stillman's tongue-in-cheek allusion to "heads of parties" was almost certainly a thinly veiled reference to Jefferson. He also indicted Jefferson's religion as the true culprit behind political and social anarchy. Identifying France as "a very important pillar of Popery" and the violent overthrow of King Louis XVI as the culmination of "the progress of vice and infidelity," Stillman and other Baptists saw in the French Revolution the inevitable end to a Christ-less society.[21]

Other Baptists were more severe in their denunciation of the evils of the French Revolution and the residual effects of infidelity in America. For Jonathan Maxcy, the precocious successor of president James Manning at Rhode Island College, the dangers of foreign religion were not always distinguishable from the foreigners themselves. He railed against "the pernicious effects of infidelity," "the arrows of infidelity," and the "cargoes of infidelity . . . imported into our country."[22] Like so many other Federalists in the aftermath of the Alien and Sedition Acts (1795), Maxcy's nativism colored his Christianity. In a Fourth of July sermon in 1799, Maxcy warned, "Never has our country been exposed to greater danger; never has our government been assaulted with greater violence, by foreign foes and domestic traitors; never have been more insidious, persevering and malevolent attempts to corrupt public opinion; to undermine the foundations of religion, to cut asunder the sinews of moral obligations, and to cover this happy land with

---

Baldwin at Second Baptist Church: "Dr. Stillman and [Baldwin] were fast friends and true yoke-fellows in every good work. As politicians, Stillman was a firm Federalist and Baldwin as firm a Jeffersonian Democrat, and generally on Fast Day and Thanksgiving-day they preached on the points in dispute here . . . On these days, the Federalists of both their congregations went to hear Dr. Stillman and the Democrats went to Baldwin's place" (Armitage, *History of the Baptists,* 2:852).

20. Stillman, *Thoughts on the French Revolution,* 10.

21. Stillman, *Thoughts on the French Revolution*, 17, 23.

22. Maxcy, "Address, Delivered to the Graduates of Rhode Island College," 310; Maxcy, "Address, Delivered to the Candidates for the Baccalaureate of Rhode Island College," 326; Maxcy, "Oration, Delivered in the First Congregational Meeting House, in Providence, on the Fourth of July, 1799," 392.

carnage, desolation and ruin."[23] After describing the irreligion of France, Maxcy insisted,

> We must rank among our disgraces as well as among our misfortunes, the existence of a set of men in our country, who have derived their political principles from foreign influence and foreign intrigue; who exert their utmost efforts to ruin our government, and to prostrate all permanent establishments. These men discard, as the effects of superstition, all ancient institutions; and, instead, of adhering to a uniform order of things, delight in perpetual revolutions. Their system of rights, like their system of government, is metaphysic and fantastical. They do not consider that government is a science derived from the experience of ages, and that it ought to embrace the rights and welfare, not of the present age only, but of all posterity.[24]

Maxcy clearly accused the Francophile Jefferson and his "set of men" with importing subversive ideas of "foreign influence" epitomized in the French Revolution. In a 1798 graduation sermon at the college, Maxcy derided the "intruding arm of foreign domination" and the "pernicious effects of infidelity, atheism, and unbridled ambition" that razed the "sacred institutions" of America.[25] For the young college president, the purpose of government was not simply to protect individual rights for rights' sake, but to secure those rights for the public good and for the glory of God over generations. Baptist Federalists were intent on eliminating religious establishment but not at the expense of public religion.

Baptist Federalists continually reminded their hearers that tyranny was just as oppressive in a democracy as it was in a monarchy. Portending the age of Jackson, Maxcy scoffed at "our levelling democrats" and the "reeking demagogues" who inevitably came to power in their midst.[26] In a Fourth of July sermon in 1802 entitled "America's Deliverance and Duty," Richard Furman voiced the same concern. Furman, who cultivated a friendship with Southern Federalist and Presidential candidate Senator Charles Pinckney, sounded remarkably like Timothy Dwight when he declared,

---

23. Maxcy, "Oration, Delivered in the First Congregational Meeting House, in Providence, on the Fourth of July, 1799," 381.

24. Maxcy, "Oration, Delivered in the First Congregational Meeting House, in Providence, on the Fourth of July, 1799," 382–83.

25. Maxcy, "An Address, Delivered to the Graduates of Rhode Island College," 309–10.

26. Maxcy, "Oration, Delivered in the First Congregational Meeting House, in Providence, on the Fourth of July, 1799," 389, 392.

> The influence of demagogues, and the artifice, or fury of party, too often mislead and convulse governments of this form; and sometimes, as in the case of the Roman, and more ancient republicks of Greece, overwhelm them in final ruin. To guard against these very pernicious evils should be our care: and in the exercise of it, particular attention should be given to the principles and conduct of those who are invested with public trusts by the votes of the people. The virtuous and wise, alone, should be chosen. The man of ambition, and bad principles, who in a monarchy would solicit royal favor with fawning adulation, will not fail, among us, to court the people with strongest professions of his regard to liberty; and by a conformity in his manners to popular sentiments and prejudices.[27]

By "virtuous and wise" rulers, Furman usually meant Federalists. For Baptists, a so-called "democratic religion," the potential for American demagoguery was just as frightening as the looming specter of British tyranny.[28] If the Deist Jefferson forced Baptists to sacrifice public religion in order to gain freedom of religion, the cost was certainly too great.

Better an imperious yet orthodox establishment with a virtuous citizenry, Baptist Federalists reasoned, than a society of "bad principles" in the hands of an infidel who denied the deity of Christ. According to Henry Holcombe, the pastor of First Baptist Church of Savannah, Georgia, "The sons and daughters of infidelity and vice talk of bliss, which is much more than mere peace, but experience woe. Long observation confirms what the Bible asserts, that, 'they know not the way of peace.' The only source of this important knowledge, among men, is the word of God."[29] In order to keep the peace, Holcombe believed in the Bible and Federalism. Years later, as pastor of First Baptist Church of Philadelphia, Holcombe charged, "the prevalence of infidelity, and its issues, require more than ordinary power to counteract their deleterious effects."[30] What will it profit a nation, Holcombe asked, to gain independence yet forfeit its soul?[31]

27. Furman, "America's Deliverance and Duty," 405–6.
28. Wills, *Democratic Religion*.
29. Holcombe, "Letter XIX," 150.
30. "Appendix," in Holcombe, *First Fruits*, 226.

31. The life of Adoniram Judson, the first American Baptist overseas missionary, illustrates the perceived dangers of infidelity. As a student at Brown University (1804–1807), Judson, not yet a Baptist, was influenced by his classmate Jacob Eames of Belfast, Maine. Eames was a Deist and succeeded in turning Judson away from traditional Christian beliefs for a time, to the later dismay of his father Adoniram Judson Sr., who was a Congregationalist pastor and Federalist in Massachusetts. According to Courtney Anderson, "if Adoniram's father had even suspected he was dabbling in

In a chapel address that same year, Federalist and Professor of Learned Languages at Rhode Island College Asa Messer framed the question another way: "Hume and Paine are infidels. Locke and Newton are Christians. Does not the difference of their belief arise wholly from the difference of their moral tempers? But which of them is the most worthy of your notice? Will you believe David Hume, or will you believe John Locke? Will you believe Thomas Paine, or will you believe Sir Isaac Newton?" While Locke and Newton were hardly Peter and Paul in terms of Christian orthodoxy, Messer's rhetorical questions reveal that, for many Baptists, infidelity struck at the heart of credibility. A man who would not adhere even to the broadest claims of Christianity could not be trusted to lead a country. Later in the sermon Messer contemplated the "splendor" of "George Washington and John Adams."[32] Not surprisingly, Jefferson was never mentioned.

This endemic obsession with infidelity and Deism was so strong among Baptist Federalists that it imbued their interpretation of the Bible. Hezekiah Smith, a founding father of the Warren Association and the pastor at First Baptist Church of Haverhill, Massachusetts, preached to the First Massachusetts Brigade from Psalm 52:7 ("See the man who would not make God his refuge"). In the wake of Benedict Arnold's defection to the British in 1780, Smith took stock of Doeg the Edomite and speculated, "I am apt to think he was a Deist, or an Atheist, who made not God his strength, but trusted in his riches, and strengthened himself in his wickedness."[33] Sometimes Baptist Federalists appeared to locate infidelity behind every rock and tree. Between Deism and atheism there was but little difference in the minds of most Baptist leaders in the new republic. Even in 1780, the future Federalist Smith warned, "It is to be feared that our land is infested with too many similar characters, whose mischievous designs are covered with the veil of deceitfulness, and whose dissolute principles are pregnant with the greatest evils, both in religion and in politics." Baptist Federalists identified Deism, specifically Thomas Jefferson's Deism, as the source of religious, social, and political anarchy both in Europe and in America. In their efforts to combat

---

Deism he would have ridden posthaste to Providence and removed him from Brown at once" (Anderson, *To the Golden Shore*, 32–33). Ironically, Judson's "dabbling with Deism" was the means by which he eventually believed in the gospel and by which he realized his call to international missions, converting to the Baptist faith. Although Judson later spent time in a French jail and enumerated "many of the evils which infidelity had brought upon France and upon the world," it is unclear whether Judson ever favored one party over another (Anderson, *To the Golden Shore*, 93).

32. Messer, "Discourse Delivered in the Chapel of Rhode Island College," 427, 430.
33. Smith, *Chaplain Smith and the Baptists*, 274.

irreligion, Baptist Federalists not only preached the deity of Christ, but the sanctity of the Constitution.

The Divinity of the Constitution

Despite the persistent accusations that Federalists were pseudo-loyalists (and with Morgan Edwards that was true), Baptist Federalists were some of the most ardent patriots in their denomination.[34] Hezekiah Smith was a chaplain in the Continental Army and friend of George Washington, stationed with him in New York City in 1776.[35] Smith's friend, Princeton classmate, and Rhode Island College co-founder James Manning was a delegate from Rhode Island to the Continental Congress in 1786. (Princeton President John Witherspoon served as a delegate to the Second Continental Congress and was the only clergyman to sign the Declaration of Independence.) As shown, Richard Furman was obviously well known in the Charleston area for his patriotism and by British General Cornwallis as a "notorious" rebel. As Kristopher Maulden explains, "Federalists may have been accused of trying to recreate British government in the new nation, but they imagined themselves the true defenders of American republicanism."[36] In *Federalist No. 37*, James Madison identified one of the challenges faced by the Convention in "combining the requisite stability and energy in government, with the inviolable attention due to liberty and to the republican form."[37] In defending the need for public order in the new republic, Federalists believed they were creating a nation where republican ideals could be protected and nourished.

For Baptist Federalists, political stability and a maximalist style of governance was the best way to safeguard their new-found religious liberty from those who would seek to return their villages and towns to the Puritan establishment. An enlarged state was the friend of the church, ensuring that the First Amendment "separation" remained in place. If Jeffersonian Baptists like John Leland welcomed a "wall" to keep back the establishment, Baptist Federalists contended for a semi-permeable membrane, porous enough to encourage civil religion yet thick enough to filter out infidelity.

---

34. As James P. Byrd notes, "Despite their avowed dedication to the most thorough ideas of liberty, Baptists gained a reputation for loyalism. Such claims were mostly false, though there were notable exceptions, including the well-known Baptist historian Morgan Edwards" (Byrd, *Sacred Scripture, Sacred War*, 136).

35. Smith, "Wednesday, June 5, 1776," 439.

36. Maulden, *Federalist Frontier*, 52.

37. Madison, "Federalist No. 37," 223–24.

The primary way that Baptist Federalists demonstrated their support for an administration that protected rather than profaned their religious liberty is in their belief that the United States Constitution was of God.

The debate among Baptists about the First Amendment concerned who or what would stand guard at the Jeffersonian wall. For Baptist Federalists, it was the Constitution. According to Jonathan Maxcy, whose younger brother Virgil was also a well-known Federalist, the Constitution "reflected so much honor on Americans."[38] In many ways, it was a divinely inspired document. One of the staunchest Baptist defenders of the Constitution was also one of the greatest Baptist leaders in Revolutionary America as well as one of the boldest activists for religious liberty: Oliver Hart. Originally sent from the Federalist-laden Philadelphia Association, and as "a fervent advocate for the American Revolution," Hart served churches in both South Carolina and New Jersey.[39] His 1789 Thanksgiving Day sermon, *America's Remembrancer, with Respect to her Blessedness and Duty*, is, in the words of one scholar, "a classic, Providential interpretation of American exceptionalism."[40] In the sermon, Hart applied Numbers 23:23 directly to America - "Surely there is no inchantment against Jacob, neither is there any divination against Israel: according to this time it shall be said of Jacob, and of Israel, What hath God wrought!" In his eyes, America was a shining spectacle for the entire world. For Hart, a co-framer of the *Charleston Confession*, the hand of Almighty God was behind the entire Constitutional Convention. He reflected, "however much divided with regard to locality, religion, personal interests, tempers and prejudices, they all united as one man," and "who, but the Being who governs the heart, could effect this?"[41] The sermon was nothing less than an apology for the Constitution itself.

Even as a Baptist, Hart had no suspicion of the newly centralized authority. He praised "the mature production of the most wise and approved patriots, legally chosen as our representatives, from whom we had everything to expect and nothing to fear." Ultimately, America's federalized government was "open, free, and generous, although energetic—calculated to render the citizens of the United States happy, as it secures unto them all their rights and privileges, upon the most permanent basis."[42] This was, in essence, the Baptist case for the Constitution: the preservation of

---

38. Maxcy, "Oration Delivered in the Baptist Meeting House in Providence, July 4th, 1795," 374.
39. Yarnell, "Early American Political Theology," 64.
40. Smith, *Oliver Hart and the Rise of Baptist America*, 343.
41. Hart, *America's Remembrancer*, 3–13.
42. Hart, *America's Remembrancer*, 12–14.

religious liberty. Baptist Federalists could not be certain that their freedom of religion would be secure in their new republic until the republic itself was secure. Perhaps more than any other group in America, Baptist Federalists demonstrate what C. Bradley Thompson has called "American-style republicanism." According to Thompson, the difference between Federalists and Anti-Federalists was not in the priority of individual rights, but in the amount of power they were willing to allot to the federal government in order to protect those rights. "American-style republicanism was unique because of the emphasis it put on limiting the political power of those who rule—including the rule of the majority—so that individuals could rule themselves more efficaciously . . . It meant the people controlling the growth and power of government so that individuals could have greater freedom to be left alone and govern themselves."[43] Baptist Federalists embodied this Americanized principle when they contended for greater federal control in order to protect what they believed to be the greatest freedom of all: the freedom of conscience.

Baptist Federalists also attended the Constitutional Convention. Hart's protégé Samuel Stillman attended both the Convention in Philadelphia as well as the Massachusetts Constitutional Convention. Henry Holcombe, who formerly served in the cavalry during the Revolutionary War, was also a delegate at the Convention to ratify the Constitution in 1788. Having served as chaplain in the Continental Army during the war, Baptist Federalist William Rogers even gave the opening prayer for the Convention on the Fourth of July.[44] Rogers's patriotic piety left no doubt of his belief in the divinity of their work that day:

> As this is a period, O Lord! big, with events, impenetrable by any human scrutiny, we fervently recommend to thy fatherly notice, that august Body assembled in this city, who compose our Federal Convention; will it please Thee, O Eternal I Am! to favor them from day to day with thy immediate presence; be thou their wisdom and their strength! Enable them to devise such measures as may prove happily instrumental for healing all divisions, and promoting the good of the great whole; incline the hearts of all the people to receive with pleasure, combined

---

43. Thompson, *America's Revolutionary Mind*, 278.

44. McLoughlin records, "Several of the more prominent urban Baptists . . . such as Samuel Stillman and Thomas Gair in Boston and James Manning in Providence, favored the new Constitution. The Federalist leaders in Boston brought Manning to the convention there in hopes that he might persuade Baptist delegates to vote for ratification. (John Hancock asked Manning to deliver the closing prayer at the convention)" (McLoughlin, *Soul Liberty*, 192–93).

with a determination to carry into execution, whatever these thy servants may wisely recommend; that the United States of America may furnish the world with one example of a free and permanent government, which shall be the result of human and mutual deliberation, and which shall not, like all other governments, whether ancient or modern, spring out of mere chance, or be established by force.—May we triumph in the cheering prospect of being completely delivered from anarchy; and continue, under the influence of republican virtue, to partake of all the blessings of cultivated and civilized society![45]

Still, as Jill Lepore has described, "Each of the states was a laboratory, each new constitution another political experiment."[46] From New England to the South, Baptist Federalists encountered their own unique constitutional challenges because every state possessed its own social and political milieu. Southampton pastor William Van Horne, who would eventually join the Continental Army at Valley Forge and later serve as chaplain, was a member of the Pennsylvania constitutional convention in 1776. As one of eight men representing Bucks County, Van Horne was part of a three-man committee that prepared the final draft of the preamble of the constitution, a committee which also included the convention's president: Benjamin Franklin.[47] Pennsylvania's constitution, the most radical in terms of its democracy, began with a Declaration of Rights that echoed the preamble to the Declaration of Independence.[48] The second was the "inalienable right to worship Almighty God according to the dictates of their own consciences and understanding: And that no man ought or of right can be compelled to attend any religious worship, or erect or support any place of worship, or maintain any ministry, contrary to, or against, his own free will and

---

45. Morris, *Christian Life and Character of the Civil Institutions of the United States*, 253.

46. Lepore, *These Truths*, 112.

47. Van Horne, "Revolutionary War Letters of the Reverend William Van Horne," 105–6. With a unicameral legislature and without an executive branch, the original Pennsylvania Constitution was not without its critics. In a 1779 letter, Van Horne opposed these "Anti-constitutional Gentlemen" (Van Horne, "Camp at Croton October 27th, 1779," in Van Horne, "Revolutionary War Letters of the Reverend William Van Horne," 135).

48. Lepore, *These Truths*, 112. According to Gordon Wood, "Equality became the rallying cry of the Pennsylvania radicals in the spring and summer of 1776." Wood later adds, "The new government which they formed in the late summer of 1776 was permeated, more so than any other government created in the Revolution, by the principle of rotation of office" (Wood, *Creation of the American Republic*, 86–87).

consent." At the state-level, Baptist Federalists like Van Horne were remarkably Jeffersonian even in their constitutionalism.[49]

However, the Constitution of the United States did not originally proscribe religious establishments at the state level. As a result, Baptists were forced to contend for church-state separation in their respective states even after 1787. For example, in 1792, Baptist Federalist Caleb Blood became the very first non-Congregationalist to deliver an election sermon in Vermont, a state that continued to provide for the public support of religion.[50] While insisting that "virtue should be considered as a necessary qualification for a civil ruler" and that an unbelieving magistrate could neither please God nor promote the good of the nation, the pastor from Shaftsbury nevertheless condemned "religious establishments by law" that "never fail of pernicious consequences both to church and state." Blood declared, "As to the aid of the civil power to force men to support gospel ministers, I humbly conceive that it never can be necessary."[51] One year later, Vermont completely removed religious tests from its Constitution.

In the years after 1787, Baptist Federalists stretched as far as south as Georgia and as west as Ohio preaching their gospel of order and stability. James Manning's nephew, Stephen Gano, whose father John was alleged by some to have baptized George Washington, helped constitute the very first Protestant church in the Northwest Territory in Columbia, Ohio in 1790.[52] Seth Stafford, one of Henry Holcombe's parishioners from his church at Pipe Creek, was a delegate to the South Carolina Ratifying Convention in 1788 from St. Peter's Parish. One of the larger slaveowners in the Parish with eighteen slaves, Stafford was a frontier farmer who voted in favor of

49. Hezekiah Smith, for instance, led the opposition in Haverhill to the town's approval of an article in the proposed Massachusetts constitution in 1780 upholding the establishment of the Congregationalist churches. In a petition to the General Court of Massachusetts, Smith and other Baptists charged that the third article "asserts a right in the people to give away a power they never had themselves; for no man has a right to judge for others in religious matters" ("Appendix F," in Broome, *Life, Ministry, and Journals of Hezekiah Smith*, 645).

50. Curry, *First Freedoms*, 189–90; Zvesper, *Political Philosophy and Rhetoric*, 26–28.

51. Blood, *Sermon Preached Before the Honorable Legislature of the State of Vermont*, 28, 34–35.

52. Kidd and Hankins, *Baptists in America*, 79–80. In a sermon commemorating George Washington's death in 1800, after praising the fallen hero for presiding over "the formation of our excellent constitution," Gano later exhorted his hearers, "It is not expected that we should all be generals, presidents or rulers; but we should all be good citizens—peaceable, industrious, virtuous and faithful, in our several stations; 'rendering to Caesar the things that are Caesar's, and unto God the things that are God's.'" (Gano, *Sermon on the Death of General George Washington*, 9, 16–17).

ratifying the Constitution with Holcombe.[53] In ascribing divine status to the Constitution, Baptist Federalists were simply treating the proceedings in Philadelphia as the logical conclusion to what God had already miraculously achieved for the American people in their independence from Britain. Like the nation of Israel in the Old Testament, Yahweh had borne them up on eagle's wings and given them a law. (Exod. 19:4)

On the last day of the Constitutional Convention, James Manning was asked to "close the solemn convocation with thanksgiving prayer."[54] The prayer was reportedly so awe-inspiring that Manning became renowned for his patriotism and devotion. Although Rhode Island was the only state not to originally ratify the Constitution, Manning represented many Baptist Federalists who rejoiced at its ratification in other states. So convinced was Manning that the Constitution was the work of the Almighty that he rebuked the "deliberately wicked" rulers of "our wicked state."[55] The social and political instability of the Articles of Confederation was not sufficient to operate any enlightened country in Manning's mind. According to Reuben A. Guild, Manning's biographer, "The fears and forebodings of Dr. Manning in regard to the Confederation proved but too well founded. Notwithstanding the efforts of the wisest statesmen, it was found inefficient to promote social order, and all those paramount interests which it is the design of government to foster and protect."[56] For Baptist Federalists, union was next to godliness, and the kingdom of God was opposed to political and social anarchy. The Constitution was thus a gift from God himself, no less inspired than the victory over Britain. In order to fortify the union between themselves and with their new countrymen, Baptist Federalists became the leading advocates for denominational and educational institutions.

Entities and Education

In many ways, Baptist Federalists were replacing establishment with ecumenism. While Baptist Republicans like Leland and the Danbury Association had developed a kind of siege mentality against Anglicans and the Standing Order, Baptists in Rhode Island, Pennsylvania, and South Carolina—the three centers for Baptist Federalism—enjoyed a degree of religious tolerance that did not breed the same kind of antagonism toward the established church. In these states with lighter or no establishments, less

---

53. Rowland et al., *History of Beaufort County, South Carolina*, 1:299–301.
54. Guild, *Life, Times, and Correspondence of James Manning*, 404.
55. Guild, *Life, Times, and Correspondence of James Manning*, 411.
56. Guild, *Life, Times, and Correspondence of James Manning*, 402.

inter-denominational hostility allowed many Baptists to adopt the Federalist vision of stability and order without the inveterate distrust of authority that characterized so many Republicans. This Baptist-Federalist alliance was often along theological lines. For instance, Jonathan Maxcy was the leading American Baptist proponent of New Divinity theology, the theological tradition stemming from Jonathan Edwards's successors in the Congregationalist Church, most of whom were Federalists. Maxcy was even recognized by these Congregationalists as someone who promoted the most pristine form of their doctrine of atonement.[57] In New York City, First Baptist Church suffered a split due to the New Divinity theology of Federalist Benjamin Foster.[58] Oliver Hart was converted under the preaching of Anglican George Whitefield and relished the writings of Jonathan Edwards, as opposed to the Arminian John Leland who resisted "the metaphysical, long-winded Mr. Edwards."[59] Baptist Federalists were not afraid to align themselves theologically and politically with members of the established church, even while seeking to eliminate the establishment of religion in America.

With a spirit of cooperation and the goal of forging a reputable denomination that demanded the attention of their peers, Baptist Federalists composed the vanguard of Baptist education in the new republic. Brothers John and Nicholas Brown, two of the founders of what would become their namesake Brown University, were active Federalists along with their fellow Baptist merchant Daniel Jenckes. The Browns and Jenckes were instrumental in establishing the city of Providence as one of only two Federalist centers in the state of Rhode Island. They relocated the College of Rhode Island from its original site in Warren and ensured that James Manning replaced the unlettered Six-Principle Baptist Samuel Winsor as pastor of FBC Providence. Winsor was a rural farmer who held to the more provincial beliefs and customs of the Six-Principalists, including their distinctive "laying on of hands." In his work on rural Rhode Island, Daniel P. Jones explains, "Dominated by the Baptists, and more especially by the General Six-Principle sect, rural Rhode Islanders were religiously a rustic and provincial lot, egalitarian and obscurantist in their customs and highly suspicious of outsiders."[60] By ousting Elder Windsor, the well-known Baptist merchants were securing a more learned, cosmopolitan pulpit and distancing their Federalist haven from a group of Baptists who had long been hostile to formal education. In

57. Park, *Atonement*.

58. Disosway, *Earliest Churches of New York and its Vicinity*, 195.

59. Leland, "Part of a Speech, Delivered at Suffield, Connecticut, on the First Jubilee of the United States," 524. Isaac Backus, however, was a follower of Edwards.

60. Jones, *Economic and Social Transformation of Rural Rhode Island, 1780–1850*, 17.

the state of South Carolina, "No man except Furman himself had done more for the cause of education."[61] Furman's educational vision not only served as the foundation for Furman Academy (and eventually the Southern Baptist Theological Seminary); he also led in the creation of an educational fund for Baptist ministers in the South similar to the kind envisioned by James Manning in the North.[62] Not surprisingly, Furman was known to enjoy the theological writings of Yale President and fellow Federalist Timothy Dwight, the grandson of Jonathan Edwards.[63]

When Jonathan Maxcy interviewed to become the first president of South Carolina College in 1804, he was only thirty-six years old. Yet, amazingly, Maxcy had already presided over two other colleges by the time he arrived in Columbia. At just twenty-four, he had become the youngest college president in America, succeeding the deceased James Manning at Rhode Island College in 1792. After spending just two years at Union College in Schenectady, New York, Maxcy had traveled south to find a better climate for his sickly health. In addition to his reputation as "one of the most learned men which our country has produced," Maxcy's politics also helped bring him to Columbia.[64] Pastor of First Baptist Church of Charleston and fellow Federalist Richard Furman had wielded his political influence in the state to recommend Maxcy for the inaugural office.[65] Nevertheless, Maxcy's Federalism was an issue with some of the trustees who were determined to "have a republican at the head of the college or all is lost."[66] They devised a plan to test the young scholar:

> There was some prejudice on the part of some of the friends of the new College against Dr. Maxcy, and they were not satisfied that he was the man for the place. It was accordingly agreed before hand that in this reception meeting the subject should be

61. Furman, "Letter From Dr. Furman of Charleston, to Dr. Rippon of London," 416–17; King, *History of South Carolina Baptists*, 172.

62. Guild, *Chaplain Smith and the Baptists*, 329–30.

63. "Extracts from Dr. W. T. Brantly's Sermon Delivered in 1825," in Foster, *Life and Works of Dr. Richard Furman, D.D.*, 221.

64. Elton, "Memoir," 21.

65. Rogers, *Richard Furman*, 132. According to Tupper, "It may not be improper to state here that Dr. Furman suggested to the Board of Trustees of the South Carolina College the name of Dr. Maxcy, its first president, whose magnetic power over students was never surpassed. We have seen tears in the eyes of the late Chief Justice O'Neal, and heard the tones, all tremulous with emotion, of the elder Dr. Manly, as they alluded to the strains of wisdom and eloquence which in the class-room poured from the lips of their singularly gifted instructor" (Tupper, *Two Centuries of the First Baptist Church of South Carolina 1683–1883*, 210).

66. Hollis, *University of South Carolina*, 1:34.

proposed for discussion: "Is might right?" and that Dr. Maxcy should be asked to take the affirmative—that might is right. When the time came, without a moment's premeditation, Dr. Maxcy arose and with an audacity perfectly startling, and eloquence that was overwhelming, and a sophistry that would have deceived the very elect, argued that might was right and made the worse appear the better reason. When he sat down not one dared to reply. When he saw that no one was going to take up the negative, he arose and said: "Gentlemen, might is not right," and then proceeded with thunderbolts of eloquence, logic and truth to knock down the fabric of sophistry and falsehood he had just set up. That was all of the discussion. He was the only speaker. When he took his seat they whispered to one another: "What a grand man! He is the very man to launch our College." And they arose right there and gave him their hands and their hearts.[67]

Eventually, Maxcy would attract other Federalists to Columbia. Five years after Maxcy arrived in South Carolina, when his disciple William B. Johnson led the fundraising effort for the very first meetinghouse in Columbia, the future first president of the Southern Baptist Convention encountered opposition to the project due to his own Federalist views.[68]

More than most, Baptist Federalists were self-conscious of the fact that Baptists had long been perceived as a disorderly and uneducated people. Therefore, their actions were often oriented toward the goal of political and social respectability. For instance, when Oliver Hart wrote to Richard Furman in 1777 encouraging him to attend South Carolina's Constitutional Assembly in order to advocate for religious liberty, he confessed, "I fear some of the Baptists on the Frontiers will be deemed unfriendly to the Government. Therefore let all of us who are willing to stand up in Support of our happy Constitution unite together in one band; we shall Thereby be the more respectable in the eyes of the Government."[69]

Richard Furman's vision for Baptist education was grounded in the very same idea. Without a learned class of clergymen, Baptists would never be taken seriously in the new republic and their liberties almost certainly compromised. In a 1791 letter to Samuel Pearce of Birmingham, England, Furman wrote,

---

67. Hungerpillar, "Sketch of the Life and Character of Jonathan Maxcy, D.D.," 24–25; Williams, "Historical Sketches—No. 2," 1. According to Williams, William B. Johnson's son Frank recounted this story.

68. Wills, *First Baptist Church of Columbia, South Carolina, 1809 to 2002*, 95.

69. Hart, "To Richard Furman," 133.

> Our liberty, religious as well as civil is unrestrained and those who have liberty and worth of every denomination are eligible to places of civil trust, which makes a considerable difference between our temporal situation and that of our brethren in Britain where a partial establishment prevails. For this we ought to be thankful. But a great part of our ministers as well as members are very illiterate men; which is a great hindrance to the Baptists having that weight in the State they would be entitled to, and has in many instances, in the interior parts of the country, opened the door to enthusiasm and confusion among them . . . [70]

In other words, Furman believed that Baptist education not only helped to advance the gospel; it safeguarded order and religious liberty in their newly constituted nation. Furman understood well the political importance of education and class in America. Having been raised in the humble South Carolina high country and subsequently called to pastor the Southern Baptist "mother church" in Charleston, Furman eventually "made such progress as would have ranked him among men of the first intelligence in any country."[71] Baptist Federalism often fell along lines of social status and literacy. For example, Hezekiah Smith actually owned five houses (four of which he rented to tenants), more than anyone else in the town of Haverhill.[72] Pastors like Samuel Stillman and William Van Horne received a classical education from an early age.[73] Brown University, of which Smith was a co-founder, Stillman a trustee, and Van Horne a graduate, became a kind of Federalist headquarters in the early republic.[74] Federalists even came from overseas to serve the Baptist educational cause. William Staughton, who was baptized by the so-called "Baptist Brainerd" Samuel Pearce in Birmingham and assumed the pastorate in Georgetown, South Carolina

---

70. Furman, "To Mr. Pierce," 116–17.

71. Albert Mohler has called the First Baptist Church of Charleston "the source of a theological river that runs through the center of Southern Baptist life and gave birth to the Southern Baptist Theological Seminary" (Mohler, "Foreword," xi); Armitage, *History of the Baptists*, 813.

72. Broome, *Life, Ministry, and Journals of Hezekiah Smith*, 101.

73. "Biographical Sketch of the Author's Life," in Stillman, *Select Sermons on Doctrinal and Practical Subjects*, 523.

74. That is not to say that Brown University was an exclusively Federalist institution or that it did not welcome Republicans into its leadership. For example, Isaac Backus joined John Brown and Nicholas Brown (both Federalists) and several others as trustees for the chartering of the College in the English Colony of Rhode Island and Providence Plantations (the original name for the school) in 1764. Thomas Baldwin also joined the trustees in 1807.

upon Richard Furman's request, became the first president of Columbian College in 1821.[75]

In addition to education, perhaps the most lasting legacy of Baptist Federalism were the permanent institutions they constructed in order to unify Baptists and to marshal their resources for the cause of Baptist missions. Henry Holcombe, for instance, was the founder of the Savannah River Baptist Association. Oliver Hart was the architect of the very first Baptist association in the South, in Charleston. Richard Furman helped establish the first Baptist state convention in America and became its first president. In 1814, Furman was unanimously elected the inaugural president of the Triennial Convention, the first national Baptist denomination in America (and was re-elected in 1817).[76] However, Furman was not the only Federalist leading the new General Missionary Convention. For the board of foreign missions, with the Republican Thomas Baldwin replacing Furman who declined the presidency due to distance, Henry Holcombe was elected first vice president, William Rogers second vice president, and William Staughton corresponding secretary.[77] As Sam Haselby notes, "deprived of their party, many former Federalists threw their energies into missionary and moral improvement associations."[78] In 1814, the very same year that the Federalist party began its precipitous decline culminating in the seemingly treasonous Hartford Convention, Baptist Federalists were instead forging a different kind of voluntary society, one that would seek to Christianize not only American culture, but the entire world. The Triennial Convention was by no means a Federalist creation, but its leadership and its vision were largely engineered by Baptist Federalists who, despite the death of their own party, summoned their centralizing and mobilizing instincts in order to unite their fissiparous denomination for missions and to re-constitute American Baptists in the new republic.[79] These Baptists stood with Thomas Jefferson as the champions of religious liberty in America, but their belief in the value of political and social stability to protect that liberty led them to the Federalist party.

75. Carey, *Samuel Pearce*, 1913.

76. The General Missionary Convention of the Baptist Denomination in the United States of America for Foreign Missions was nicknamed the "Triennial Convention" because it met every three years.

77. *Proceedings of the Baptist Convention for Missionary Purposes*, 12.

78. Haselby, *Origins of American Religious Nationalism*, 201.

79. As history would have it, the Triennial Convention also built upon the work of the Baptist Missionary Society in Northamptonshire, England, who were already sending their own missionaries to India.

Chapter 5

Race and Removal

In his oration before the Massachusetts Assembly and Governor Caleb Strong in 1802, Thomas Baldwin concluded, "If we are not a free people, I confess it surpasses my ingenuity to conceive how a people can be so."[1] But by "people" he meant only one race of people. Baldwin's concept of freedom, like most of his Baptist brethren at that time, was narrowed by his own ethnocentrism. In their zealous pursuit of civil and religious liberty, Baptists had done relatively little to abolish the enslavement of an entire people in the so-called "empire of liberty." Years earlier, in a Thanksgiving Day sermon in 1795, Baldwin urged, "May the day soon arrive, when not a difference of climate or features, nor the color of the skin, when nothing but crimes shall consign any of the human race to slavery."[2] While such statements were not uncommon in the earliest years of the republic, white Baptists were far more hopeful than helpful. New England Baptists, who were the first to oppose the institution, did not appear to take umbrage with slavery before the revolutionary era.

In 1773, the Ashfield Baptists had been the first and only Baptist congregation to publicly denounce slavery before the war.[3] In the statement, Rev. Ebenezer Smith appealed to Americans' Whiggish politics and to their basic sense of compassion. He beseeched, "We complain of Bondage, and shall we at the same time keep our fellow men in bondage?" He later added, "Which of us would love to be treated or have our Children treated as we

---

1. Baldwin, *Sermon, Delivered Before His Excellency Caleb Strong*, 14.
2. Baldwin, *Sermon, Delivered February 19, 1795*, 22.
3. McLoughlin, *Soul Liberty*, 152–56.

treat them?"[4] Whereas Smith used civil liberty to argue for abolition, some Baptists leveraged abolitionism to argue for religious liberty. In the preface to *A Fish Caught in His Own Net* (1768), Isaac Backus pointed to the inconsistency of those British "lords in the state" who denounced slavery in the colonies and yet upheld religious establishment (and profited from slavery).[5] Nevertheless, as Thomas Kidd and Barry Hankins observe, "most white Baptists spoke reverentially of the Revolution's significance for universal liberty, but they avoided the Revolution's (or the gospel's) implications for slavery."[6] White Baptists were much more concerned with their own quest for liberty. 1773 was the same year that Backus issued a call to all of his fellow Baptists in New England to stop submitting certificates and to refuse to pay religious taxes. 1773 was also the year that British Baptist John Allen's *An Oration Upon the Beauties of Liberty* was published in Boston, including some statements against slavery in a three-page appendix. However, it is unclear to what degree this tract shaped the Baptist politics of slavery. Hezekiah Smith and Samuel Stillman, for instance, owned slaves during this time.[7] The Brown family, key patrons of Rhode Island College of whom both Smith and Stillman were trustees, were involved in the business of shipping slaves.[8]

"The Negro Question"

Between 1776 and the 1830s, liberty-loving Baptists accepted, tolerated, and then justified the institution of slavery. As Edmund S. Morgan has demonstrated in his study of Virginia, "The rise of liberty and equality in America had been accompanied by the rise of slavery. That two such seemingly contradictory developments were taking place simultaneously over a long period of time, from the seventeenth century to the nineteenth, is the central paradox of American history."[9] Due to their beliefs about church membership, Baptists encountered this paradox more than any other denomination in America. According to Janet Moore Lindman, it was part of the Baptist experience in the early republic. "In molding their evangelical ideal to the boundaries of the institutional church, Baptists grappled with

4. "Ebenezer Smith's letter about Negro's, Oct. 16, 1773. Received Nov. 6. I.B. [Isaac Backus]," In McLoughlin, *Soul Liberty*, 154–55.
5. Backus, *Fish Caught in His Own Net*, 177–78.
6. Kidd and Hankins, *Baptists in America*, 99.
7. McLoughlin, *Soul Liberty*, 148.
8. Kidd and Hankins, *Baptists in America*, 99.
9. Morgan, *American Slavery, American Freedom*, 4.

how to incorporate a corporeal and egalitarian spirituality into a society based on unequal relations. A paradox of piety transpired; spiritual parity and social inequity coexisted within Baptist communities."[10]

In the early days of the republic, religious liberty proved to be a barrier that Baptists used not only to separate the church from the state, but also to distance themselves from the issue of slavery. As historians have shown, in the 1790s, Baptist associations in Virginia began to contend that the albatross of slavery was a discussion best left to the "legislative body" rather than the ecclesiastical, contributing to the so-called "spiritualization" of the church and insulating Baptists from the divisive issue of slavery.[11] According to this rationale, slavery was a political issue, not a spiritual one. In neighboring Kentucky, the Salem Association received a query from Rolling Fork church in 1798 about the ownership of slaves, to which it responded that it was "improper to enter in to so important and critical matter at present." Rolling Fork soon after withdrew from the Association. Mill Creek did the same after a similar situation in nearby Jefferson County. In 1791, the Elkhorn Association "appointed a committee of three to draw up a memorial to the Convention to be held on the 3d day of April next, requesting them to take up the subject of Religious Liberty and Perpetual Slavery, in the formation of the constitution of this District, and report at the 'Crossing,' on the 8th of September." Although the memorial was read and approved at the next meeting, the churches themselves opposed it. The following meeting the Association disapproved of the memorial.[12]

Baptists' awkward stance on slavery was a reflection of the state of the republic, and the church in Portsmouth, Virginia demonstrated just how awkward it could be. After Elder Thomas Armistead moved away in 1794, a black preacher from Northampton County named Jacob Bishop moved to town. His preaching was so "admired by saints and sinners" that friends in the community even bought his and his wife's freedom. However, by late 1796, the congregation remained without a pastor "and the church seemed at a low ebb." When the church sought counsel from neighboring churches, they were advised that, "whereas the black brethren in the church seemed anxious for a vote in conference, that it would be best to consider the black people as a wing of the body, and Jacob Bishop to take the oversight of them, as this church, at that time consisted of a number of black people." However, this only seemed to worsen the problem. While the whites were willing to essentially allow for two congregations and two pastors within the same

---

10. Lindman, *Bodies of Belief*, 181.
11. Irons, *Origins of Proslavery Christianity*, 72.
12. Spencer, *History of Kentucky Baptists*, 1:183–84.

church, the black members wished for one body, even with its racial division: "The black people at first seemed pleased with the proposition, but soon repented and came and told the Deacons they were afraid that matters might turn up disagreeably to them and dishonoring to God, and said they would be subordinate to the white brethren, if they would let them continue as they were; which was consented to."[13] Baptized blacks were eager to participate in the business of the church, but the white members were not willing for them to do so, at least not as it pertained to the church at large. In the early republic, it seemed, everyone was "anxious for a vote." Liberty and slavery could not be reconciled in the Baptist church.

Of course, in most parts of the country, low-church Baptists were known for their ministry to all classes and colors, including slaves.[14] Established ministers, for example, mocked their *extempore* preaching style that appealed to the unlearned.[15] The Presbyterian educator Charles C. Jones recorded, "In general the Negroes were followers of the Baptists in Virginia, and after a while, as they permitted many colored men to preach, the great majority of them went to hear preachers of their own color."[16] This no doubt contributed to the suspicion that Baptist churches were too sympathetic and accommodating to slaves. Even the most pro-slavery Baptist churches sometimes took political action in order to help slaves honor the Sabbath and obey the commands of God. In South Carolina, where forty percent of Baptist preachers owned slaves in the late eighteenth-century, the Charleston Association petitioned in 1801 and 1802 against a state law which "forbade slaves meeting even in the company of white persons for instruction or religious worship before sunrise or after sunset." Due in large part to the Baptist petitions, the law was modified in 1803 to allow that "religious assemblages with a majority of whites would not be disturbed by officers."[17] Oddly enough, religious liberty could serve both as an ideal by which Baptists insisted that slavery was extraneous to the church, and as the principle by which Baptists welcomed slaves *into* the church.

As Matthew Mason has argued, "there was never a time between the Revolution and the Civil War in which slavery went unchallenged."[18] In fluctuating numbers and in various groups, Baptists were consistently

---

13. Burkitt and Read, *Concise History of the Kehukee Baptist Association*, 258–59.
14. Hatch, *Democratization of American Christianity*, 102.
15. Osgood, *Wonderful Works of God Are To Be Remembered*, 1218, 1220.
16. Jones, *Religious Instruction of the Negroes*, 49.
17. Townsend, *South Carolina Baptists, 1670–1805*, 255; Kidd and Hankins, *Baptists in America*, 100.
18. Mason, *Slavery and Politics in the Early American Republic*, 5.

part of this avant garde in the early republic. Calls for emancipation among Baptists eventually came from both the North and the South, though far more in the former than the latter. After 1783, James Manning had joined the abolitionist efforts of Moses Brown, the former Baptist-turned-Quaker.[19] Manning even corresponded with London Baptists who drew up petitions to Parliament to end the British slave trade.[20] Baptists also used their largest platforms to speak out on the issue. On February 7, 1789, in his speech to the Massachusetts constitutional convention, Isaac Backus expressed his hope that one day America would bring an end to "the practice of making merchandise of slaves and souls of men."[21] In the 1790s, Baptist Associations from New England to Georgia publicly condemned the practice and business of slavery, like the Shaftesbury Association in New York when it declared in 1792 its "detestation of the SLAVE TRADE."[22] Such public condemnations of slavery by Baptists and other religious groups contributed to what Matthew Karp has described as "the anxious, if not paranoid, temper of slaveholding classes across the Age of Revolution."[23] They had good reason to be anxious. In the slave rebellion led by a man named Gabriel in 1800, a revolt which "reflected slaves' keen, if incomplete, awareness of the political context of the times," a number of the rebels attended the Baptist Hungry Meeting House in the Richmond area.[24]

By the so-called "Era of Good Feelings," slavery had not yet begun to explode the nation as it would in the Jacksonian era, but Baptists perceived its volatility. Reflecting back to his childhood in the late 1810s, Jeremiah Bell Jeter recalled, "At that period there was a prevalent opinion in Virginia not that slavery was in all cases sinful, but that the system imposed great responsibilities, and was fraught with many evils, economical, social, political, moral, and should as soon as possible be abolished."[25] Slavery was not yet considered a "positive good" as John C. Calhoun described it in 1837.[26] Similar to Thomas Jefferson's view, Baptists during this time believed that slavery was not inherently evil, though its effects were undeniably so.[27]

---

19. McLoughlin, *Soul Liberty*, 148.

20. "Rev. Dr. Rippon of London to James Manning, Feb. 14, 1788," in Guild, *Life, Times, and Correspondence of James Manning*, 407.

21. Elliot, *Debates in the Several State Conventions*, 1:149.

22. *Minutes of the Shaftesbury Association*, 11.

23. Karp, *This Vast Southern Empire*, 28.

24. Scully, *Religion and the Making of Nat Turner's Virginia*, 129.

25. Jeter, *Recollections of a Long Life*, 69.

26. Elder, *Calhoun*, 337–38.

27. Jefferson, *Notes on the State of Virginia*, Query XVIII, 169–71.

As a result, Baptists did not ask slave-owners to manumit their slaves, but to simply treat them well, like the article entitled "Anecdote of an American Negro Slave" in an 1817 issue of *The American Baptist Magazine and Missionary Intelligencer:*

> A poor ignorant negro came to a minister, with a melancholy and dejected look, and desired him to come and baptize his master again. "Why, Sambo," replied the minister, "what is the matter with your master?" "O, my massa been one good massa when you baptize afore; but now he forget all his religion, and scold, and vex, and whip poor negro!" What a cutting reproof does this convey to all those who, having been "buried by baptism into the death of Christ," are, nevertheless, not "walking in newness of life!" The *lives* of professors are books, which the most ignorant, and the most depraved, can read and understand![28]

In the South, if Baptists opposed slavery at all, they were much more likely to support colonization efforts than to advocate for abolitionism. As historians have shown, in Virginia, where nearly half the nation's enslaved and free blacks resided, colonization eventually became part of the proslavery agenda. "The ACS in Virginia began as essentially antislavery in the older gradual-emancipation tradition," Marie Tyler-McGraw notes, "but was always monitored from within by proslavery and states' rights persons whose power grew over the decades."[29] Due to the "great inconvenience" of the growing free black population, slaveholders believed the ACS could alleviate the tension that inevitably arose when enslaved blacks were exposed to free blacks. In secret correspondence with President Thomas Jefferson, Governor James Monroe had even once considered the removal of all free and emancipated blacks from Virginia.[30] Indeed, Old Dominion was a leader in colonization from the beginning. Virginia Congressman Charles Fenton Mercer took a primary role in the founding of ACS.[31]

The ACS thus became a way for Chesapeake-area Baptists who were wary of Northern abolitionism yet eager to see African Americans govern themselves to exercise their anti-slavery beliefs in a less controversial manner. Allison Burgess, chaplain of the House of Representatives, served as one of the founding members of the American Colonization Society in 1816.[32]

28. "Anecdote of an American Negro Slave," 1:20.
29. Tyler-McGraw, *African Republic*, 4.
30. Tyler-McGraw, *African Republic*, 12, 14.
31. Tomek, *Colonization and its Discontents*, 5.
32. Wilson and Fiske, *Appleton's Cyclopaedia of American Biography*, 1:58; Staudenraus, *African Colonization Movement*, 258n14.

Obadiah Buel Brown, the first pastor of First Baptist Church in Washington, D.C. and chaplain of both the U.S. House and Senate, did as well. William Staughton, the first president of Columbian College, was president of a local auxiliary of the colonization society in 1823 (as well as one of the founding members of the Philadelphia auxiliary).[33] Robert Semple and Andrew Broaddus were vice-presidents of another auxiliary society.[34] William Crane, who founded the Richmond African Baptist missionary society, was a member of the Richmond auxiliary.[35] Also noting later figures such as Jeremiah Bell Jeter, Aaron Menikoff has observed, "Colonization appealed broadly to Virginia's Baptists."[36] In Georgia, Jesse Mercer endorsed the idea in *The Christian Index*.[37] William Rabun, the governor of Georgia from 1817 to 1819 and a member of the Baptist choir in Powelton, was a member of an auxiliary in Milledgeville.[38] (Jonas Galusha (NH), Stephen Gano (RI), William Colgate (NY) were members of Northern auxiliaries.)[39] In 1819, the Baptist endorsement of colonization was manifest when black ministers Colin Teague and Lott Carey were appointed by the Triennial Convention in cooperation with the American Colonization Society as missionary colonists to West Africa.[40]

In wealthier South Carolina, however, white Baptists were a bit more apprehensive to colonize their slaves.[41] According to Beverly C. Tomek, "Though colonization remained popular in the North and border South, it began to face greater opposition not just from immediatists but from the planters of the lower South, especially as the cotton gin made slavery

33. Staudenraus, *African Colonization Movement*, 39.

34. Wilson and Fiske, *Appleton's Cyclopaedia of American Biography*, 1:548; *Dictionary of American Biography*, 2:555.

35. Wilson and Fiske, *Appleton's Cyclopaedia of American Biography*, 2:1; Staudenraus, *African Colonization Movement*, 109, 128. See also Tyler-McGraw, *African Republic*, 48.

36. Aaron Menikoff, *Politics and Piety*, 73.

37. Mercer, "African Colonization," 372.

38. Wilson and Fiske, *Appleton's Cyclopaedia of American Biography*, 5:157; Staudenraus, *African Colonization Movement*, 71.

39. Wilson and Fiske, *Appleton's Cyclopaedia of American Biography*, 2:584, 589; 1:688–69; Staudenraus, *African Colonization Movement*, 40, 84, 86, 132.

40. As John Saillant notes, colonization ultimately served to further deteriorate black-white relations in the states. "Colonizationists never separated the races geographically, as was their initial aim, but they did help to reify racial separation in civic and cultural life. Colonization, in its geographical aims, failed but, in a cultural sense, triumphed" (Saillant, *Black Puritan, Black Republican*, 153.)

41. For an excellent social history of slavery and the Afro-American population in colonial South Carolina, see Wood, *Black Majority*.

increasingly profitable."[42] In general Baptists followed, rather than fought, this trend. In 1821, a year after the Missouri Compromise, Basil Manly Sr. expressed his hesitations about emancipation and colonization in a college speech. Manly would eventually own as many as forty slaves, but he also appeared to have misgivings. More than most, Manly exemplified the internal conflict and paradox of slavery among a freedom-loving people. Admitting that slavery was "utterly repugnant to the spirit of our republican institutions," he confessed that "the inconsistency between slavery and a perfect equality and freedom can never be removed so long as those terms embrace the same ideas they do at present." Manly even recognized the contradiction in the Constitution itself. "While the framers of our constitution recognized most distinctly the principle that all men are naturally free and equal, with the very hand that subscribed to it, and fought to maintain it, they held the chain that bound a portion of their fellow men to perpetual servitude." Nevertheless, he was not willing to indict the founders for something he believed could not be avoided: "The stigma which attaches to hypocrisy and tyranny is indeed wiped away in this instance by the reflection that to them slavery was unavoidable."[43] On the subject of colonization, Manly reasoned,

> The difficulty and expense of the colonization system are indeed matters of serious moment. It is not however expected that the plan can be carried into complete and full operation at once. It must be the work of time. The period has not yet arrived when a direct and extensive interference on the part of government would be prudent. All that can now be asked of government is just to admit the principle, to encourage the formation of benevolent societies which have in view this grand object, and to protect with their flag these sons of misfortune as they are returning to their long lost home. When the principle of colonization is once admitted, the work will of itself go on. A cause of so much benevolence and justice will rarely fail to command the energies of the good. And I cannot avoid indulging the pleasing anticipation, that in the progress of civilization, of liberty and religion which are all engaged to support this cause, the time may yet arrive when this government may with propriety declare herself the friend of universal emancipation.[44]

Like so many white Baptists in the infant nation, and unlike his fellow Southern Baptists decades later, Manly's faith was in the future of America.

---

42. Tomek, *Colonization and its Discontents*, 12.
43. Manly, "On the Emancipation of Slaves," 63.
44. Manly, "On the Emancipation of Slaves," 63, 66–67.

Whether civil or religious, any challenges an oppressed people faced in the new republic could be overcome by the sheer "progress of civilization." The politics of optimism that drove Baptists to contend for their own liberty could sometimes have the opposite effect when it came to emancipation. In Manly's case, he was standing directly in the way of that progress. As a Democrat, Manly's vision of America would face its own challenges during the Nullification Crisis, when he supported his fellow South Carolinian John Calhoun against Andrew Jackson and the power of the federal government.[45]

Richard Furman was not as conflicted about slavery. In fact, Manly's predecessor at First Baptist Church of Charleston laid the groundwork for later Southern Baptists who would justify the great southern evil. Furman's influence and legacy in the Baptist South were substantial. In 1841, when William B. Johnson was welcomed to the floor after being voted the fourth president of the Triennial Convention, he began his acceptance speech by paying homage to his childhood hero, "the sainted Furman."[46] Four years later, when Johnson became the first president of the Southern Baptist Convention, Furman was the first person to be referenced in his convention address.[47] Manly, who was present in Augusta, Georgia in 1845, had called Furman "the wisest man I have ever known."[48] With the Southern Baptist Theological Seminary growing out of the theology faculty at Furman Academy, one could certainly make the case that Furman, the inaugural president of the Triennial Convention, was the most influential Baptist in Southern (and perhaps American) history.[49]

Therefore, unsurprisingly, Furman's influence on the issue of slavery was also considerable. For instance, according to Mark A. Noll, Furman's private correspondence helped to keep "proslavery texts alive" in the early nineteenth century.[50] His treatise on slavery, *Exposition of the Views of the Baptists, Relative to the Coloured Population of the United States, in a Communication to the Governor of South Carolina*, was a document of enormous consequence. Not only did Furman throw his political and moral weight

---

45. Fuller, "Song of Mercy and Judgment," 8.

46. Woodson, *Giant in the Land*, 98; In his "Reminiscences," Johnson recalls, "My acquaintance with this man of God began when I was a boy, and I well remember the deep and solemn impression which his grave and ministerial appearance made upon my mind, young as I then was; an impression which was deepened by a more familiar knowledge of his character" (Cited in King, *History of South Carolina Baptists*, 212.)

47. Johnson, "Address of the Convention," 205.

48. Friend, "Biography of Richard Furman, Sr.," 29.

49. Todd, "Sainted Furman," 99–120.

50. Noll, "Missouri, Denmark Vesey, Biblical Proslavery, and a Crisis for *Sola Scriptura*," 101.

into the most flammable debate in the country in one of the most volatile moments in South Carolina history, he did so on behalf of the newly formed South Carolina Baptist Convention—the convention he architected, presided over, and the first of its Baptist kind in America.[51] In one sense, that such a treatise was written by a Baptist is unsurprising. Monica Najar has noted how "Baptist churches consistently claimed authority over *all* aspects of their members' lives, including marriage, slavery, business practices, child rearing, and leisure activities. No issue, decision, or behavior was defined as private or outside of the purview of the church."[52] In another sense, Furman's *Exposition* was an example of how religious liberty should function in his particular vision of the republic: the state could not speak authoritatively to the church, but the church could do so to the state.

In the address, Furman delivered one of the first written defenses of slavery and paternalism in the United States and set forth arguments that Southern Baptists would use to justify slavery for decades to come. After plans for a slave revolt led by free carpenter Denmark Vesey were discovered in 1822 and thirty-five conspirators put to death, Furman wished to bring "the intended Insurrection into view by publicly acknowledging its prevention to be an instance of the Divine Goodness." South Carolina certainly must have felt like a social, racial, and political tinderbox. As a result, the exposition was both a word of support to the fearful white citizens of South Carolina and a word of warning to its black inhabitants. In response to those who argued that a Day of Public Thanksgiving would only provoke another insurrection, Furman insisted "that the Negroes should know, that however numerous they are in some parts of these Southern States, they, yet, are not, even including all descriptions, bond and free, in the United States, but little more than one sixth part of the whole number of Inhabitants."[53] On this occasion, Furman's concern was the "public peace of the State," rebuking "certain writers" who had "advanced positions, and inculcated sentiments, very unfriendly to the principle and practice of holding slaves."[54]

As a whole, Furman's treatise must be interpreted as the conservative voice of a Charleston Federalist lion in the twilight of his career, affirming the pro-slavery position of a denomination that had been suspected of being overly amenable to slaves, and summoning the power of the church to quell the instability of the very state he had helped create. Insisting that "the

---

51. Basil Manly Sr. and William B. Johnson helped write the constitution for the new state convention with Furman.

52. Najar, *Evangelizing the South*, 6.

53. Furman, *Exposition of the Views of the Baptists*, 3–4, 6.

54. Furman, *Exposition of the Views of the Baptists*, 7.

right of holding slaves is clearly established in the Holy Scriptures, both by precept and example," Furman called upon a host of proof texts, including the *locus classicus* of the pro-slavery position: 1 Timothy 6:1 ("account their masters worthy of all honour").[55] Amazingly, Furman even appealed to Lockean principles to argue that slaves had become slaves by their own choice! To the vexing question of how slaves had arrived in America in the first place, Furman asserted that "the Africans brought to America were, in general, slaves, by their own consent, before they came from their own country, or fell into the hands of white men." He concluded, "the man made a slave in this manner, might be said to be made so by his own consent, and by the indulgence of barbarous principles."[56] As Furman demonstrated, white Baptists were able to use revolutionary principles to argue for their own liberty *and* to trample upon the liberty of others. When Harriet Beecher Stowe published *A Key to Uncle Tom's Cabin* (1853) to defend the veracity of her famous novel, she included a pro-slavery memorial from the Charleston Baptist Association to the South Carolina legislature in 1835 which stated, "The right of masters to dispose of the time of their slaves has been distinctly recognized by the Creator of all things, who is surely at liberty to vest the right of property over any object in whomsoever he pleases."[57] But the Revolution could be invoked on both sides of the slavery issue. In 1831, Baptist Nat Turner led the most violent slave revolt in American history under the very same banner of liberty. As James P. Byrd has concluded, "Turner had planned his attack for July 4—it would be his Independence Day—but logistical problems forced a delay. Still, we cannot miss his plan to connect his "revolution" with that of 1776, nor can we miss his connection with the Bible."[58]

By the late eighteenth and early nineteenth centuries, slavery had already drawn lines in the new nation—and among Baptists. On one hand, Richard Furman had established a network of like-minded Baptists like William B. Johnson and Basil Manly Sr., even recruiting fellow gentlemen to the South like Jonathan Maxcy who shared the same aversion to a "system of equality."[59] On the other hand, there were still a multitude of Baptists even in the South who openly opposed the institution of slavery, and no two Baptists in America appeared as diametrically opposed as did Richard Furman

---

55. Furman, *Exposition of the Views of the Baptists*, 7–8.
56. Furman, *Exposition of the Views of the Baptists*, 11.
57 Stowe, *Key to Uncle Tom's Cabin*, 385.
58. Byrd, *Holy Baptism of Fire and Blood*, 25.
59. Maxcy, "Oration, Delivered at the First Congregational Meeting House, in Providence, on the Fourth of July, 1799," 388.

and John Leland. Upon leaving Virginia, Leland condemned slavery using his own brand of Lockean philosophy. "Slavery," Leland declared in his Resolution for the General Committee of Virginia Baptists in 1789, "in its best appearance, is a violent deprivation of the rights of nature, inconsistent with republican government, destructive of every humane and benevolent passion of the soul, and subversive to that liberty absolutely necessary to ennoble the human mind." The Baptist preacher then implored, "let me ask whether Heaven has nothing in store for poor negroes better than these galling chains? If so, ye ministers of Jesus, and saints of the Most High, ye wrestling Jacobs, who have power with God, and can prevail over the angel, let your prayers, your ardent prayers, ascend to the throne of God incessantly, that he may pour the blessing of *freedom* upon the poor blacks."[60] As someone who had lived in both Virginia and Massachusetts, Leland had a unique view of the American situation and the so-called "Negro Question."[61] In his view, emancipation and religious liberty were two sides of the same republican coin. Conversely, slavery and establishment were the twin evils of civil and religious tyranny. Just as Leland had praised the South for its revivalism and religious liberty, so he also viewed slavery as a predominantly Southern evil. In 1802, from Cheshire, Massachusetts, Leland explained, "As personal slavery exists chiefly in the southern states, so religious slavery abounds exclusively in three or four of the New England states."[62] Politically speaking, from John Leland's vantage point, each region of the country had its burden to bear.[63] In just a couple decades, slavery would permeate the farthest reaches of Southern and Baptist society. Even among the Cherokees in Georgia, Baptist political leaders like Jesse Bushyhead fought against the tyranny of the United States in Jackson's removal program but also owned black slaves, some of which were Baptist.[64]

As scathing as John Leland's critiques could be against the Congregationalists, his public rebuke of slavery was just as severe. For instance, Leland was not afraid to mock the infamous Three-Fifths Compromise of the Constitution using his experiences from the Baptist church:

---

60. Leland, "Letter of Valediction," 174.

61. Leland, "Address Delivered at North Adams, on the 4th of March, 1831," 612.

62. Leland, "Oration, Delivered at Cheshire, July 5, 1802, on the Celebration of Providence," 268.

63. This is not to say that New England did not grapple with slavery and that the issue did not split Baptist churches in New England. By 1840, "not a few" churches in Maine were "rent in twain" due to the issue of slavery and the "sweet fellowship of former years was sadly marred" (Burrage, *History of the Baptists in Maine*, 314.

64. McLoughlin, *Cherokees and Christianity*, 78. By some accounts, as discovered by missionary Evan Jones, Bushyhead was not known for mistreatment of his slaves.

> They [slaves] are not considered in a complex character, in the United States, possessing *three-fifths* of humanity and *two-fifths* of animal property. I have spent fifteen years of my life in a slaveholding state (Virginia), calling led me to mingle with the slaves, as well as with their masters: and I believe there are as many of the slaves (in proportion to their numbers) who join the Christian churches, as there are of the whites. Some of them can read—others hear and believe, and a number of them are zealous preachers and exhorters. Redemption by the blood of Christ—a gracious change of heart—and holiness of life, are their favorite topics. The slaves generally put more confidence in the preachers of their own color, than they do in the whites, from a belief tha they are less likely to deceive them. Of course, should they be removed into a section assigned them, there would be neither need nor propriety for government to furnish them with religious teachers.[65]

Even Leland entertained the idea of removing slaves to another land, but his plan was distinct from the traditional concept of colonization, which he called "sacrilegious" for its ripping apart of families and traditions.[66] On more than one occasion he suggested a "section of territory" or "sisters states" on the American continent to which slaves could be educated and provided for by their masters for three years with the help of the United States treasury.[67] Although Leland's proposal belied certain prejudices of his own, it speaks to his consideration of the needs and rights of the slaves as well as to his understanding that most slave-owners would not simply emancipate their slaves.[68] At times, Leland could be both a realist and an idealist. Regardless, he was consistently a Baptist. "One of the greatest injustices of slavery, in his view, was the denial of slaves' rights to freedom of conscience."[69]

---

65. Leland, "Free Thoughts on Times and Things," 673.

66. Leland, "Address Delivered at North Adams," 612.

67. Leland, "Address Delivered at North Adams," 612, Leland, "Free Thoughts on Times and Things," 672.

68 Eric C. Smith has argued, "Though infused with evangelical theology, Leland's position was virtually identical to Jefferson's in substance. Both men were what have now come to be called 'conditional terminators' — proponents of emancipation under the 'right' conditions" (Smith, *John Leland*, 201).

69. Scully, *Religion and the Making of Nat Turner's Virginia*, 110.

Freedom on the Frontier

On the frontier, white Baptists confronted the issue of slavery in a number of ways. Thomas Lincoln, the father of Abraham Lincoln, moved his family from Kentucky to Indiana in December of 1816 because of the ban on slavery in the Northwest Ordinance. Decades later, his son claimed that Thomas left Kentucky "partly on account of slavery, but chiefly on account of the difficulty of land titles in Kentucky."[70] Such overlap of moral principle and personal advancement was not uncommon on the Baptist frontier. In Ohio, Baptists shaped the politics of slavery directly. Rev. John Smith of Virginia, identified as the first full-time Baptist preacher in Ohio, was a member of its constitutional convention in 1802 that banned slavery, becoming one of the state's first two U.S. Senators. (One of Thomas Jefferson's former slaves, Peter Fossett, eventually moved to Ohio and became a Baptist pastor.[71]) During his time in the Senate, the staunchly Republican Smith became acquainted with Vice President Aaron Burr, who presided over the assembly. By 1808, however, Smith was forced to resign from office under allegations of his participation in Burr's scandal to allegedly secede American land to Spain.[72] A Senate committee chaired by John Quincy Adams had investigated Smith's actions and recommended expulsion from the Senate. Although the resolution fell one vote short of the required two-thirds majority, Smith resigned from Congress with no small degree of shame, eventually moving to Louisiana.[73]

But Smith's legacy also had a bright side. While in Columbia, a young Thomas Morris became a clerk in Smith's store. Morris's father was a Baptist pastor who had moved his family in 1795 to the Baptist community of Columbia, the church of which was co-founded by Stephen Gano. Although it is not clear if Morris remained in the Baptist church, his wife was a member for thirty years, and Morris himself would still associate himself with the Baptists. He once praised the abolitionism of a Virginian named Obed Donham, who in 1802 donated two lots in Williamsburgh, Ohio to the Baptist church "who do not hold slaves, nor commune at the Lord's Table with those who practice such tyranny over their fellow creatures."[74] Morris would go on to become the first abolitionist Senator in the history

---

70. Burlingame, *Abraham Lincoln,* 1:21.

71. Kidd, *Thomas Jefferson,* 238.

72. Cheathem, *Andrew Jackson and the Rise of the Democratic Party,* 40–41, 45–46, 58, 100; Cheathem, *Andrew Jackson,* 46–48.

73. Dunlevy, *History of the Miami Baptist Association,* 96–119.

74. Morris, *Life of Thomas Morris,* 24.

of the United States. In 1844, he was the Vice-Presidential nominee for the anti-slavery Liberty Party.

In 1810, at the age of twenty-six, Jesse Lynch Holman moved from Kentucky to Indiana largely due to his aversion to slavery.[75] Holman, who would become one of the first three justices on the Indiana Supreme Court, had freed his wife's slaves upon arrival to Indiana, where slavery was prohibited. Years later, he served as one of the three judges that ruled on *Lasselle v. State* (1820), an Indiana Supreme Court case that resulted in all slaves being held within the state to be freed. Holman and his father were advocates of eventual emancipation, and Holman himself was an active member of the Indiana Colonization Society, presiding over its organization meeting in Indianapolis on November 4, 1829. According to I. George Blake, "it appears that he was only a moderate abolitionist."[76] However, when Holman was appointed to the federal judgeship, a faction within the Democratic party began to oppose his confirmation, and slavery was a key issue. The fracas prompted Holman to travel to Washington in early 1836 to seek an audience with President Jackson. His description of the meeting is revealing of just how significantly the issue of slavery shaped American politics:

> I was fortunate to find him alone. He conversed freely on a great variety of subjects. Talked some on the subject of my appointment, & the opposition that was got up against me. . . . He mentioned the charge of abolition . . . which I had answered in several letters, which I had shown him. I satisfied him completely on that subject, & especially by repeating my decision in the first Negro case I acted on a few days after I rec'd my commission, & which I gave a certificate for removal of the slave to Kentucky. I stated the principles upon which I decided. It gave him entire satisfaction & . . . the Gen'l was particularly pleased with my decision. . .[77]

Holman was later confirmed unanimously as a United States District Judge, proving that Baptists in the west were capable of upward mobility in a way they were not in other parts of the early republic, but not without a degree of politicking. Dependent on one's personal views, slavery could pose a large and sometimes insuperable obstacle to political advancement.

---

75. Cady, *Origin and Development of the Missionary Baptist Church in Indiana*, 92.
76. Blake, "Jesse Lynch Holman," 48.
77. Blake, "Jesse Lynch Holman: Pioneer Hoosier," 49.

Friends of Humanity

Baptist David Barrow encountered his own obstacles, but mostly from Baptists themselves. After freeing his own slaves in 1784 due to his "conviction of the iniquity, and a discovery of the inconsistency of heredity slavery, with a republican form of government," Barrow's abolitionist views compelled him in 1798 to leave Virginia for Kentucky, where he believed that an agrarian lifestyle could be profitable without slave labor. Before leaving, Barrow wrote a *Circular Letter* to his congregation in Southampton, Virginia defending his departure. Barrow believed "the business of speculation" to be "incompatible with the work of the ministry" and slavery to be "contrary to the laws of God and nature."[78] As a summary of Barrow's "religious and political faith," the letter is significant not only for its bold stand against slavery, but also for its wedding of Baptist theology and politics. Amazingly, the Baptist minister listed 26 political principles but only 15 theological doctrines. The result, in the words of one historian, was "a summary of the political philosophy of the Jeffersonian Republicans as it was popularly understood."[79] From the natural equality of man to the civil compact of government to the universal right of suffrage, Barrow left no doubt of his Republican politics. As a Baptist Jeffersonian, religious liberty was not far from his mind:

> 13. That all religious tests, and ecclesiastical establishments, are oppressive, and infringing the rights of conscience.
> 14. That civil rulers have nothing more to do with religion, in their public capacities, than private men; save only, that they should protect its professors in the interrupted enjoyment of it, with life, property, and character, in common with other good citizens.[80]

Ultimately, Barrow's abolitionism was as republican as it was Baptist. He implored "that all masters, or owners of slaves, may consider how inconsistently they act, with a Republican Government, and whether in this particular, they are *doing, as they would others should do to them!*"[81]

Barrow was no stranger to a little opposition. In fact, his Baptist views prepared him well for the political and religious hatred he would face on the frontier. In 1778, he and fellow Baptist minister Edward Mintz were assaulted by a group of men while preaching near the Nansemond River in Virginia. Dragging the two preachers from the stage to the river, the

---

78. Allen, "David Barrow's *Circular Letter* of 1798," 445.
79. Allen, "David Barrow's *Circular Letter* of 1798," 440.
80. Allen, "David Barrow's *Circular Letter* of 1798," 448.
81. Allen, "David Barrow's *Circular Letter* of 1798," 450.

gang repeatedly dunked Barrow and Mintz into the muddy water, holding them underneath for nearly a minute at a time. Mocking their baptism by immersion, the gang swore "as [the preachers] loved *dipping*, to give them enough of it." When Barrow was brought up each time, they asked him if he believed.[82] Such harrowing experiences of persecution no doubt steeled the young Baptist for a life of abolitionism and unimpeachable conviction.

When Barrow arrived in Kentucky, however, he faced several church schisms because of his views. In 1807, when he was expelled from the North District Association (and the same year that the African slave trade was banned), he led messengers from nine churches to form the "Baptized Licking Locust Association, Friends of Humanity." Although the group was relatively short-lived, disbanding not long after Barrow's death in 1819, the Friends of Humanity was a trailblazing venture in the West. Carter Tarrant, a fellow member and self-professed "Emancipator in principle," had resigned from his church in Hillsborough, Kentucky due to his anti-slavery views, founding with seventeen others the Regular Baptist Church of Christ at Craig's Creek in Woodford County, Kentucky. In an 1806 sermon in the town of Versailles, Tarrant appealed to both the Virginia and federal constitutions in order to make his case for emancipation.[83] Through the Friends of Humanity, Baptists contributed a significant chapter in the rise of abolitionism in America and in the tumultuous road to civil war. In Illinois, Baptists like the future Whig John Mason Peck attended conferences for the Friends of Humanity, praising the "valuable things in this society" and accepting their support for his seminary at Rock Spring.[84] (Peck was one of the leading Baptist antislavery voices in the West, establishing schools for slaves in Illinois and Missouri.) Historians have even speculated as to the influence of the Friends of Humanity on a young Abraham Lincoln.[85]

During his time with the Friends, David Barrow also published an important antislavery tract in 1808 and helped to organize the Kentucky Abolition Society. So impassioned was Barrow for emancipation, and so deeply rooted his Jeffersonianism, that in 1815 he decided to send a letter to former President Thomas Jefferson to advocate for abolition. Although

---

82. Scully, *Religion and the Making of Nat Turner's Virginia*, 50.

83. Menikoff, *Politics and Piety*, 93.

84. Peck, *Forty Years of Pioneer Life*, 209–10; 228, 293–94; Carwardine, "Evangelicals, Whigs and the Election of William Henry Harrison," 64.

85. McBeth, *Baptist Heritage*, 383—84. Slavery eventually became the most divisive issue between Whigs and Democrats. As William J. Cooper Jr. explains, "Although the Whigs continuously berated the Democrats for politicizing slavery, the Democrats, in turn, castigated the Whigs for attempting to make the slave issue their own" (Cooper, *South and the Politics of Slavery, 1828–1856*, 67.)

his fellow Virginian had long been opposed to any efforts at ending slavery and had never claimed the faith of historic Christianity, the Baptist minister nevertheless appealed to the teachings and example of Jesus:

> I trust that Bigotry, that tarnishes the Aspects & sours the Tempers of so many of the Professors of Christianity, has never influenced your Prejudice so as to bias your Judgment, relative to the great Subject of Religion: and I live under flattering Expectations that the Tolerance of our Government, will ultimately have the goodly Effect to remove those Animosities & party Spirit, that is too visible among the different Christian Sects, and that they will be led under the Influence of that "Charity that never fails" to meet & embrace one another upon pure Apostolic Grounds, and thereby manifest to an admiring World, the native Beauty and Utility of the Doctrines & Morality of the Lord Jesus.
>
> The enclosed Scraps [of antislavery writings] will furnish you with a more general Idea, of some Things that have been agitated in this Quarter, than I have time or Room at present to insert.—I forward them with a Hope that at some leisure Hour, you may find Freedom to drop me some Hints, that your Knowledge, Feelings, & Observations on the Subjects of Slavery & emancipation may dictate, which may be helpful to us in our present Struggles.
>
> And now Dear Sir, I most sincerely pray, that after a Life of public Toil & Usefulness you may through Divine Grace, be found among the heavenly Songsters, rendering "Blessing, and Honour, and Glory, and Power unto him who sitteth upon the Throne, and unto the Lamb, for ever and ever.[86]

Barrow's epistle illustrates, rather ironically, how Baptists who fought for their liberty in the name of Jesus Christ *with* Thomas Jefferson could then defend the liberty of Africans and the name of Jesus *to* Thomas Jefferson, who believed in neither. Nevertheless, Jefferson responded to the letter:

> Unhappily it is a case for which both parties require long and difficult preparation. The mind of the master is to be apprised by reflection, and strengthened by the energies of conscience, against the obstacles of self interest, to an acquiescence in the rights of others; that of the slave is to be prepared by instruction and habit for self-government and for the honest pursuits of industry and social duty. Both of these courses of preparation

---

86. "David Barrow to Thomas Jefferson, 20 March 1815," in Looney, *Papers of Thomas Jefferson*, 8:364–65. Also see Kidd, "Baptist Abolitionist Appeals to Thomas Jefferson."

require time, and the former must precede the latter. Some progress is sensibly made in it; yet not so much as I had hoped and expected. But it will wield in time to temperate & steady pursuit, to the enlargement of the human mind, and its advancement in science.

We are not in a world ungoverned by the laws and the power of a superior agent. Our efforts are in his hand, and directed by it; and he will give them their effect in his own time. Where the disease is most deeply seated, there it will be slowest in eradication. In the Northern states it was merely superficial, & easily corrected. in the Southern it was incorporated with the whole system, and requires time, patience, and perseverance in the curative process. That it may finally be effected and its progress hastened will be the last and fondest prayer of him who now salutes you with respect & consideration.[87]

Thomas Jefferson did not believe in a three-in-one God, a vicarious atonement, or in emancipation. But he did believe in providence, prayer, and progress. Therefore, while Baptists and Thomas Jefferson were seemingly worlds apart theologically and even socially, they shared a mutual belief in the kinetic energy of the American experiment. While Baptist views on slavery were not monolithic, they were almost always couched in the rhetoric of the Revolution. Not surprisingly, the themes of progress and improvement that attended the "Negro Question" also imbued the debate over Native Americans.

"Civilizing of these Indians"

Although the Indian removal controversy did not begin in earnest until the 1820s, the precarious relationship between colonists and Native Americans dated as far back as King Philip's War and even to the earliest Puritans.[88] John Leland, for example, praised Roger Williams's unpopular kindness to the Indians in Massachusetts Bay Colony. In addition to his controversial views concerning religious liberty, when Williams declared "that it was unjust to take the land of the Indians without a satisfactory reward, he was banished from Massachusetts Bay, and fled south to the Indians, who gave him a tract of land which he named Providence."[89] Baptists like Leland could therefore

---

87. "Thomas Jefferson to David Barrow, 1 May 1815," in Looney, *Papers of Thomas Jefferson: Retirement Series*, 8:454–55.

88. See Lepore, *Name of War*. Also see Horn, *1619*, 85–118.

89. Leland, "Address at a Democratic Meeting Held at Cheshire, August 28, 1834," 655. Roger Williams's first and most popular book concerned the Indians. Published in

take some form of pride in their earliest Baptist ancestors' ministry to the Native Americans. However, Baptists were also a forward-minded people, and their sense of manifest destiny did not typically create a space for people they deemed to be intellectually and morally inferior.[90] Isaac Backus had a slightly different take on Roger Williams, boasting that he "did the most to prevent the ruin of all these colonies by the Indians of any one man in the country."[91] In other words, by defending religious freedom, Williams did not just defend the Indians; he also defended America *from* the Indians. When Jonathan Maxcy (who ironically pastored and presided institutions in Providence, Rhode Island) contemplated America's future, the west was not far from his mind: "When these extensive western regions shall be filled with people, the whole habitable world will have been surrounded and settled by civilized man." Remarkably, Maxcy even predicted when this migration would happen. "This event will probably occur in the seventh grand Millenary from the creation. Then the kingdoms of this world, will become the kingdoms of our Lord. All nations shall bow to his scepter, all enemies shall fall under his feet."[92] The Baptist vision of America included the civilization—and conversion—of the west. As a nation appointed by God to bring freedom to the world, America was commissioned to conquer and evangelize the heathen. As William G. McLoughlin has shown, for Baptists, "To Christianize was to Americanize."[93] However, as a people of religious liberty, Baptists inevitably had competing visions of how to liberate Native Americans from their sin.

Not surprisingly, John Leland located the source of white racism against Native Americans in religious establishment. "The early settlers of New England had a strong notion of a Christian commonwealth," Leland recollected, "that Christians had the same pre-eminence over the heathen that the Israelites had over the inhabitants of Canaan; that as God gave the tribes the land of the Canaanites, so also it was his will that Christians should take away the land of the Indians."[94] As a Baptist, Leland placed a strong em-

---

1643, *A Key into the Language of America* is, according to Gaustad, "an early and valuable example of cultural anthropology" (Gaustad, *Roger Williams*, 29).

90. Some scholars, however, have critiqued the entire idea of manifest destiny. Alan Taylor contends, "During the 1780s, the United States lacked any evident 'Manifest Destiny' to dominate the West." He has even called it "the most misleading phrase ever offered to explain American expansion" (Taylor, *American Republics*, xxiv, 32).

91. Backus, *Government and Liberty Described*, 355–56.

92. Maxcy, "Discourse, Delivered in the Chapel of South Carolina College, July 4th, 1819," 294.

93. McLoughlin, *Cherokees and Christianity, 1794–1870*, 38.

94. Leland, "Address at a Democratic Meeting Held at Cheshire, August 28, 1834,"

phasis on the newness of God's new covenant with his people. Since God's covenant was no longer secured by ancestry but by faith, and his covenant sign no longer made by circumcision but by baptism, Christians should not look to Old Testament Israel to inform their purpose and identity in the New Testament church. Therefore, America was not the new Israel and the Native Americans were not the new Canaanites. Lives and property were at stake in this important distinction between church and state. According to Leland, if any people in America suffered from this unbiblical kind of covenant theology, it wasn't just the Baptists. It was the Native Americans.[95] The evils committed by the earliest settlers against the Indians were enough for Isaac Backus to question their Christianity and to insist that the stain of racism was a "poison whereof we are not yet thoroughly purged."[96]

Like the Revolution itself, the Baptist debate over the plight of Native Americans was a conversation with, and often an endorsement of, John Locke.[97] According to C. Bradley Thompson, "The revolutionary generation learned to ground property rights in self-ownership from John Locke's chapter on property in the *Second Treatise*," and thus they viewed "liberty and property as indissolubly connected."[98] According to Locke, "every man has *property* in his own person" so that no man "has any right to but himself." Each man, he reasoned, is "master of himself, and *proprietor of his own person*, and the actions or labor of it." This principle of self-ownership transfers to property when he applies the "labour of his body, and the work of his hands" to material things, such as land. By virtue of cultivating or improving the soil, man has inserted a part of himself into the land, thereby giving him the right to "preserve his property."[99] In the early republic, this is exactly what many claimed that the Native Americans had *not* done to the American soil. But John Leland pushed back against this form of white entitlement. Leland asked,

> Did not the Creator of the earth give the whole of it to all the inhabitants of it? Does the law of nature give to an individual

---

654.

95. Harry S. Stout expounds, "However harsh these sentiments ring to modern ears, they were what justified early Americans in their audacious land grab. Backed by biblical precedent and America's resurrected identity as the New Israel, the process of Indian removal made perfect sense to them" (Stout, *American Aristocrats*, 22.)

96. Backus, *Policy As Well As Honesty*, 371.

97. According to Gordon S. Wood, "few American ministers saw any need to deny the Enlightenment for the sake of religion" (Wood, *Creation of the American Republic*, 8).

98. Thompson, *America's Revolutionary Mind*, 196, 199.

99. Locke, *Two Treatises of Government*, para. 27, 44, 87.

any more of the earth than his body can cover? What gives men a moral right to any portion of the earth, except the improvement which they have put upon it? If one improves a section of the earth, by building on it, or fencing it, how far does his exclaim extend? To the sea—to the mountains—to a certain degree of latitude, or how far? If two settlements begin at the same time, being a thousand miles distant, do their claims run to the centre? Or has another an equal right to build and possess between them? I am still waiting for an elucidation of these and similar questions.[100]

While Leland was waiting for a reasonable explanation, other Baptists like fellow Republican David Jones employed Locke's principles to argue *against* Native American sovereignty and *for* white land distribution for the purpose of "civilizing" the Indians. "Providence seems to point out the civilizing of these Indians," he observed, "for a farming life will lead to laws, learning, and government, to secure property."[101] For Jones, who served as chaplain under Major General Anthony Wayne in both the Revolutionary War and the Indians Wars in the Old Northwest Territory, the only legitimate way to "secure property" was not to live on the land, but to cultivate it (i.e. "a farming life"). Having spent time evangelizing Indians in the Ohio River valley and even publishing a journal from his two visits, Jones confidently applied the Lockean idea of social contract to argue his case. In an article from a series entitled "Indian Affairs" in the *Philadelphia Aurora* in 1811, Jones told the story of a conversation with an Indian about land boundaries. "They laughed at me," Jones wrote. Then they added,

> When the Great Manitto made man, he gave him a right to three things, viz, he had a right to as much air as he wanted, and to use as much water as he wanted, and he had a right to cultivate as much land as would support him; but he had no right to forbid a brother to do the same. From these principles it is evidence that all right to landed property arises from civil compact, and that every man as a legal right to as much as he can purchase.[102]

John Locke also supplied Americans with a way of understanding the Native American situation when he explained the pre-civilized state of humanity as a "state of nature," a condition in which many saw the American west. Thompson explains, "The idea of a state of nature was not a fiction

100. Leland, "Address Delivered at North Adams," 611.

101. Jones, *Journal of Two Visits Made to Some Nations of Indians on the West Side of the River Ohio*, 81.

102. Jones, "Indian Affairs."

or a hypothetical construct for American revolutionaries. It described their social reality and explained much of their lived experience throughout the colonial period. As long as there was an American frontier, there would be something like a state of nature along the western boundaries of the provinces or in those places where the long arm of British or provincial law did not extend."[103] In his dealings with the Native Americans, David Jones fully subscribed to this thinking. In a letter to President James Madison in 1815, Jones concluded, "To me it is as plain as two and three makes five, that neither Whiteman or Indians has any property in Soil. All right to soil arises from civil compact, in a State of Nature [one] can therefore have no right to land. The Phrase Indian Country is common Nonsense, never examined. By Nature we have no property in Land."[104] Jones's beliefs fully supported his Jeffersonian politics and his own brand of white supremacy. Jones disclaimed the necessity of making written agreements of any kind with Native Americans, a view similar to that of Georgia Governor and Baptist Wilson Lumpkin years later during Andrew Jackson's removal controversy.[105] Two years earlier, he wrote to Secretary of State James Monroe, calling treaties with Indians "foolish" and suggesting that a full-scale war was the only solution for peace.[106]

The Indian wars on the frontier inevitably shaped the way that Baptists viewed Native Americans and their enemies abroad. Behind the fighting in Ohio, David Jones saw the long arm of Britain. Calling the Indian-British warfare on the frontier a "tory war," Jones insisted that the Indians were "well paid by the British to commit the murders on our defenseless frontiers."[107] Some Baptists even played a significant role in the military campaigns that shaped the American west. Having arrived in Ohio with his father John Gano, John Stites Gano eventually became one of "the pioneers of Cincinnati" and enjoyed a tremendous military career that culminated

---

103. Thompson, *America's Revolutionary Mind*, 257.

104. David Jones to James Madison, March 8, 1815, MS in the American Baptist Historical Society, Rochester, New York. Also see Wolever, *Life, Journal and Works of David Jones, 1736–1820*, 102–3.

105. According to Theda Perdue and Michael D. Green, "Lumpkin had broadcast his opinion that Cherokees should be treated like orphan children incapable of making decisions, and instead of continuing to fool around negotiating a removal agreement, the government, either his or Jackson's, should simply legislate their expulsion" (Perdue and Green, *Cherokee Nation and the Trail of Tears*, 107).

106. Terry Wolever concludes, A full-scale war against the natives was thus suggested by Jones, a war lasting as long as required for the Indians to accept the complete terms of the white men" (*Life, Journal and Works of David Jones*, 112).

107. Jones, "Old Indian School Must Be Abandoned," 2.

in his being promoted to General of the Ohio Militia in 1806.[108] In 1791, Gano was involved in the defeat of Arthur St. Clair's regiment in the Battle of the Wabash River.[109] Led by Little Turtle of the Miamis, Blue Jacket of the Shawnees, and Buckongahelas of the Delawares, the coalition of Native Americans delivered what was to be the United States' worst ever defeat by the American Indians. By 1813, Gano's enmity for the Indians of the Ohio Territory had not diminished. In an October 16th letter, General William Henry Harrison commanded Gano, "You will take the command of all the posts upon the frontier of the State of Ohio. You can establish your quarters at Fort Meigs, Lower or Upper Sandusky. You will afford all the security possible to the frontiers as well by repelling any invasion of the savages as by preventing any depredation upon them."[110]

Nevertheless, by the time that Baptists had convened for the sake of domestic and foreign missions, and the subject of Indian removal had taken center stage in Washington under President Andrew Jackson, certain Baptists made arguments against their mistreatment, including the concept of religious liberty. For instance, in *Remarks on the Practicability of Indian Reform, Embracing their Colonization* (1829), Isaac McCoy boldly asserted "that, in a comparison of religious sentiments with the Indians, some refined people in christendom ought to blush at their own bigoted attachments. I suppose the natives have always been in the habit of killing witches; but I very much question if ever there was a man upon the continent chased out of his country, imprisoned, or whipped, for his religion, before the settlement of the whites in it."[111] For McCoy, religious liberty was not simply for Baptists, but for Native Americans as well. And if the Indians suffered from their own form of ignorance, so did whites.

According to Daniel Williams, "the issue of removal divided Baptists as deeply as it did the rest of the nation. Within the Baptist Triennial Convention, one can not only see two sides of the social reform movement in one denomination but also regional divisions that the debates over slavery and abolition would later exacerbate into a final schism."[112] Instead of simply removing the Indians, Isaac McCoy pushed for colonization in lands west of the Mississippi, a plan not endorsed by most of his Baptist brethren when met with political resistance. McCoy, who was probably influenced

---

108. Cist, *Cincinatti Miscellany, or Antiquities of the West*, 1:255.

109. Wolever, *Life and Ministry of John Gano, 1727–1804*, 1:422.

110. "Wm. Henry Harrison to Major Gen. John S. Gano," in Wolever, *Life and Ministry of John Gano, 1727–1804*, 1:433.

111. McCoy, *Remarks on the Practicability of Indian Reform, Embracing their Colonization*, 16.

112. Williams, "New Era in Their History," 57.

by David Jones, shared Jones's vision for Indian agriculture.[113] According to McCoy's plan, every native who migrated to the territory would be given a tract of land where he could establish his family and learn to farm. The plan even included a centralized government, a Constitution, and a legislature comparable with other states in the union. The Board of Foreign Missions initially consented to McCoy's plan in 1824, even preparing a memorial to present to Congress in 1828 which was referred to the Committee on Indian Affairs. In 1829, under the new Jackson administration, when the Convention prepared another memorial, McCoy disapproved because "it did not present a prayer in favor of settling the Indians in the West, but merely asked the Government, in event of Indian removal, to provide for them in the future."[114] The Board and McCoy could not come to an agreement over the ambiguous memorial.

By 1832, "the Convention's refusal to present the prospect of the Indians obtaining land rights and becoming a part of the republic was a political statement . . . The Convention likewise bowed to the political reality of removal, despite the protests and influence of at least some of its delegates. It did not, however, put its weight behind the political steps necessity in McCoy's estimation to ensure that the Indians could survive and thrive once they were removed."[115] In the age of Jackson, McCoy's vision for Native Americans would not be achieved. Perhaps history might have unfolded much differently had his plan of colonization been adopted. Tragically, Baptists would play a much greater, more sinister role in the Indian removal controversy when Georgia Governor Wilson Lumpkin, a future vice president of the Southern Baptist Convention, would take the leading role in Indian removal in the so-called "Trail of Tears" behind President Andrew Jackson.[116] Lumpkin, who had initially supported McCoy's "collocation" plan, was more eager to be free of the Cherokee than to protect their life, liberty, and pursuit of happiness.[117]

---

113. Wolever, *Life, Journal and Works of David Jones*, 175.

114. McCoy, *History of Baptist Indian Missions*, 395–96.

115. Williams, "New Era in Their History," 61.

116. In an 1824 article of *The American Baptist Magazine* entitled "Indian Reservations in Georgia," a document from President James Monroe to Congress was published, indicating the political leanings among Baptists on the issue of Native Americans. "An attempt to remove them by force, would, in my opinion, be unjust," Monroe stated. He later added that it would be best "if they could be prevailed on to retire west and north of our states and territories, on lands to be procured for them by the United States, in exchange for those on which they now reside" (Monroe, "Indian Reservations in Georgia," 342).

117. McLoughlin, *Cherokees and Christianity, 1794–1870*, 70.

Still, neither Lumpkin nor McCoy matched the tenacity and perseverance of Baptist Evan Jones, arguably the most successful missionary to the Cherokees. Serving the tribe from 1821 to his death in 1872, Jones worked predominantly with full-blooded Cherokees, sided with the majority of Cherokees against Andrew Jackson's removal program, and even walked with them on the infamous Trail of Tears. Unlike Congregationalists Samuel A. Worcester and Elizur Butler, who initially refused to sign the oath of allegiance to the state of Georgia (Chief Justice John Marshall sustained their appeal to the Supreme Court in *Worcester v. Georgia* [1832]) and then gave up their opposition, Jones's defense of Cherokee freedoms never waned. His support for Cherokee resistance was so vigorous that in 1836 federal officials actually banished him from the Nation. But Jones continued to itinerate throughout Cherokee country, ministering alongside Cherokee Baptists like Jesse Bushyhead, a political leader in the tribe who also resisted the push for removal and who translated parts of the Bible for Jones. Due to his support for the tribe, Jones was given the unique honor of being admitted as a full member.

As a Baptist, Jones would not swear allegiance to a state that suppressed the basic liberties—civil or religious—of individuals. In addition to opposing other Baptist missionaries who signed the oath, Jones also strongly condemned slavery, and in 1832–33 actually persuaded some slaveholding Cherokees to emancipate their slaves.[118] He helped organize antislavery groups among the Cherokees, including the most notable, the Keetoowah Society.[119] When the nation divided during the Civil War, Jones served as chaplain for the Union Cherokees, further entrenching himself on the side of liberty. However, Jones was not typical of most Baptist missionaries to the Native Americans after 1832. In 1844, when Georgia Baptists recommended slaveholder James E. Reeve to the Home Mission Society as a missionary to the American South, the conflict that erupted in the Triennial Convention would precipitate the fracturing of the denomination and the birth of the Southern Baptist Convention (1845).[120] Missions to the Cherokee played a significant role not only in the national political landscape but in the life of the Baptist denomination itself.

White Baptists were as fervent in their quest for religious liberty as any other group in the new nation. Yet, tragically, they did not always apply this principle in the same way to Africans and Native Americans. Even amongst the mission-minded, Baptists such as David Jones refused to make treaties

---

118. McLoughlin, *Cherokees and Christianity, 1794–1870*, 30–31, 117.

119. Smithers, *Cherokee Diaspora*, 127, 151.

120. See Gardner, *Decade of Debate and Division*.

with Native Americans and advocated their conquest. On the other hand, Isaac McCoy insisted, "We found the natives living in those modes of life which they, as a free people, chose for themselves; and we should be found by our invaders in the exercise of the same liberty."[121] Most Baptists would not have described Native Americans as a "free people," although, like Thomas Baldwin in 1802, they were more than willing to do so for themselves. But such was the inherent diversity among Baptists, and their politics of race and removal belied just how diverse their concepts of religious liberty could be. From the Friends of Humanity to state constitutions to Supreme Court decisions, Baptists left their mark along the turbulent road to Civil War and the remaking of America, following their principle of religious liberty to its most natural, universal conclusion.

---

121. Wolever, *Life, Journal and Works of David Jones*, 114–15; McCoy, *Remarks on the Practicability of Indian Reform*, 5.

Chapter 6

Missions, Nationalism, and Foreign Policy

THE REVOLUTION WAS A resounding affirmation to Baptists that the cause of conscience was of God. After helping the United States gain its independence from Britain, white Baptists enjoyed the spoils of patriotism by raising their collective voice even louder in favor of religious liberty. In 1779, when Samuel Stillman delivered the first election sermon in Boston by a Baptist, he chose as his text Matthew 22:21: "Then saith he unto them, 'Render therefore unto Caesar, the things that are Caesar's; and unto God, the things that are God's.'" In the unprecedented sermon, Stillman contended for the "indispensable necessity of a Bill of Rights."[1] By the end of the war in 1783, James Manning happily reported that "a spirit of toleration more universally prevails throughout New England, and the doctrines of religious as well as civil liberty are better understood by the people at large, against any infractions of which they are determined to guard." Nevertheless, with twelve students at Rhode Island College and more expected soon, Manning insisted on soliciting "further benefactions" so that the school could continue to be "instrumental in greatly promoting Baptist principles, and the spread of civil and religious liberty throughout New England."[2] For Baptists, the struggle for liberty was not finished. As the Apostle Paul wrote to the Galatian church so Baptists advocated in the new nation: "For freedom Christ has set us free; stand firm therefore, and do not submit again to the yoke of slavery."[3]

---

1. Stillman, *Sermon Preached Before the Honorable Council*, 5, 10.
2. Manning, "Reply to Samuel Stennett, Providence, Nov. 8th, 1783," 313–14.
3. Gal 5:1 (ESV).

Most Baptists, however, were not college-educated and did not enjoy the toleration of Rhode Island. In Virginia, Baptists faced their own challenges, as they encountered fellow Christians who had actually *intensified* their hostility to religious liberty after 1783. Baptist Andrew Broaddus experienced persecution even in his own home. His father, John, was a schoolteacher and farmer who was devoted to the Episcopalian establishment and "bitterly opposed to all dissenters." As a commissary in the Continental Army, John once dispatched his son, then only a boy, to hide his military papers in the woods after hearing of approaching British troops. After the war, Mr. Broaddus's disdain for Baptists only increased due to "the exertions they had successfully made for the overthrow of the Episcopal Establishment." Broaddus was not like some Episcopalians in Virginia who were willing to support disestablishment as long as a general assessment was substituted in its place.[4] Andrew was thus forbidden by his father from attending the Baptist church. Nevertheless, during the services, Andrew would listen to the hymns from outside the church building, describing it as "the music of heaven." In 1789, much to his father's chagrin, Andrew was baptized by Elder Theodoric Noell, his "father in the gospel." As a result of his experiences in Virginia, throughout his life, Broaddus would challenge those "High-handed Protestants" who "persecuted for conscience' sake."[5] Baptists did not relent in their pursuit of religious liberty after the war. Ironically, they were often forced to advocate more vehemently for liberty of conscience against those who had just finished fighting with them for that very liberty.[6]

Therefore, due to this social and religious hegemony, Baptists were generally more concerned about the tyranny they faced next door than the tyranny that loomed overseas. However, they did not completely separate the two. Baptists in America could not always distinguish between their problems at home and abroad. For example, Richard Furman believed that infidelity was one of the greatest dangers to American religious liberty because it sought to "copy after the principles and measures of France," a nation that had been engulfed in anarchy and anti-religious sentiment.[7] In 1797, a Rhode Island College student from South Carolina reported to Furman

---

4. Semple, *History of the Rise and Progress of the Baptists in Virginia*, 27.

5. Broaddus, *Sermons and Other Writings of the Rev. Andrew Broaddus*, 3, 11–12, 501.

6. Virginia hosted its fair share of lower class Baptists. For example, Abner Clopton joined Shockoe Baptist Church in Virginia in August of 1812. Jeremiah Bell Jeter then writes, "He might have entered a communion more distinguished for numbers, wealth, and literature, and more esteemed and admired by the world; but he sought to please God, and not men" (Jeter, *Memoir of Abner W. Clopton, A.M.*, 34).

7. Furman, *Death's Dominion Over Man Considered*, 242.

that, due to "the European War" and the precipitous decline in crop prices at home, patrons "could spare but little money toward the promotion of" the minister's education fund.[8] Conversely, issues in America often led Baptists to focus on events overseas. On October 17, 1795, the Goshen Association in Virginia recommended to its seventeen churches a day of fasting and prayer for "the treaty of amity and commerce, between Great Britain and America." The attention paid to Jay's Treaty by the Baptist churches, according to Robert Baylor Semple, "arose from the violent party heat, which, at that time, agitated the minds of American generally, and which it seems, frequently made its way into the pulpit and religious assemblies."[9] From politics to pulpits, from prayers to peace treaties, national and international interests often overlapped for Baptists in America.

The idea of a Baptist "foreign policy" is therefore a slippery concept because Baptists did not share the same domestic experiences and thus did not view the world in the same way. The "uneducated" Andrew Broaddus, for example, interpreted Matthew 24:5–29 and the signs of the end of the age differently than some of his more erudite brethren.[10] In his opinion, unlike that of Bostonians Samuel Stillman and Thomas Baldwin, the passage did not refer to nineteenth century America, but rather to first century Israel. Phrases like "you will hear of wars and rumors of wars" could not be applied to American diplomacy on the Atlantic because they described the destruction of Jerusalem, a very specific moment in history.[11] Due to their belief that God established covenants with individual believers rather than with nations, Baptists who endured an especially cruel amount of persecution under the religious establishment or who experienced a higher degree of marginalization in society were less prone to view their incipient nation as an American Israel in any political sense. No Christian state, demurred John Leland, could be brought upon "the same footing with the commonwealth of Israel," for this kind of typology had caused "the European nation to make a seizure of America."[12] Baptists like Leland and Broaddus were unable or unwilling to develop a robust foreign policy that centered the United States in a strategic, worldwide campaign to Christianize the nations and to

---

8. J. B. Cook to Richard Furman, July 13, 1797: "I am sorry to hear of the low state of the fund. Money is a very scarce article everywhere, owing, I presume, to the European war. Farmers cannot obtain a full price for their produce and, on that account, can spare but little money toward the promotion of such a laudable institution" (Foster, *Life and Works of Dr. Richard Furman, D.D.*, 166–67).

9. Semple, *History of the Rise and Progress of the Baptists in Virginia*, 143.

10. Broaddus, *Sermons and Other Writings*, 13.

11. Broaddus, *Sermons and Other Writings*, 269–70.

12. Leland, "Yankee Spy," 217.

defeat the powers of the Antichrist. This was, at least in their view, strictly the mission of the church. In other words, America was John Winthrop's city on a hill, not Augustine's city of God. Nevertheless, regardless of their class or their politics, most Baptists believed that America was to become a sanctuary or "theatre" of religious liberty that would eventually redeem the world from spiritual tyranny, either by example or by extension.[13] In this sense, Baptists paid close attention to the special role of the United States in the Atlantic and on the frontier. This unique call to be a light to the nations began with the ground beneath them.

"We Are a World within Ourselves"

Although the Baptist definition of religious liberty was much different than the kind that had motivated the earliest Pilgrims, their view of the American continent had changed relatively little over two centuries. In 1621, amidst scurvy and mortality and the threat of Native attacks, one Plymouth settler wrote back to England, "A better place cannot be in the world." In terms of its fishing and furs, America was "nature's masterpiece."[14] Two hundred years later, in 1824, John Leland spoke to the local Republican party in Pittsfield, Massachusetts and expressed the same wonder at the beauty and bounty of the American landscape:

> Compare the United States with most of the nations, and we enjoy a paradise. Yes, our extensive country, reaching from Yellow Stone to Passamaquaddy, and from the Atlantic to never—containing all the soils, climes, lakes and rivers necessary for life, we are a world within ourselves, and by attention to agriculture, manufactures and inland commerce, under the fostering hand of government, and smiles of Divine Providence, we need not go abroad for joy. And with a million of well-trained militia we have not much to fear, by land, while our navy guards us from unfriendly visitors.[15]

Leland was once again articulating the Jeffersonian ideal: freedom, farms, and frontier. Instead of a trans-Atlantic worldview, Leland counseled his fellow Republicans to look inward, to the west. Rather than globalism, he emphasized "inland" commerce. As opposed to a standing army to defend their sylvan "paradise," he promoted a "well-trained militia" and a navy that

---

13. Manning, "To Thomas Llewelyn, LL.D., London; Providence, Nov. 8, 1783," 319.
14. Turner, *They Knew They Were Pilgrims*, 78, 128.
15. Leland, "Address at Pittsfield," 505.

would protect them from their enemies. "We are a world within ourselves," Leland insisted, celebrating the vast domain of verdant mountains and lakes that anchored Baptists' foreign policy. While he may not have believed that America was a new Israel, John Leland and his Baptist countrymen certainly viewed their "extensive country" as a kind of new Eden, teeming with freedom and opportunity.

Thomas Jefferson's Louisiana Purchase was the political realization of his yeoman vision of America, and Baptists adopted this westward, agricultural plan for the United States in various ways. Yellowstone National Park, in which Leland boasted in his Pittsfield Address, was made possible by Jefferson's purchase from France in 1803. While Napoleon, whose regime Jefferson had once described as "enlightened," needed to recoup losses from his European wars, Jefferson himself eyed more land to satisfy thousands of Americans, including Baptists, who sought new lives on the seemingly virgin soil that God had supposedly given them.[16] Although the phrase "manifest destiny" would not be coined until 1845 by *Democratic Review* editor John L. O'Sullivan, the expansionist spirit of the early national period beckoned Baptists almost from the very beginning of the American experiment. Indeed, by the end of the Revolution, Baptists were already describing the frontier in words similar to the prophet Isaiah, like a desert in bloom. James Manning wrote in 1783 that "the wilderness has blossomed like the rose, and the Baptist principles have greatly prevailed there."[17] Baptists saw the western frontier as the beginning of a new harvest of souls. For Manning, the abundance of "pious illiterate ministers" in the "vast, extended frontiers" demanded a learned clergy from the college.[18]

Under Jefferson's administration, even those Baptists who were unsettled by the political upheaval of 1800 were still optimistic about western expansion. Less than a month before the Louisiana Purchase and just a month after Ohio had become the seventeenth state in the union, Col. John Stites Gano wrote an old friend in Providence, Rhode Island, where his brother Stephen pastored First Baptist Church. From his vantage point in Cincinnati, Gano envisioned a growing western frontier with more people and greater wealth:

---

16. Savannah *Columbian Museum*, November 2, 1803, quoted in Broussard, *Southern Federalists*, 74.

17. Manning, "To The Rev. John Ryland; Providence, Nov. 8, 1783," in Guild, *Life, Times, and Correspondence of James Manning, and the Early History of Brown University*, 309.

18. Manning, "Reply to Samuel Stennett," in Guild, *Life, Times, and Correspondence of James Manning, and the Early History of Brown University*, 316.

Yours of February last came to hand this week, for which please to accept my thanks—it has not been for the want of esteem that you have not had a line before this from me, but the great revolution and change in our government, and politics has left everything respecting offices and, at an uncertain and precarious issue, and what effect it will have on the minds of the people at present I cannot inform you, and have delayed writing on that account; but as our legislature is now in session, and have a number of important appointments to make, it will soon be known, when the new government comes into full operation, whether the change will be of advantage or not. I am in hopes it will encourage population and add to the prosperity and happiness of the people of our new State.[19]

Nervousness at the "great revolution" was shared by many officials and officers who had served under the Adams administration. Gano's apprehension most likely reveals his party affiliation, as Jefferson's patronage policy was believed by most Federalists to be a shameless attempt to rid every person or department which stood opposed to the Republican party.[20] Nevertheless, with better infrastructure and more settlement, Gano anticipated greater "prosperity and happiness" in Ohio.

On the coast, Baptists viewed the Atlantic Ocean both as an international highway by which to increase the wealth of the infant nation and as a natural barrier that God had established in order to protect them from attack. Depending on one's political party, it was usually one more than the other. Although Jonathan Maxcy described the American continent as a "delightful garden of Eden" and stressed the importance of agriculture, true to his Federalist politics, he did not adopt a strictly Jeffersonian economic vision of America. Maintaining that "we stand by our own strength, disconnected from foreign influence and foreign power," he also avowed, "Commerce in the present advanced state of society, is of the highest importance." Maxcy pushed for "commercial treaties" with foreign countries and "the encouragement of exportation."[21] Whereas Republicans like Leland celebrated the oceanic bulwark *between* America and Britain, Maxcy believed that the Atlantic allowed them to *become like* Britain, foreseeing "a country

---

19. Colonel John Stites Gano, "Cincinnati, April 3d, 1803," in Wolever, *Life and Ministry of John Gano, 1727–1804*, 1:428.

20. For an examination of Jefferson's patronage policy, see Malone, *Jefferson the President: First Term, 1801–1805*; Cunningham, *Jeffersonian Republicans in Power*.

21. Maxcy, "Oration Delivered Before the Providence Association of Mechanics and Manufacturers, at the Annual Election, April 13, 1795," 354, 357.

whose ports open to every quarter of the globe, and whose fleets will one day cover the ocean."[22]

As a Bostonian, Thomas Baldwin could not ignore the importance of international trade to the east. However, when the Republican Baldwin reflected on the eastern shores, he described America less as a global crossroads and more as an idyllic, impenetrable, independent refuge. "The wide Atlantic laves our eastern board, and forms one barrier to the progress of invasion," Baldwin cheered, "and at the same time wafts to our shores the fruits and treasures of every clime. On its bays and inlets our ancient towns and cities are planted. Here, the busy multitude throng; and trade, and commerce collect their immense stores of wealth." He then speculated, "Should a foreign enemy attempt to invade our country, he would meet a phalanx of veterans more impenetrable than walls of granite. Our dependence is not on foreign auxiliaries or mercenary aid; but under God, we rely on the skill and bravery of our citizens."[23] Baldwin's foreign policy was typical of most Baptists in the early republic who believed that Divine Providence and the continent itself, not skillful diplomacy and economics, would protect the American people from infidelity and despotism. They were, after all, a "world within" themselves. Similar to what Russell E. Richey has observed among early American Methodists, Baptists in the new nation "experienced America as geography" before they experienced it as statecraft, and the physical character of the continent colored their own view of the world around them.[24]

Whereas the Federalist Maxcy promoted commerce on the Atlantic and manufacturing on the eastern seaboard, as a Republican who adopted Jefferson's yeoman vision of America, Baldwin tended to look west more than east. In a sermon to an artillery company in 1807, he described Europe as a volcano with "rivers of burning lava . . . running in all directions, marking their progress with desolation and death!"[25] However, in a Thanksgiving sermon in 1795, like scores of Baptists before and after him, Baldwin described the American continent using Old Testament imagery: "Heaven had undoubtedly designed this beautiful part of creation, for noble purposes than to lie an uncultivated waste, for beasts and savages to roam over. It was evidently marked out by Divine Providence, as the favored spot, on

22. Maxcy, "Oration Delivered in the Baptist Meeting House in Providence, July 4th, 1795," 374.

23. Baldwin, *Discourse, Delivered Before the Ancient and Honourable Artillery Company*, 23–24.

24. Richey, *Early American Methodism*, 37.

25. Baldwin, *Discourse, Delivered Before the Ancient and Honourable Artillery Company*, 25.

which Liberty (which had long been imprisoned in other parts of the globe) should erect her spacious temple."[26] To Baldwin, Europe was a volcano and the United States was a garden. The American wilderness was not simply a new Canaan; it was a "temple" where God himself dwelled, where the special presence of the Creator blessed his chosen people.[27] Unlike the anticlerical Jefferson, Baldwin conceived of his country in religious and even sacerdotal terms. However, like Jefferson, Baldwin believed that this sacred wilderness was to become a *white* west. In the early republic, foreign policy did not begin in Europe with English or French ambassadors; it began on the American frontier with the very people that had inhabited their "spacious temple" for thousands of years.

An Emergent Religious Nationalism

The most significant factor that shaped Baptist foreign policy is which nation or group a Baptist identified as the greatest threat to religious liberty. From missionary societies to frontier evangelism to temperance societies to higher education, almost every aspect of Baptist public life was shaped by the way ministers responded to popery and paganism in their international context. As previously shown, when David Jones encountered Indian warfare on the frontier while ministering to the Natives in the Midwest, he framed the conflict as a war with Britain, stating, "In short, the present war is a tory war, for if England had not been courage by a dependence on them, we should have had no war at this time." According to George Truett Rogers, "his animosity toward the British apparently blinded his thinking," leading him to blame the British for a number of woes with the Indians while omitting American transgressions. Jones scoffed, "The Indians themselves do not accuse us with any acts of injustice. No—they own they are well paid by the British to commit the murders on our defenseless frontiers." Conveniently, Jones made no mention of Indians' hostility toward his own countrymen who had settled on land they occupied. He stated matter-of-factly, "During our revolutionary war, it is well known that most of the savage tribes of

---

26. Baldwin, *Sermon, Delivered February 19, 1795*, 13.

27. James Madison Pendleton's father, a Virginia Baptist, was likely a Republican because he named his son after the fourth president, also from Virginia. Recalling the trials of his parents in their westward journey Pendleton writes, "When I remember that my parents left the land of their birth, encountered the perils of what was then called the 'wilderness' on their way to Kentucky, suffered the inconveniences and hardships of a sort of pioneer life—all this that their children might enjoy better advantages than they had enjoyed—no language can express the grateful admiration I feel for them" (Pendleton, *Reminiscences of a Long Life*, 7).

Americans united the savages of Great Britain, to distress and harass the citizens of the United States, by every means in their power."[28] When the jingoistic Jones witnessed Indian atrocities, he saw the invisible hand of Britain, the nation against which he had fought almost sixteen years as army chaplain. Jones nearly laid the blame for the entire conflict at the feet of the British, refusing to accept his own nation's culpability in fueling the war. Eventually, Jones took a militant approach to the very people he had once tried to save, as his own disdain for British tyranny brought him to view the Natives more as "lords of the soil" and less as converts to the gospel.[29] Jones was not the only western Baptist to take this kind of hostile approach. William Whiteside Jr., a Revolutionary War veteran from North Carolina, eventually became a well-known Colonel in the Illinois Militia who served during the War of 1812. Whiteside was known as a leader among the early Baptists in Illinois *and* as a leading Indian fighter.[30]

Conversely, Native American Baptists sometimes encountered a different kind of struggle for religious liberty, faced with the challenge of resisting the traditional religion of their ancestors on one hand and opposing forced resettlement by their white brethren on the other. According to Dan B. Wimberly, Chief Jesse Bushyhead's ministry was shaped by the way he responded to white speculators and their greed for more land. For example, Bushyhead "favored temperance for spiritual and political reasons. In the past, whites had used liquor as an incentive to induce chiefs to sign land-grab treaties." Bushyhead sided with the so-called "National party" or "Patriot party" in his tribe, lobbying in Washington D.C. *against* removal. Eventually, he walked hand-in-hand with his fellow Cherokee as they were forced from their land by the Jackson administration, migrating west to present-day Oklahoma in 1839 along with Baptist missionary Evan Jones in the infamous Trail of Tears. Nevertheless, baptized into the Baptist faith in 1830, Bushyhead served as "an important bridge in the conversion of Cherokees to Christianity," evangelizing his own people and forming interpersonal relationships with whites despite the oppression of the United States government. For Bushyhead, who eventually became chief justice of the Cherokee supreme court, Christianity "offered hope not found in the old Native religion."[31]

28. Jones, "Indian Affairs."
29. Jones, "Old Indian School Must Be Changed," 2.
30. Peck, *Forty Years of Pioneer Life*, 96.
31. Wimberly, *Cherokee in Controversy*, 36, 198, 35. Smithers, *Cherokee Diaspora*, 62.

More refined Baptists like James Manning had a different take on the western frontier. Rather than fighting the English, Manning preferred to fraternize with them. In a 1772 letter to an English Baptist, Manning showed his drab view of the west when he wrote, "I have visited the western provinces this fall, and find there but dead times in religion, except in Virginia, where God still continues to do wonders amongst the people." Nevertheless, in the same letter, Manning reported on the work of his former Hopewell Academy classmate David Jones between the Ohio and Mississippi Rivers, calling him "an apostle amongst Gentiles." The somewhat incredulous Manning then penned, "He thinks there is a great prospect of many turning to God amongst them; and who knows but they may? I believe it is the first instance of the Baptists going among them for that purpose."[32] Manning then expressed his doubt that Jones would find sufficient funds for his journey from the Association. Although years later Manning would agree that God was at work in the wilderness, he believed that education, not evangelism, was the greatest need. Rather than enmity for England, Manning spoke of his "affection" for his British brethren and his willingness to work with them to redeem souls.[33] The college president much preferred to imitate the English in their institutions than to fight against them on the battlefield, even writing to an English Baptist in 1777 that "the saints of God do not mean to wage war against each other."[34] Within the same Association, the difference between the anti-British, agricultural, Republican Jones and the pro-British, academic, Federalist Manning foreshadowed a growing chasm among Baptists in the next generation between frontier evangelism and international missions, between a less educated, rural revivalism and a more literate Convention life.[35] Ultimately, this division would be most visible with the formation of the Triennial Convention, the first nationwide Baptist denomination and missionary convention in American history—led mostly by educated, pro-British Baptists.

Focusing mainly on Congregationalists like Timothy Dwight and the Connecticut Wits, Sam Haselby has located a "new, nationalist missionary movement" that emerged in the infant American nation. In *The Origins of American Religious Nationalism*, Haselby "presents the primary conflict in

---

32. Manning, "To the Rev. Dr. Stennett; Providence, Nov. 13, 1772," 205.
33. Manning, "To the Rev. John Ryland," 309.
34. Manning, "To the Rev. Benjamin Wallin, Nov. 12, 1776," 245.
35. This is not to suggest that David Jones was uneducated. He was, after all, classmates with Manning at Hopewell Academy in New Jersey, America's first Baptist secondary school. (Jones entered in late 1758) Jones also studied with Abel Morgan, an outstanding Greek scholar. However, Jones had a rural upbringing, growing up on a Delaware farm.

American religion during the early republic as one between frontier revivalism and a nationalist missions movement—in other words, not as denominational but as social and geographic."[36] According to Haselby, the missions movement in America was not simply a coordinated plan to reach the lost but an attempt at nation-building. While these organizations promoted a narrative of a "providential, Christianizing nation, overseen by paternalistic leaders," the more egalitarian frontier revivalists found the wealth and ambition of these missionaries to be contrary to their vision of America and to Christianity itself.[37] Certain elements of this interplay between homespun revivalism and the more refined missions movement were present in Baptist life, and Haselby identifies primitive Baptists, "Hard-Shell" Baptists, "anti-effort" preachers, and anti-mission Baptists as part of the resistance to this nationalist movement. In other words, these Baptists were motivated by more than sheer anti-intellectualism, but by anti-elitism. From the lack of Southern-funded Baptist tract societies to Kentucky Baptists' reluctance to support seminaries, Baptists provide for Haselby an enticing foil to the patrician missionary centers in Massachusetts and Connecticut.

However, what Haselby neglects in his study of religious nationalism is that Baptists themselves contributed to this nascent nationalism in various ways. Not every Baptist was a low-church, frontier-style, self-learned evangelist. Some were even Dwightian. While they opposed Timothy Dwight's establishmentarian worldview, many Baptists nevertheless cast their own vision of America and believed their missions strategy to be consonant with it. For example, Richard Furman, who would forge the first Baptist state convention in America and would become the inaugural president of the Triennial Convention, utilized voluntary societies instead of establishment in order to forge his own vision of a Christian society. In 1795, Furman led the formation of a "Society" in Charleston "for encouraging Emigration of virtuous citizens from other Countries." In a letter to his sister on April 1, 1795, Furman wrote, "It has met with remarkable success; most of the notable characters in Charleston having embarked in the Design . . . The exertions of Dr. Ramsay have however had great influence in forwarding the Design. Judge Grimke, John Rutledge, Jr., Mr. Dessaussure, the lawyer, and myself were on the Committee which formed the rules and the Paper of Information which accompanies this."[38] Furman partnered with the most

---

36. Haselby, *Origins of American Religious Nationalism*, 3.

37. Haselby, *Origins of American Religious Nationalism*, 17.

38. Furman, "Charleston, April 1, 1795," 119. Mr. Sessaussure is presumably Henry William Dessaussure. For a look into Dessaussure's Federalist politics, see Den Hartog, *Patriotism and Piety*.

notable Federalists in the South to regulate the influx of "those about to leave Europe" whom he deemed undesirable to American society.

Like Timothy Dwight, who according to W. T. Brantly exercised more influence over Furman's thinking than any other American theologian, Furman too had a nationalist agenda for the United States.[39] The plantation owner believed in reaching the lost *and* in regulating immigration in order to secure his own patriarchal vision of America. Not surprisingly, Furman was also a primary leader in the cause of Baptist education, attracting New England Federalists like Jonathan Maxcy to the South in order to promote the same ideals. Furman, who advocated for the education of blacks in his 1822 slavery treatise, believed in missions *and* slavery, a fact that provided no small amount of fodder for anti-mission Baptists.[40] These seeming contradictions in Furman's social theory were part of his comprehensive plan for a Christianized and Christianizing America.

However, this early Baptist nationalism was not necessarily relegated to Federalists. Thomas Baldwin, the first president of the Baptist Board of Foreign Missions and the inaugural secretary of the Triennial Convention, promoted the same causes as his southern cohort. Baldwin could think of nothing "more deserving of legislative attention, than the education of youth and children."[41] Years later, after the formation of the Triennial Convention, Baldwin bragged that a "laudable zeal for the missionary cause is everywhere apparent; and societies auxiliary to the 'Board of Foreign Missions,' are forming from Maine to Georgia, and from the Atlantic to the Mississippi."[42] Indeed, Baldwin was not simply saving the lost; he was establishing a nationwide network of Christian missionaries, educators, and activists. Consistent with Haselby's thesis, Baldwin shared the same aristocratic sensibilities as his fellow Boston clergymen and as Furman in Charleston. Nathan Hatch records,

> When the rustic preacher Elias Smith was called to pastor the Baptist church in Woburn, Massachusetts, in 1798, the "very fashionable" Baldwin tried to persuade the young man to put

---

39. W. T. Brantly, "Extracts from Dr. W. T. Brantly's Sermon Delivered in 1825," in Foster, *Life and Works of Dr. Richard Furman, D.D.*, 221; Fitzmier, *New England's Moral Legislator: Timothy Dwight, 1752–1817*, 162. According to Sam Haselby, Timothy Dwight was "the nation's most preeminent anti-Jeffersonian" (Haselby, *Origins of American Religious Nationalism*, 29).

40. Furman, *Exposition of the Views of the Baptists*, 12–14; Parker, *Public Address*, 58–59. "Now my dear brethren is not the soul of a negro as precious in America as in Africa?" (59).

41. Baldwin, *Sermon, Delivered Before His Excellency Caleb Strong*, 16.

42. Baldwin, "Editor's Address," 4.

aside his plain attire and dress "in fashionable black, a large three cornered hat, and black silk gloves." Shocked by this emphasis on externals, Smith asked Baldwin if Baptists "were going back to the place where from whence we came out." Baldwin replied, "We wish to make our denomination respectable as well as the rest."[43]

In the eyes of at least some revivalists, pro-missions Baptists appeared to be imitating Congregationalist clergy more than Christ himself. While they were certainly not interested in joining the Standing Order in their unholy union of church and state, many Baptists nevertheless desired to Christianize their new nation with organizations led by elite, educated, and "very fashionable" men, sometimes to the disdain of their less sophisticated peers. Religious liberty and religious nationalism were by no means mutually exclusive in the early American nation.

Although Haselby's observations of Baptist anti-intellectualism are well attested, this should not at all suggest that *every* Baptist on the frontier was engaged in the kind of unlearned revivalism promoted by the likes of John Taylor and Daniel Parker. Some pro-missions Baptists who moved westward and southward actually came indirectly from Timothy Dwight and his circle of Congregationalists. From 1817 to 1818, Adiel Sherwood studied at Andover Seminary under renown textual scholar and New Divinity professor Moses Stuart, who was educated and converted under Dwight at Yale. While at Andover, Thomas Baldwin encouraged the young Sherwood in his efforts in the missionary society and recommended him to the Savannah Missionary Society in Georgia, where Sherwood would spend the majority of his career. According to Jarrett Burch, "The Savannah Missionary Society (a mixture of Congregationalists, Presbyterians, and Baptists) provided missionary-minded Baptists with a means of founding benevolent institutions. This society's purpose centered on the propagation of the gospel at home and later abroad."[44] As a stalwart of Sunday school education, a co-founder of the Georgia Baptist Convention, an organizer of local temperance societies and manual labor schools, and president of Shurtleff College in Illinois, Adiel Sherwood illustrates well the nation-building conducted by pro-missions Baptists according to their comprehensive vision for America.[45] Sherwood would eventually become one of the leading opponents of the anti-mission movement. In his *Strictures on the Sentiments*

---

43. Hatch, *Democratization of American Christianity*, 94.
44. Burch, *Adiel Sherwood*, 12–13, 17–18.
45. Burch, *Adiel Sherwood*, 163–66.

of the Kehukee Association (1828), Sherwood sought to clarify his exact position on Baptist education:

> We do not mean here by *learned*, men who have received a diploma *merely*, for one is no test of ripe scholarship; but we mean men of *education—men who know something*, and we care not *where* or *how* they obtained it, whether in a College, or at home over a pine knot light. Nor do we intend by *unlearned* all who have not shared the advantages of a collegiate life; for we know many men self-taught, who better deserve the appellation of scholars, than many who have been "*graduated*." Our opinion is, that a College is the *best place* to acquire a thorough education, and a Theological Seminary the most suitable nursery for Biblical knowledge.[46]

As will be shown, missions and education were inextricable in early Baptist politics because they were both grounded in a particular nationalist vision of the United States that sought to establish civil religion alongside freedom *of* religion. The men who advocated these ideals naturally led the organizations that promoted them, like state and national conventions. Pro-missions Baptists were seeking to redeem souls *and* society. They wanted to change Americans as a whole, "to make them moral," and this is why they encountered so much opposition to their Herculean efforts.[47] Anti-mission Baptists were certainly not against spreading the gospel and biblical knowledge; they were against *those spreading* the gospel and such knowledge, and the degree of authority they wielded in order to do so.

For Sherwood, the debate over colleges and seminaries was directly connected with America's own international context, as he believed that the Kehukee Association had dangerously imbibed 5 things: (1) a spirit of avarice, (2) the spirit "which lords it over God's heritage," (3) a spirit of pride, (4) a spirit of popery, (5) and a spirit of infidelity.[48] In response to those who accused pro-mission Baptists of greed and tyranny, Sherwood accused his Kehukee brethren of their own brand of ambition and despotism. After boasting that the Baptist denomination "has been four times doubled both in England and America, since these Seminaries exerted their benign and happy influence," Sherwood charged those who opposed mission societies with their own form of self-seeking nationalism: "It fears all the money will be sent out of the country for 'distant objects' and therefore none will flow into the pockets of the resident ministers." Those who opposed missions,

---

46. Sherwood, *Strictures on the Sentiments of the Kehukee Association*, 19.
47. See Burch, *Adiel Sherwood*, 23.
48. Sherwood, *Strictures on the Sentiments of the Kehukee Association*, 20–22.

Sherwood argued, had absorbed a nativist spirit. However, Sherwood possibly reflected his own nativism, and the burgeoning Anti-Catholicism in the 1820s with new waves of European immigration, when he warned that "in opposing Bible Societies, he . . . manifestly takes sides with the Pope." Comparing the Kehukee Association's tract to a papal bull, Sherwood later charged, "Though one was written in Rome by Pope Pius VII, and the other by a Protestant Association in North Carolina, yet they both oppose the spread of God's word—this is Antichrist."[49]

Perhaps most revealing of the emergent nationalism of the Baptist missions movement is Sherwood's association of anti-mission groups with infidels in the new republic, referring back to an instance "when 14 churches in North Carolina protested against Missions two or three years ago" and "infidel papers rejoiced and said the Baptists were coming over to their principles." Sherwood even mentioned the two newspapers by name: *Plain Truth* (1822–28) and *The Reformer* (1820–35), periodicals that Sherwood believed were "set up to slander down missions and other benevolent institutions" and "supported by infidels, universalists, a few cold-hearted professors, who have not religion enough to pray in families, and scores of drunken apostates from various denominations!" Clearly, the debate over missions involved more than evangelism. But what interest would these non-Baptist papers have in the mission strategy of North Carolina Baptists? More importantly, why would Sherwood have accused these Baptists of infidelity? The answer almost certainly lies in the fact that mission groups were tied to certain nationalistic initiatives and institutions that stood contrary to the goals of Enlightenment liberals who envisioned a post-Christian or non-evangelical republic. In these two newspapers, Sherwood saw the worst of philosophical religion and the inevitable devolution of those Baptist churches that repudiated organizational ministry.

A bi-weekly magazine published out of Canandaigua, New York, *Plain Truth* was co-edited by Lyman A. Spalding, a Quaker merchant and abolitionist who also established a newspaper entitled *Priestcraft Exposed and Primitive Christianity Defended*. The anticlerical Spalding rejected both evangelical religion and really any form of Christianity that sought to establish itself outside the church walls. According to John Fea, "no religious periodical was more caustic" than *The Reformer*, an anti-mission newspaper out of Philadelphia mostly under the editorship of Theophilus Gates.[50] An intellectual who, like fellow printer Benjamin Franklin, disavowed his own Calvinist upbringing, Gates held that true Christianity should be divested

---

49. Sherwood, *Strictures on the Sentiments of the Kehukee Association*, 22.
50. Fea, *Bible Cause*, 59–60.

of all external structures in favor of Christ's moral teachings. Therefore, the extra-ecclesiastical nature of mission groups and their "benevolent institutions" deeply troubled him. Although far less totalitarian than those who wished to join together church and state, Baptist voluntary societies and social reform efforts were so large in their societal scope that they provoked the hostility of Baptists and non-Baptists alike who believed that hierarchical reform was simply religious establishment by another name. Thus, in many ways, at the heart of the anti-mission controversy was the conflict between two differing visions of religious liberty. For some, any determination of society made by Christians (i.e. education, temperance, anti-gambling) was an infringement upon their most basic right to pursue their own happiness. For others, to influence the very fabric of society was simply a Christian's duty. Sherwood explained,

> Infidel papers cry down the cause of Missions and other means of improvement and virtue, because they know in proportion as these gain upon the feelings and affections of the community, their theatres, and gambling houses, and dram shops, and brothels will be deserted; therefore they have played up the old tune, "money, money," when we have asked for the support of a few men, going to tell of a crucified Savior to a world lying in wickedness . . . The expense of the theatres in our great cities are threefold more than that of all the benevolent institutions in our country. The expense of our spirituous liquors are annually about forty-five millions—more than ninety times as much as is given for all our charitable objects! Now who cannot discover that the objections of the opponents to our cause, do not lie in their *economy*, but in a *settled, deadly* hostility to the kingdom of Christ?[51]

Pro-mission Baptists were converting both society and sinners according to their own definition of religious liberty. In the American south and west, Sherwood's nationalist approach to missions would continue through the antebellum period in the ministry of Baptists like R. B. C. Howell, pastor of First Baptist Church of Nashville. Howell was one of the staunchest opponents of the anti-mission movement during his era and even helped lay the groundwork for the Southern Baptist Theological Seminary. Not surprisingly, he also considered Timothy Dwight's systematic theology to be one of the best ever written.[52]

---

51. Sherwood, *Strictures on the Sentiments of the Kehukee Association*, 23.
52. Howell, *Terms of Communion at the Lord's Table*, 192.

In addition to the divergent ecclesiologies and social predilections between mission and anti-mission Baptists were their competing visions of the future of America.[53] With the birth of the Triennial Convention in 1814, an organization inspired by the missionary efforts of Andrew Fuller, William Carey, and the Baptist Missionary Society in Northamptonshire, England, the lines that were drawn in the anti-mission controversy were nearly as political as they were theological. Due to their partnership with British Baptists in an era of tense international conflict and evidenced in the fact that their very first overseas missionary, Adoniram Judson, was himself a former Congregationalist with family ties to the Standing Order, the leaders of the Triennial Convention developed more of a sympathy for English interests and for Old World culture than their anti-mission counterparts. In short, because of their social and theological links with Old and New England, pro-mission Baptists defined religious liberty and American-British relations much more conservatively than their more unrefined, revivalist brethren.

During the "democratization" of the Second Great Awakening, these differences between missionary and anti-mission Baptists were especially pronounced in the West because the frontier became a spiritual, social, and political battleground where Baptists shaped churches as well as entire communities.[54] In 1820, from Clark County, Illinois, Daniel Parker became the first Baptist to publicly criticize the mission movement in *A Public Address to the Baptist Society, and Friends of Religion in General, on the Principle and Practice of the Baptist Board of Foreign Missions for the United States of America*. Parker's pamphlet was a powerful rebuke to those in Baptist power, condemning everything from the salary of Luther Rice (another former Congregationalist) to the use of the dandified title of "President" for its leaders. The Primitive Baptist and soon-to-be Illinois senator unequivocally charged pro-mission Baptists with erecting a kind of Baptist Standing Order when he chided,

> Just look at the simile between the rise of popery and the principles and practice of our beloved brethren in the mission system,

---

53. According to Leon McBeth, "The antimission movement had several leaders, of whom the most prominent were Daniel Parker, John Taylor, Joshua Lawrence, and Alexander Campbell. Parker (1781–1844) was the great enemy of missions on the frontier" (McBeth, *Baptist Heritage*, 373).

54. According to Charles Sellers, "Baptists institutionalized most fully the egalitarian localism of the subsistence culture. Against both state and wider church, they defended fiercely the independence of their democratic congregations. The only denominational organization they could tolerate was voluntary regional associations" (Sellers, *Market Revolution*, 159). However, sometimes Baptists even resisted these!

and I have no doubt but Constantine appeared to possess as great zeal as our brethren now do, and what awful consequences attended that establishment. I can truly say, O, solemn thought, I feel like the time is not far distant when God will chastise His people for their pride and folly. And I fear the mission establishment is the way this distress will come.[55]

In the eyes of many frontier Baptists, the mission movement was a "mission establishment," drawing its political power not from taxes but from collections and offerings. From their non-elitist beginnings, Baptists had created an oligarchy in the name of evangelism. For this reason, according to Joshua Guthman, Primitive Baptists like Parker identified strongly with the ideals of Thomas Jefferson. "When the Primitives surveyed their past, they saw themselves walking the old paths, lonely truth-bearers in a fallen world, guardians of the doctrine of election, and hard-working husbandmen whose labor preserved Jefferson's Republic against encroaching aristocracy."[56]

That same year, John Taylor of Kentucky exhibited the same populist censure of Baptist missions in his *Thoughts on Missions* (1820). Like Parker, Taylor believed that the entire mission movement was inimical to Protestantism and to Christian character. Moreover, Taylor objected to the British origins of the movement, concluding that "the English Baptist Mission to Calcutta" was nothing more than a front for English imperialism. He reasoned, "for there England has many subjects, and though the natives are but sparingly benefitted as yet, their other subjects, and especially their soldiery, have been." In the Triennial Convention, the abolitionist Taylor detected Baptists' complicity in a new kind of empire, one that robbed Baptist churches of their autonomy and natives of their dignity. Taylor even poked at the correspondence between Adoniram and Ann Judson, speculating that "in the first report of the Board of Foreign Missions . . . it would look as if her husband had the same taste for money that the horse leech has for blood."[57] Beneath anti-mission ideas was a groundswell of Baptist populism.

In stark contrast with Daniel Parker and John Taylor who opposed seemingly everything that smelled of Old and New England, John Mason Peck, the first domestic missionary for the Triennial Convention, was a New Englander who was fond of working with British Baptists. Originally converted in the Congregationalist church in Litchfield, Connecticut, Peck would be appointed with James E. Welch to the "Missouri Territory," where

---

55. Parker, *Public Address to the Baptist Society*.
56. Guthman, *Strangers Below*, 35.
57. Taylor, *Thoughts on Missions*.

they co-founded the First Baptist Church of St. Louis. As an organizer of the first missionary society in the West, Bible and Sunday School societies, Rock Springs Seminary (later renamed Shurtleff College), the Illinois Baptist Education Society, publication societies, and a host of other initiatives, Peck's ministry embodied all of the values and ideals of his "long-confiding friends" in the Massachusetts Baptist Missionary Society.[58] Believing that the "one prime essential for the religious welfare of the West was the establishment of a seminary," Peck insisted upon "a good, thorough, practical English education" for those on the frontier. Occasionally, British Baptists would even travel out West to spend weeks with Peck, who, unlike his anti-mission counterparts, was very fond of the British Baptist mission in India.[59] Peck represented the group of men that, according to Richard J. Carwardine, "upheld the evangelical values of both Old and New England. Wherever they carried this Yankee culture the Whig party was assured a constituency, particularly through upstate New York, into the Western Reserve and other parts of the Old Northwest, and beyond."[60]

Peck also passed his educational ideas and his affinity for Britain to former slaves who imitated his vision for the West. Freedman John Berry Meachum began teaching slave children in St. Louis through a day school instituted by Peck. Between 1818 and 1822, blacks and whites worshipped together under Peck's leadership. However, as the number of black members grew, Peck and others believed it was best for the blacks to have their own congregation. Formally ordained in 1825, Meachum assumed leadership of the congregation and helped establish the First African Baptist Church of St. Louis. Due to local opposition to black literacy, the Sheriff arrested Meachum and a white Englishman who had been hired as a teacher to instruct students in the basement of the church. Eventually, the school was forced to shut down as Meachum and Peck faced repeated threats against the institution of black learning.[61] Identified by Gayle T. Tate as a black nationalist figure, Meachum shared Peck's belief in an educated foundation to a Christian society. Years later, Meachum posited,

> In order that we might do more for our young children, I would recommend *manual labor schools* to be established in the different states, so as the children could have free access to them. And I would recommend in these schools pious teachers, either white or colored, who would take all pains with the children

---

58. Peck, *Forty Years of Pioneer Life*, 237.
59. Peck, *Forty Years of Pioneer Life*, 225, 315, 261.
60. Carwardine, *Evangelicals and Politics in Antebellum America*, 117.
61. Durst, "Reverend John Berry Meachum (1789–1854)," 2–3.

to bring them up in piety, and in industrious habits. We must endeavor to have our children look up a little, for they are too many to lie in idleness and dishonor.[62]

As demonstrated by Peck's and Meachum's leadership and their British pedagogy, Baptist nationalism offered a vision for both whites and blacks in America, albeit in separate congregations and corners of society.[63]

In June 1822, Peck recorded his encounter with Daniel Parker at the meeting of the Wabash Association in Indiana. Baptists in the southwestern corner of the Indiana Territory had questioned the biblical basis of mission boards since 1818, well before the Kehukee Declaration of 1827.[64] Although Peck was originally not allowed a seat at the Princeton Court House due to "strong prejudices and jealousies on account of my missionary character," he was asked to preach the following night by the Association. When amendments to the constitution were proposed, the topic of missions arose. After a five-hour discussion with the man he described as a "conscientious, well-meaning, though greatly-mistaken brother," Peck then wrote, "A large assembly seemed unwilling to stir from the place till the decision was reached. I have never before met with so determined an opposer to missions in every aspect. But the decision gave a decided victory to the cause of missions, fully sustaining the church which had contributed to their support." While pro-missions Baptists scored a victory among their brethren in Indiana, even more telling of Peck's influence in the region and his nationalistic approach to ministry is what he recorded next: "In the evening preached again on missions, and received a generous collection in aid of the cause at Princeton court-house. Passed the night with Judge Prince."[65] The judge to which Peck was referring was William Prince, a state circuit judge and member of the Indiana House of Representatives—after whom the town of Princeton was named. Prince had served as a captain in the Battle of Tippecanoe, where William Henry Harrison had earned his heroic reputation on the way to being elected President by Whigs like Peck.[66]

---

62. Tate, "Free Black Resistance in the Antebellum Era, 1830 to 1860," 770; Meachum, *Address to all the Colored Citizens of the United States*, 19.

63. Indeed, Peck's influence extended to multiple generations. On a September night in 1823, Peck preached in Carollton, Illinois from Heb 10:25 ("not forsaking the assembling of ourselves together, as the manner of some is; but exhorting one another: and so much the more, as ye see the day approaching") to a young Thomas Carlin, who was converted. Years later, Carlin would become the sixth governor of Illinois (Peck, *Forty Years of Pioneer Life*, 178).

64. Guthman, *Strangers Below*, 5.

65. Peck, *Forty Years of Pioneer Life*, 173–74.

66. Carwardine, "Evangelicals, Whigs and the Election of William Henry Harrison,"

Ultimately, anti-mission Baptists like Daniel Parker stood so vehemently against men like John Mason Peck not just because they allegedly conducted their ministry outside the bounds of Scripture, but because they stayed in the homes of judges and left town with "generous" amounts of money in hand. (Some affluent, pro-mission Baptists in Indiana like Jesse Lynch Holman actually *were* judges.[67]) For simple Baptists' taste, they appeared far too wealthy and far too yoked with local government officials to warrant the name "Baptist" or even "Protestant." Parker and others were convinced that "the principle and practice of the mission system is according to the spirit of this world, and not according to the spirit of the gospel."[68] "To me," derided John Leland, "it appears more like religious parade than humble piety."[69] The anti-mission controversy was thus a deeply theological issue because it pertained to the nature and role of the Baptist church and even issues of divine sovereignty, and it was also an inescapably political issue due to its relevance to the question of religious liberty and the relationship between church and state.[70]

The leadership of the Triennial Convention was largely composed of refined, New England-style, cosmopolitan Baptists who believed that civil religion was not incompatible with religious liberty and that war with Britain did not preclude *working with* Britain. One historian, for instance, has described Richard Furman as "a Southern embodiment of the best of Puritanism" and another has called him a "leading American Baptist identified with the work of William Carey and the English Baptist missionary initiative."[71] He was, according to G. William Foster Jr., "America's most influential Baptist" and one of the most well-known in England.[72] In fact, Furman surrounded himself with Baptist Englishmen who transplanted to South Carolina and who shared his aversion to the French. Edmund Botsford, a mentor to William B. Johnson and one of Furman's closest friends in the ministry, was born in Bedfordshire in 1745. Having once prepared for war with France in the British military, Botsford apparently never lost his

64.

67. Blake, "Jesse Lynch Holman," 44–45.

68. Parker, *Public Address*

69. Leland, "Which Has Done the Most Mischief in the World, the Kings-Evil or Priest-Craft?," 495.

70. Like many others, J. B. Jeter attributed the apathy toward missions to a spirit of antinomianism and hyper-Calvinism. He documents his encounter with anti-mission antinomian Baptists in Franklin County, Virginia (Jeter, *Recollections of a Long Life*, 65).

71. Nettles, "Richard Furman," 140; Rogers, *Richard Furman*, 201.

72. Foster, "Preface," xviii; Rogers, *Richard Furman*, 100. Also see Todd, "Sainted Furman: Richard Furman as America's Most Influential Baptist," 99–118.

disdain for the French.⁷³ Reporting on the death of Methodist Bishop Thomas Coke in the East Indies in 1815, Botsford wrote to a fellow English South Carolinian Baptist, "General Washington seemed to have been raised up for a blessing to America, and Bonaparte for a curse to the whole world. What a volatile, monkey-like people the French are! They boast of themselves as being the *great nation*—of monkies and tigers! No doubt Europe will be convulsed again, and we shall have our share of trouble and perplexity. How many things turn up to wean the aged from this world."⁷⁴ If any Baptist exhibited Francophobia in the deeper South, it was certainly Botsford, who served churches in both Georgia and South Carolina. Botsford had once been called by Furman to fill the pulpit at Georgetown, South Carolina after William Staughton, another Englishman, had resigned his post. Staughton, who had immigrated to America from Birmingham, England by Furman's personal request, was one of the founding members of the Baptist Missionary Society in 1792. He was also critical of French religion and philosophy. In 1796, the year of America's first partisan election, Staughton composed a circular letter to the Philadelphia Association condemning those European nations "deluged in superstition" and "the prevalence of infidelity" in American society.⁷⁵

The life and ministry of William Staughton betokened that pro-mission Baptists in America weren't simply pro-British; sometimes they *were* British. At the inaugural Triennial Convention in Philadelphia, where he pastored, Staughton was elected the first corresponding secretary for the Baptist Board of Foreign Missions. Staughton's nationalistic agenda was obvious in his many pursuits other than missions. In 1822, he became the first president of Columbian College in Washington, D.C, serving as chaplain of the United States Congress for two sessions. Staughton was a tutor for the Baptist Education Society of America of the Middle States and was a founding member of the Bible Society in Philadelphia. Like his other pro-mission Baptists, Staughton also aimed to transform the West into a distinctly Christian society, accepting the presidency of Georgetown College in Kentucky before dying on the journey in 1829. Indeed, Furman, Staughton, and

---

73. Mallary, *Memoirs of Elder Edmund Botsford*, 21.

74. Edmund Botsford, "To Mr. Cook, Georgetown, May 11, 1815," in Mallary, *Memoirs of Elder Edmund Botsford*, 190.

75. Staughton, *Memoir of the Rev. William Staughton, D.D.*, 46. Staughton's English background, his close affiliation with Furman and other Federalists, and his denunciation of infidelity all suggest that Staughton was indeed a Federalist. This evidence is contrary to Ruth Bloch's suggestion that Staughton was a Republican because of the alleged "mildness" of his criticism of the French in 1798 (Bloch, *Visionary Republic*, 278n3).

others established a network of British and pro-British Baptists who shared their vision of an educated, morally reformed, *free* America. Joseph Cook, another Englishman, was baptized by Furman and ordained by Furman and fellow South Carolina Federalist Oliver Hart. Years later, through the Baptist ministers' education fund, Furman would send Cook's son (Joseph B. Cook) to the College of Rhode Island—under New Englander Jonathan Maxcy.[76]

Indeed, Baptist leaders in these missionary and benevolent efforts typically self-identified with the older, more British way of thinking, and this was reflected in their less separationist approach to nation-building. On one hand, Regular Baptists in Federalist-laden Charleston traced their heritage to New and Old England dissenters and eschewed the nation of France.[77] On the other, skeptics of Baptist missions like John Leland believed the real violation of human rights came not from France, but from Britain:

> The ministers of the established religion, in Massachusetts, are greatly alarmed at the growth of infidelity in France, and use all their art to prevent French influence in America. Reverend gentleman, if you wish to stop the spread of Deism, seek to remove the cause. Come forth upon the plan of the gospel, and trust God and his word for your support. Renounce the scheme that Mr. Cotton first introduced in Massachusetts.[78]

Even in the deeper South, Baptist nationalism was more British and less separationist. In early 1836, a series of letters were published in Georgia's *Christian Index* in defense of what many Georgia Baptists were calling "*new movements, new plans, and new schemes.*" Jesse Mercer, the leading advocate for Baptist education in the state, simply referred to them as "the various social operations of these days."[79] In response to the idea that the "new plans" were evil because they were new, Mercer attempted to show that they were not in fact new at all. Theologically speaking, Mercer argued that pro-mission Baptists held to the old ways, and were "more generally on the doctrine of the covenant and predestination, and less practical." He later added, "By far the great majority of those engaged in *benevolent efforts are strictly Calvinistic.*" Mercer himself identified strongly with the British school of Baptist theology, carrying Andrew Fuller's works along with him

---

76. See correspondence between J. B. Cook and Richard Furman on July 13, 1797 in Foster, *Life and Works of Dr. Richard Furman, D.D.*, 166–67. Evan Jones, Baptist missionary to the Cherokees, was born in Wales.

77. Rogers, *Richard Furman*, 15.

78. Leland, "Blow at the Root," 253.

79. Mallary, *Memoirs of Elder Jesse Mercer*, 193.

on his ministerial journeys and making one of the strongest defenses of Fuller's theology ever made in the South.[80]

As president of the Georgia Baptist Convention for nineteen years, editor of a temperance newspaper, and the eponym for Mercer University, Mercer was a notable citizen with no small amount of professional aspiration, even running unsuccessfully for state senator in 1816. Mercer understood that at the heart of the missions debate was the issue of ambition. He reported, "when they condemn the promoters of them, it is by censuring their motives or designs, so as to make them wicked."[81] Certainly, the ambitious Mercer was himself the object of such criticism. (By 1833, Mercer had even entertained a serious proposal to run for governor of Georgia, but he eventually declined.[82]) In the midst of a war with Britain, and with such strong motives to lead both ecclesiastical and civil governments, pro-missions Baptists like Jesse Mercer were destined to encounter the so-called "Anti-ism" that "prevail[ed] much in the western part" of his state.[83]

Having written the article in the 1798 Georgia constitution guaranteeing religious liberty, Mercer was an ardent defender of Baptist principles. However, as Baptists moved from interlopers to insiders in southern society, he believed that church and state should work *together* rather than at loggerheads. When Mercer served as President of the Powelton Baptist Society for Foreign Missions in 1815, his recording secretary was William Rabun—the governor of Georgia.[84] In 1832, when two Congregationalist missionaries to the Cherokees were convicted of violating Georgia state law which prohibited non-Native Americans from entering Native lands without a license, Mercer vehemently opposed the Supreme Court decision that ruled Georgia's law unconstitutional (*Worcester v. Georgia [1832]*). According to Mercer, because "the United States have had a governmental agency over the Cherokees," Georgia rightly disapproved of "the establishment of an independent, national government within the limits of Georgia." Mercer took exception with those newspapers that compared the imprisonment of the missionaries to those of Adoniram Judson in Burma or John Bunyan in England because Georgia had made no law prohibiting freedom of conscience. The missionaries had simply not obtained a license or permit from the governor, he argued. In Mercer's view, the state was responsible for

---

80. Mallary, *Memoirs of Elder Jesse Mercer*, 85. For a look into Mercer's defense of Fuller's doctrine of atonement, see Mercer, "Ten Letters, Addressed to the Rev. Cyrus White, in reference to the Scriptural View of the Atonement."

81. Mallary, *Memoirs of Elder Jesse Mercer*, 201–2.

82. Mallary, *Memoirs of Elder Jesse Mercer*, 100–101.

83. Mallary, *Memoirs of Elder Jesse Mercer*, 135.

84. Mallary, *Memoirs of Elder Jesse Mercer*, 189.

encouraging religion and Christians were responsible for registering with the state before practicing their ministry. However, such an arrangement seemed to have more in common with the certificate laws in Massachusetts than with traditional Baptist views of religious liberty. Nevertheless, as a self-professed "unionist," Mercer's nationalist ideal of a Christian America included the concept of religious liberty so long as it was compatible with governmental authority.[85] "These men were not sentenced to the penitentiary, merely for residing among the Indians," Mercer contended, "but for residing within the jurisdiction of Georgia, in defiance of her laws."[86]

The tension of Mercer's argument embodied the rising struggle between union and liberty that would call into question the very idea of the *United* States in the 1830s with the Nullification Crisis (1832–33) and the issue of states' rights. This tension was felt by all Americans in the Jacksonian period, including Baptists. John Leland, for instance, could see "no radical difference between the tendency of the Hartford Convention and the ordinance of South Carolina," between "the doctrine of the Nullifiers" and eventual civil war.[87] Just as the Standing Order proved in Hartford that nationalism did not preclude a strong stance on states' rights, Baptists like Mercer proved the very same thing in Georgia in the 1830s when they argued for *more* regulation of religion by the state and *less* control at the national level. Strangely enough, missions could divide Baptists and bring them together, evoking the strongest states' rights sentiments as well as an uncharacteristic desire to unite. Long before Georgia Baptists split the Triennial Convention in 1845 over slavery and domestic missions, Baptists in Philadelphia put aside their differences on the slavery issue for the sake of foreign missions. The very same year that Congregationalists convened to condemn the War of 1812 due to their friendliness with England, Baptists convened to begin a new era of international missions for the very same reason.

The War of 1812

As a whole, Baptists in America were not immune to the diplomatic alliances that divided the first two parties after Jay's Treaty in 1795. Federalist Hezekiah Smith was among those citizens of Haverhill, Massachusetts who corresponded with John Adams in 1798 to express their support for his

---

85. Mallary, *Memoirs of Elder Jesse Mercer*, 222–23.

86. Mallary, *Memoirs of Elder Jesse Mercer*, 218–20.

87. Leland, "Address Delivered at Cheshire, on the Eighteenth Anniversary of the Battle of New Orleans, January 8, 1833," 630.

policy against the French.[88] A year later, fellow Federalist Jonathan Maxcy described a similarly pro-British, anti-French perspective of the Atlantic:

> Britain first smote us with her gigantic arm, she listened to our remonstrances, and redressed our wrongs. France, irritated at our success in preserving peace, determined on revenge. She renewed with additional vigor those secret, insidious arts, which she had long practiced to control our public councils, and to destroy the confidence of the people in the government of their choice. Detected and disappointed by the vigilance of our rulers, she threw aside the mask, and disclosed her vengeful countenance on the Atlantic. Our commerce fell prey to her all-devouring jaws. The overtures made by our government have been neglected with the most haughty disdain, and our messengers of peace treated like the representatives of a nation destitute of wisdom and power. We have now no resource left to vindicate our honor and our rights, but our courage and our force.[89]

Maxcy was referring to the so-called XYZ Affair that vindicated Federalists' aversion to the French. However, strictly speaking, Baptists were not necessarily *for* one nation or another so much as they were *against* those who they believed could potentially violate their liberty, namely religious liberty.[90] Remarkably, in 1784, James Manning and Chancellor Stephen Hopkins actually wrote to the King of France, asking for a donation for French literature and a French language professor, and thanking him for France's aid during the war. (Ambassador to France Thomas Jefferson eventually replied back to the Baptists that he did not believe it "prudent" to deliver the letter to the King.)[91] Before the French Revolution (1789–99), Baptists were not necessarily wary of French infidelity as they came to be after the storming of the Bastille. In fact, like most Americans, Baptists originally believed that France's Revolution would replicate their own. Likewise, Baptist Republicans like Daniel Merrill were by no means Francophiles like Thomas Jefferson so much as they were extremely suspicious of British tyranny. In 1815, Daniel Merrill called Britain "the scourge of the world," denouncing the New England ministerial "infatuation" with America's enemy in the War

---

88. Broome, *Life, Ministry, and Journals of Hezekiah Smith, 1737–1805*, 103.
89. Maxcy, "Oration, Delivered in the First Congregational Meeting House," 382.
90. For the disputed character of the war, see Den Hartog, "War of 1812," 74–96.
91. "Sire," in Guild, *Life, Times, and Correspondence of James Manning, and the Early History of Brown University*, 301–3.

of 1812. For Merrill, the idea that Britain was the "bulwark of their religion" was simply ridiculous.[92]

Therefore, as Aaron Menikoff has noted, "When it came to the War of 1812, Baptists did not remain neutral."[93] In fact, some Baptists departed for the war immediately after church! In Hartford, New York in 1814, Elder Amasa Brown's regiment received the order to march to Plattsburgh on the Sabbath. According to a young boy who attended the service, Brown arrived at the church building in his epaulettes, preaching a sermon on patriotism. After the sermon, Brown "marched on with his regiment in the afternoon, evincing that his love of country was true-hearted."[94] A young John L. Dagg was notified about British vessels coming up the Potomac while attending an Association meeting in nearby Fauquier County. Days later, after marching over with his local militia, Dagg "saw the light of the burning capitol, which the British had fired the day before."[95] During the war, some Baptists were taken prisoners by the British, where they further demonstrated their loyalty to the American cause. In Northern Neck, Virginia, after Deacon Epaphrus Norris was captured by the enemy as a supposed scout and questioned about the position of the American forces, he replied defiantly, "You may kill me, but you cannot make me tell you anything about our army."[96] Singing hymns by Isaac Watts to keep his spirits up, the older Norris purportedly won over the crew of the British ship and was later released.

In a predominantly Republican denomination, most rank-and-file Baptists openly supported "Madison's War." David Jones even wrote James Madison in 1813, bragging, "I possess a Talent, to make an army fight."[97] So committed was John Taylor to the necessity of the War of 1812 that he conceived of it as another "revolutionary war," referring to the War of Independence as "The Old Revolutionary War."[98] Even Federalist Richard Furman supported the cause. According to a fellow Baptist, Furman encouraged soldiers "on the lines of Charleston . . . both by his prayers and by his example." According to Robert Elder, while Furman may have been the exception among Baptists in the early decades of the United States in terms

---

92. Merrill, *Balaam Disappointed*, 24, 30.
93. Menikoff, *Politics and Piety*, 61.
94. Wright, *History of the Shaftesbury Association, from 1781 to 1853*, 308.
95. Dagg, *Autobiography of Rev. John L. Dagg, D.D.*, 15.
96. Jeter, *Recollections of a Long Life*, 193–94.
97. In Wolever, *The Life, Journal and Works of David Jones, 1736–1820*, 129.
98. Taylor, *Baptists on the American Frontier*, 121.

of public service, "the way he combined sacred duties with secular influence would become a much more common ideal in the years after his death."[99]

Not surprisingly, John Leland could hardly speak on any matter pertaining to Old England without reference to New. "Spend not your time in unmeaning parade," Leland exhorted the Sons of Liberty in Cheshire, Massachusetts in 1813, "like the militia of Massachusetts, in drinking toasts of patriotism—in volunteering to stay at home—in striving for offices or disputing about politics; but arise and avenge our wrongs, and never sheath your swords, or stack your arms, until the soil and shores of North America are freed from British cruelty."[100] The real enemies of the republic were in New and Old England, Leland believed. Similarly, Daniel Merrill contended that Americans had been abused far more by Federalists than by James Madison, and that the French bugaboo was a farce. He mocked,

> These false prophets were very expert in denouncing the war, as base, wicked, unjust and ruinous. These, with the greatest effrontery, to mislead the people, kept up a huge cry of, French Influence! French Influence! and, at the same time, they could, without a blush, eulogize Britain, and, with the greatest assurance, pronounce, that she would never make peace with Madison, and that the Administration which made war would never make peace.[101]

The British and French allegiances that divided the nation during the War of 1812 no less cleaved the Baptists of America.[102] For many Baptists were as hesitant of the war as bellicose Baptists like David Jones were for it. Although Henry Holcombe was not as outspoken in his politics as his other Southern Federalists, he clearly distanced himself from War Hawks such as the fiery John C. Calhoun of South Carolina. Like Baptist pastor W. T. Brantly, who also served in the Savannah River Association, Holcombe openly opposed the War of 1812 and even grounded his pacifism in his aversion to infidelity.[103]

---

99. Elder, *Sacred Mirror*, 180–81.

100. Leland, "Address to the Association of the Sons of Liberty, Cheshire, March 4, 1813," 374.

101. Merrill, *Balaam Disappointed*, 8, 9, 11.

102. William Parkinson reasons that the war is with Britain, not France (Parkinson, *Sermon, Delivered in the Meeting House of the First Baptist Church, in the City of New York*, 25).

103. Snyder, "William T. Brantly (1787–1845)," 80.

Unlike John Leland who justified the conflict as a "defensive war," Holcombe could not find biblical justification for the War of 1812.[104] On May 12, 1812, Holcombe wrote a letter expounding upon Romans chapter 13, a classic conservative text wherein the Apostle Paul urges Christians to submit to their authorities. "These are," Holcombe declared, "in substance, the only politics which I have ever undertaken, to explain, or defend."[105] Warning against those who "paid a disproportionate attention to politics" and inevitably "descend to the comparatively petty disputes of parties," Holcombe distinguished between a defensive war and an offensive war.[106] In his mind, the conflict with Britain qualified as the latter, and was therefore unjust. He objected to the War of 1812 on moral and biblical grounds:

> To ask what the scriptures say of *offensive* war, would be to insult the common sense of all their readers. Attempts equally vain, rash and presumptuous, have been made to justify this species of war, because, under the sanction of a special warrant from the God of nations, it was waged by the ancient Jews. But what God has done in the punishment of atrociously wicked nations, by war, as well as by famine, and by pestilence, and what we may do, as bound by his revealed will, are widely different things.[107]

As a Federalist, Holcombe disapproved of an "unlawful" war with a generally lawful nation like England. As a Baptist who emphasized the newness of God's covenant to his church, Holcombe opposed any justification for war that hinged on the Old Testament. Just as John Leland had rejected this kind of typology to oppose both religious establishment and the institution of slavery, Holcombe did so in order to argue for a more isolationist approach to foreign relations. Moreover, not only did Holcombe reject Republicans' logic for war with Britain, but he identified infidelity as the culprit behind their warmongering.

Like most Republicans, however, Baptists generally could not stomach British aggression during the war. In fact, they sometimes justified the War of 1812 using many of the same arguments and rhetoric they did for religious liberty. For William Parkinson, the rights and consent of a nation are inviolable and must be defended, the same as "that which obtains among individual free men."[108] Although Baptist Republicans did not all agree on

---

104. Leland, "Free Thoughts on War," 465.
105. "Letter XVIII," in Holcombe, *First Fruits, in a Series of Letters*, 123.
106. "Letter XVIII," in Holcombe, *First Fruits, in a Series of Letters*, 127, 128.
107. "Letter XVIII," in Holcombe, *First Fruits, in a Series of Letters*, 136.
108. Parkinson, *Sermon, Delivered in the Meeting House of the First Baptist Church, in the City of New York*, 8.

the necessity of a standing army (Parkinson and Leland, for instance, were against and Thomas Baldwin was for it), most were decidedly against "the doctrine of non-resistance" in matters of international diplomacy.[109] The celebration at war's end showed Baptists' political colors. Never afraid of hyperbole, John Leland boasted, "Never, since the age of miracles ceased, was a victory more splendid than that of New Orleans," referring to Andrew Jackson's belated triumph over the British in the Crescent City.[110] Leland summarized the results of the war in Republican fashion: "The constitution endured the shock; the administration retained the confidence of the people; the physical strength of the United States was tested and found to be unshaken; the war-party became all victorious: Mr. Madison proclaimed the peace, and Federalism gave up the ghost."[111] In Eastern Virginia, 13-year-old Jeremiah Bell Jeter was sent by his grandfather to the neighboring town of Liberty to learn the reason for the celebratory canon fire. An elder Jeter remembered that, after learning of the peace between America and Britain, he raced home and "wherever I saw a person in a house, on the road, or in a field, white or colored, I cried: 'Peace! Peace! Peace!'"[112] Jeter described his small journey home in the words of Isaiah 52:7: "How beautiful are the feet of them that preach the gospel of peace, and bring glad tidings of good things." Baptists were as elated at the Treaty of Ghent as any other religious group in the young nation.[113] Remarkably, less than a year before Jeter's homeward march, Baptists had convened in Philadelphia and decided that they would actually preach the gospel of peace *during* the war.

---

109. Parkinson, *Sermon, Delivered in the Meeting House of the First Baptist Church, in the City of New York*, 12; Baldwin, *Discourse, Delivered Before the Ancient and Honourable Artillery Company*, 6, 11–12.

110. Leland, "Address Delivered at the Request of the Republican Committee of Arrangements, at Pittsfield," 502.

111. Leland, "Part of a Speech, Delivered at Suffield," 521.

112. Jeter, *Recollections of a Long Life*, 79–80.

113. Francis Wayland described a similar celebration to the news of peace during his time in New York City. He recalls, "At length a boat reached the wharf, announcing the fact that a treaty of peace had been signed, and was waiting for nothing but the action of our government to become a law. The men on whose ears these words first fell, rushed in breathless haste into the city, to repeat them to their friends, shouting as they ran through the streets, 'Peace! Peace! Peace!' Everyone who heard the sound repeated it. From house to house, from street to street, the news spread with electric rapidity. The whole city was in commotion" (Wayland, *Memoir of the Life and Labors of Francis Wayland*, 38).

War and Missions

When American Baptists formed their very first nationwide denomination in May of 1814 for the sake of organized foreign missions, they were following the lead and impetus of British Baptists who had already begun to send missionaries to India through their Baptist Missionary Society. The first two male overseas American Baptist missionaries, Adoniram Judson and Luther Rice, had been baptized by English Baptist William Ward in September and November of 1812 in India, symbolizing the trans-Atlantic partnership between American and English Baptists. In a letter in December 1812, William Carey had pushed his American counterparts to "take these two brethren under their protection," promising, "We shall not desert them, nor their companions, should they be in want." In a previous letter to Thomas Baldwin, Carey acknowledged the unprecedented moment in Baptist history when he urged, "Do stir in this business; this is a providence which gives a new turn to American relations to Oriental Missions."[114] The correspondence between Carey and American Baptist leaders like Baldwin and William Rogers and William Staughton of Philadelphia only solidified the tightening bond between English and American Baptists as they sought to collectively fulfill Christ's Great Commission in Matthew 28:18–20 on a global scale.

Therefore, when thirty-three messengers from eleven states and Washington D. C. convened in Philadelphia to inaugurate the Triennial Convention during the War of 1812, Baptists were both following and *fighting* England. They were waging international war and promoting international worship at the very same time with the very same nation. The "flush of national pride" that suffused the nation during the War of 1812 and energized Baptists to come together as Americans also led them to partner missiologically with their enemies across the Atlantic.[115] Understandably, this created for considerable tension among mission and anti-mission Baptists in America, as the Triennial Convention was inevitably framed by many as a political movement due to its ties to countries *other* than America. To begin, the timing was less than ideal because the War of 1812 loomed over the entire Convention. In May, the British navy had blockaded New England ports to the north of Philadelphia. Three months later, to the south, the British army burned the nation's capital in Washington D.C. Pastor of First Baptist Church of New York City, William Parkinson, who called his

---

114. Baker, *Southern Baptist Convention and Its People, 1607–1972*, 107.
115. Torbet, *Social History of the Philadelphia Baptist Association: 1707–1940*, 28.

countrymen to once again muster "the noble spirit of 76'" against a familiar foe, described the moribund state of affairs during wartime:

> War, especially when, like that of the American revolution and most of the modern wars in Europe, it inundates the country, always becomes an interruption of public worship, and an obstacle to learning and science, and the cultivation and improvement of all the useful arts. Houses of worship and seminaries of learning, are, under such circumstances, commonly closed and abandoned; and if taken by the enemy, usually converted into barracks for soldiers, or perhaps stables for horses. That such was the fate of public buildings in this and other cities on our continent, during the revolutionary war, is well recollected by many in this assembly.[116]

With such a paralyzing effect upon the country, and with memories of the Revolution still fresh in their minds, the fact that American Baptists chose 1814 to become a global denomination speaks as much to the progress of Baptists *in* Western civilization as it does to Western civilization itself. The United States had arrived on the scene as a global presence in the world, and so had Baptists. Even a world war could not keep America's Baptists from organizing and mobilizing for foreign missions, amazingly enough, in tandem with Baptists from the very nation laying siege to theirs. Richard Furman's journey to Philadelphia illustrates the level of social status and ambition that characterized pro-mission Baptists even during wartime. The Convention's first president and America's most influential Baptist initially decided *not* to attend the event because of the war. However, his church objected to his objection, and he eventually made the trip to Philadelphia—with a federal judge. Henry Alan Tupper records,

> The contemplated convention in Philadelphia in May, 1814 he most earnestly approved; but as, owing to the state of war, the distance could not be traversed by sea, he felt that he could not attend it. But his church overruled his objection, made a liberal appropriation for his use and gave him leave of absence until the winter. With his beloved friend, Hon. Matthias B. Tallmadge, Judge of the Federal Court for New York (whose delicate health had caused his seeing a winter home in Charleston), he went as a delegation from the General Committee of the Charleston Baptist Association.[117]

---

116. Parkinson, *Sermon, Delivered in the Meeting House of the First Baptist Church, in the City of New York*, 10, 7.

117. Foster, *Life and Works of Dr. Richard Furman*, 31.

Receiving a recess appointment from Thomas Jefferson in 1805, Furman's "beloved friend" Judge Tallmadge was a Republican. Nevertheless, like most pro-mission Baptist leaders, Furman enjoyed friendships with civil leaders that often benefited his nationalist cause, friendships that seemed to conflate church and state in the eyes of his opponents.

Most black and white Baptists, however, did not keep the company of judges, did not hail from educated, aristocratic cities like Charleston, and thus were not members of churches that could so easily support international missions in the aftermath of war with England. For rural Baptists, the impact of the war was especially profound. In Virginia, J. B. Jeter recalled, "The war was followed by a wild and reckless spirit of speculation. Tobacco commanded enormous prices, and real estate quadrupled in its estimated value. Men who were not worth a dollar were ready to contract debts to the amount of thousands."[118] For this reason, John Leland registered his own nationalistic complaint that the silver and gold necessary to fund foreign missions "drains the country of its precious metals."[119] When men like Richard Furman raised funds for the translation of the Scriptures by Carey and Marshman in India, they were diverting them *away* from where they were needed most.[120] According to Leland, missions was the result of a struggling economy, not a strong church. "It is a lucrative business for printers, and a large field for preachers, who cannot find employment at home."[121] In the decades following the war, despite its objective to evangelize the heathen, foreign missions was made less popular in many Baptist circles due to its somewhat elitist, pro-British ethos and its tendency to siphon resources and attention away from the United States. For example, Morgan Edwards, the Baptist loyalist, had been "the first known to suggest an organic union among all the Baptists."[122] Soon after returning from the war, Elder Amasa Brown's patriotism was celebrated by all in the church, but his "zeal" for missions and benevolence societies was not. Brown "met with opposition, and suffered in consequence, even from some of his own brethren." According to a local Colonel in Fairhaven, Vermont (who was likely not a friend of Brown's), the pastor had advised his congregation, "If a man would not allow his wife the means to give to such worthy objects, he thought she would be justifiable in getting into his purse and helping herself to funds." To many

---

118. Jeter, *Recollections of a Long Life*, 80–81.

119. Leland, "Extracts from a Letter to a Friend," 530; "Address at the Dedication of the Baptist Meeting-House in Lanesborough, February 10, 1829," 554.

120. Foster, *Life and Works of Dr. Richard Furman*, 31.

121. Leland, "Which Has Done the Most Mischief in the World, the Kings-Evil or Priest-Craft?," 495.

122. Foster, *Life and Works of Dr. Richard Furman*, 171.

in the church, Brown's counsel was "outrageous," proving that the missions debate was about more than the church. It was about money, apparently dividing husband and wife![123]

Sometimes pro-missions Baptists were actually treated like foreigners even in their own land. In 1823, when Jeremiah Bell Jeter and Daniel Witt visited the New River Baptist Association in Virginia, they encountered hostility to their cause. One can gather some sense of the political and social differences that divided Baptists on the issue of missions from Jeter's account: "The Association was a small body. Its ministers were plain and illiterate, of narrow views and strong prejudices. The anti-mission spirit was then just beginning to develop itself and muster its forces for the conflict which soon followed. Witt and myself were looked upon with suspicion—as spies sent to search out the resources of the country."[124] For those Baptists who "took deep interest in the first efforts made in England to convey the gospel in India," they soon learned that such an interest would come at a cost.[125] Nevertheless, the expansionist, Americanized spirit that pushed Baptists west to the frontier also drew them overseas with the gospel. The rise of missions in American Baptist life was both a sign of Baptist political strength in the United States and of the willingness of many Baptists to view the conservatism and causes of Old and New England as friendly to freedom of religion, not necessarily inimical to it. Led by educated men of more polite society, the incipient missions movement and its benevolence societies signaled that Baptists too had a nationalistic vision for America, but compatible with religious liberty, and that they were willing to partner with different groups and even former enemies in order to Christianize their nation and others. Although Baptists were not uniformly settled on the missions debate, nearly every Baptist was willing to participate in the ecumenism of the new American nation in some way in order to secure the future they envisioned for the United States.

---

123. Wright, *History of the Shaftesbury Association*, 308. According to John Leland, the sheer amount of money allocated to missions was itself a spiritual danger. He charged, "But to create large funds in advance, for the declared purpose of educating young men for the ministry, and supporting missionaries, lays a temptation before them which may be too strong for many to withstand" (Leland, "Which Has Done the Most Mischief in the World, the Kings-Evil or Priest-Craft?," 494).

124. Jeter, *Recollections of a Long Life*, 114.

125. Foster, *Life and Works of Dr. Richard Furman*, 31.

Chapter 7

Ecumenism, Education, and the Birth of a "Respectable" Denomination

THE PROCESS OF DISESTABLISHMENT in America was a long, arduous, state-by-state endeavor. As a result, it was also an ecumenical struggle for the nation's dissenters. From Presbyterians in Virginia to Episcopalians in Vermont, Baptists partnered with a number of Protestant denominations in order to oppose general assessments and religious laws of all kinds.[1] In 1784, James Manning observed that a "brotherly kindness prevails more amongst the several denominations throughout New England than heretofore, and of course the prejudices against Baptists are greatly abated." In his travels throughout the country, Manning also noted an increase in "cordial invitations into the pulpits of the Pedobaptists" extended to Baptists.[2] This was also the case in parts of the South. While in Savannah in 1795, Richard Furman was invited to preach by Rev. Edward Ellington at the Episcopal Church to over 500 people.[3] In regions across the United States, Baptists were beginning to carve out a niche for themselves in public life and polite society. In the towns of Brunswick, Woodbridge, Elizabethtown, and Newark, New Jersey, reports of Presbyterians "opening their houses of worship to the Baptists, and flocking to hear them" spread quickly in the area,

---

1. Esbeck, "Disestablishment in Virginia, 1776–1802," 149; McLoughlin, *Soul Liberty*, 290–91.

2. James Manning, "To John Rippon, Providence, Aug. 3, 1784," in Guild, *Life, Times, and Correspondence of James Manning*, 328.

3. Richard Furman, "Charleston, Sept. 28, 1795," in Foster, *Life and Works of Dr. Richard Furman, D.D.*, 120.

proving that Baptists were no longer the so-called "madmen of Munster" as they had once been branded.[4]

Like the Great Awakening decades earlier, the Revolution had an inclusive effect upon American religion, tending to ameliorate relations among certain dissenting groups.[5] The spirit of 76' had an especially strong influence upon the catholicity of those denominations who participated in the *Second* Great Awakening, the majority of whom shared a similar goal of Christianizing their infant nation.[6] In a burgeoning age of moral and social reform, Baptists aligned themselves with denominations of all kinds in order to advance public virtue in the new republic. For instance, Richard Furman and Dr. Isaac Stockton Keith of the Presbyterian church were the "chief agents" in forming the Charleston Bible Society in 1810, of which Furman remained vice president until his death.[7] Among their most important services was visiting military forts and distributing Bibles to soldiers. Five years earlier, Furman and Keith were appointed to collect donations for the translation of the Scriptures by the Baptist Missionary Society in India.[8] Occasionally, though not routinely, Baptists even established friendly relations with Catholics in order to support noble causes in their communities. After coming to New Orleans for his health in 1817 and being invited by Baptist Cornelius Paulding to preach in the city, a young William B. Johnson preached in St. Louis Cathedral for a benefit for the Poydras Orphan Asylum (Johnson also assisted in forming a mission society as a local auxiliary to the Triennial Convention).[9] Father Anthony of the diocese approved of the homily, but he cautiously requested to "see his sermon before he preaches it."[10]

In the early republic, Baptists were replacing establishment with ecumenism.[11] No less concerned about public morality than their Congre-

---

4. James Manning, "To the Rev. Dr. Smith, Providence, 18th Nov., 1790," in Guild, *Life, Times, and Correspondence of James Manning*, 437.

5. This "evangelical unionism" during the Revolutionary period is explored in depth in Alan Heimert's *Religion and the American Mind: From the Great Awakening to the Revolution*, 351–412.

6. See Todd, "Populist Puritan," 137–52.

7. Cook, "Biography of Richard Furman," 30–31. The Charleston Bible Society met at the home of Charles Cotesworth Pinckney, its first president, further demonstrating Furman's ties to Federalist leadership.

8. Cook, "Biography of Richard Furman," 102.

9. Harsch, "Who Dat Say Dey Gonna Teach Dem Saints?," 187.

10. Woodson, *Giant in the Land*, 41–42.

11. Of course, Baptist "toleration" had its limits. When Alexander Campbell recalled his experience in the Redstone Baptist Association (PA) in 1815 and their reception to his new ideas about immersion, he commented that the Baptist preachers there

gationalist and Episcopalian brethren, Baptists envisioned a civil religion forged by personal initiative rather than legal enforcement, by voluntary societies instead of the state. The "spirit of toleration" that prevailed among Baptists and other groups during this time was a corollary of the widespread belief that, once the government was gradually divested of state-sponsored religion, something other than taxes or trade was needed to hold together the cords of society. In effect, by opening themselves to ecumenical activism, Baptists were demonstrating their willingness to embrace religious liberty and to take personal responsibility for the moral fabric of their communities. They were, as Henry Holcombe wrote to the Charleston Association in 1796, engaging both "private and public, civil and religious life."[12]

Certain Baptists embraced this responsibility more than others. According to Daniel Walker Howe, "Some of the divisions among Baptists reflected social class differences; middle-class Baptists were more likely to support interdenominational co-operation on behalf of temperance, for example, while Primitive Baptists . . . warned that such reform activities were distractions and corruptions of the pure gospel message."[13] Indeed, the liberal spirit in the American nation was not always looked upon favorably by other groups or even other Baptists. In 1802, Jonathan Maxcy was appointed President of Union College, an inter-denominational institution in Schenectady, New York that characterized the inclusive nation-building that took place during the age. As one scholar has noted, Union "was not technically in New England but it was clearly in the cultural orbit and theological trajectory of the Puritan faith and outlook that had shaped the region to the east."[14] In this conservative milieu, Maxcy's presidency was not soon without controversy. In addition to his Baptist views and his militant Federalism, Maxcy's willingness to accommodate other theological positions was the source of the most concern. One of the trustees of the College, J. B. Johnson, objected to the "unsoundness" of Maxcy's opinions when the latter asked at James Manning's funeral, "Will the gates of paradise be barred against these because they did not possess the penetrating sagacity of an Edwards or a Hopkins? Or shall these great theological champions engross heaven, and shout hallelujahs from its walls, while Priestley, a Price, and Winchester, merely for difference in opinion, though preeminent in virtue, must sink

---

were "narrow, contracted, illiberal, and uneducated men" (Foster, *Life of Alexander Campbell*, 61).

12. Menikoff, *Politics and Piety*, 53.
13. Howe, *What Hath God Wrought*, 180.
14. Hart, *John Williamson Nevin*, 40.

into the regions of darkness and pain?"[15] Despite Maxcy's sanguine outlook concerning the eternal state of these men's souls, the heterodox views of Joseph Priestley, Richard Price, and Elhanan Winchester were not viewed by most evangelicals as a mere "difference in opinion." Priestley and Price, both British philosophers, adhered to deistical systems of thought that more closely aligned with that of Thomas Jefferson than anything resembling historical Christianity. Joseph Priestley, who among other things was a chemist and political theorist, authored *An History of the Corruptions of Christianity* (1782), in which he questioned everything from the Trinity to the deity of Christ to the penal substitutionary atonement to the immortality of the soul. Elhanan Winchester, a former Baptist, was a Universalist who denied that souls would be punished forever in Hell, a belief that most believed undermined public morality.[16] To Maxcy, such men were infidels and their views were deleterious to the well-being of the state. However, curiously enough, he apparently would not anathematize them. They were, in his opinion, "preeminent in virtue." Maxcy's theological ecumenism went a step beyond most Baptists in this regard.

Baptists did not always agree on the level of toleration that should be extended to other Protestant denominations, especially those in political power. Samuel Stillman exemplified the spirit of the age when he asked several Congregationalist ministers in the Boston area to participate in his ordination, much to the revulsion of rural Separate Baptists. In a similar vein, Stillman also pursued the policy of open communion (i.e. offering the Lord's Supper to non-Baptists) with Congregationalists, something that the Separates—former Congregationalists—found to be unacceptable and unbiblical.[17] A new ecumenism had steadily arisen in the new nation, both in the pulpit and in the public square. So powerful was this ecumenical spirit that the question was not whether Baptists supported religious tolerance, but to which kind of tolerance they subscribed.

Two Kinds of Ecumenism

With the birth of a religiously disestablished nation and the rise of voluntary groups, Baptists were participants in a new religious marketplace that gradually elevated their status in society and exposed them to a flux of inter-denominational activity even while pitting them against these same

---

15. Guild, *Life, Times, and Correspondence of James Manning*, 402n1.

16. For an in-depth look into Winchester's theological views and other sects of Universalism in America, see McClymond, *Devil's Redemption*, 580–607.

17. McLoughlin, *Soul Liberty*, 166.

denominations in the revivalistic contests of the Second Great Awakening. As scholars have noted, before the rising sectarianism of the late 1830s, the first several decades of the infant republic were typified by a general friendliness among denominations due to the benevolence movements of the period.[18] In the Philadelphia area alone, several national organizations were established in the early nineteenth century that were supported partly or completely by Baptists, including the American Bible Society which in 1816 brought together seven Protestant denominations.[19] Originally from the Philadelphia Association, Oliver Hart practiced what one scholar has called "evangelical catholicity" before and after 1776, working with Presbyterians during the Revolutionary war on special missions from the state of South Carolina and petitioning congress for religious liberty under the new constitution.[20] In Charleston, "the cultural Hart developed irenic relations not only with Regular Baptists, General Baptists, Welsh Baptists, and Separate Baptists but also with Independents, Methodists, Presbyterians, and Anglicans. Hart was quite comfortable with wealthy citizens of all denominations in this premiere southern city."[21] Calling his predecessor a "liberal Baptist," Richard Furman had eulogized Hart as the "prime mover" behind the education society and Baptist association in the Charleston area.[22] Furman saw himself continuing Hart's legacy of inclusive, ecumenical ministry in the city. Indeed, Hart served as a "father in the gospel" to other Baptists as well, including Samuel Stillman, Edmund Botsford, and James Ewing.[23] All four of these men adopted Hart's "evangelical catholicity" to varying degrees.

New England Baptists exhibited the same collegial spirit in their own communities. In Cavendish, Vermont, Asaph Fletcher "was for a time President of the Medical Society of his County, and delivered lectures before that body."[24] In 1784, Hezekiah Smith was the first minister to be inducted into the Haverhill Fire Club, an organization limited to thirty-six members that had the responsibility of giving fire and theft protection to the town of Haverhill. Smith was also a member of the local literary society that met in a private library in town.[25] Smith's participation in local public life was part of what William McLoughlin has called the "assimilationist approach"

---

18. Cross, *Burned-Over District*, 255.
19. Torbet, *Social History of the Philadelphia Baptist Association: 1707–1940*, 30.
20. Smith, "'Oh That All Bigotry was Rooted Out of the Earth!,'" 95–96.
21. Yarnell, "Early American Political Theology," 63.
22. Furman, *Rewards of Grace Conferred on Christ's Faithful People*, 339.
23. Furman, *Rewards of Grace Conferred on Christ's Faithful People*, 339.
24. Benedict, *General History*, 488
25. Broome, *Life, Ministry, and Journals of Hezekiah Smith*, 102.

of the so-called "western Baptists" like Smith, James Manning, and Samuel Stillman who hailed from western provinces and whose Federalist sensibilities helped them integrate into New England religious culture.[26] This was no small task, especially when, for example, Congregationalists like Timothy Dwight believed that most Separates who had become Baptists had done so merely "for the purpose of avoiding the legal obligation of supporting ministers." "They were extremely ignorant," Dwight characterized Separate Baptists, "and possessed of strong feelings and warm imaginations, in the exercise of which they chose to find religion, rather than in the faith and obedience of the Gospel."[27] Against such prejudices many Baptists labored to project a more respectable and intellectual image in New England society.[28] McLoughlin points to James Manning's request of Ezra Stiles to draft the charter of Rhode Island College in 1763 as one example of this "assimilationist view." According to McLoughlin, Baptists in New England halted this approach during the 1770s in their quest for religious liberty, but resumed it in full after 1800 "when the Baptists had more or less achieved the religious liberty they sought."[29] Eventually, Baptists permeated the various voluntary groups in the region and climbed the social ladder in the process. Of Thomas Baldwin it was said rather humorously that "no important association seemed complete unless it had enrolled him as its President."[30]

Not every Baptist, however, could tolerate such tolerance, at least not when it involved linking arms with those who defined religious liberty much differently than they did. Some Baptists made little distinction between denominations. John Taylor, for instance, simply referred to the Standing Order as "Presbyterians," a generalization that was not only historically and theologically inaccurate, but that also overlooked the fact that Presbyterians themselves had labored with Baptists to disestablish religion in several states.[31] Not surprisingly, John Leland had much to say about the voluntary societies of the age, almost all of it negative. In contrast to the reputable Baldwin who presided over numerous societies, Leland mocked

26. McLoughlin, *Soul Liberty*, 167.

27. Dwight, *Travels in New England and New York*, 4:321. Also see Fitzmier, *New England's Moral Legislator*, 135.

28. Edmund S. Morgan notes that Ezra Stiles "disliked Baptists, Quakers, Anglicans, and Timothy Dwight," while Dwight "dislike deists, democrats, and—apparently—Ezra Stiles" (Morgan, "Ezra Stiles and Timothy Dwight," 101.

29. McLoughlin, *Soul Liberty*, 167.

30. Chessman, *Memoir of Rev. Thomas Baldwin, D.D.*, 66.

31. Taylor, *Baptists on the American Frontier*, 92. The confusion was also exacerbated by the Plan of Union (1801), which united Presbyterian and Congregationalist churches for the sake of missions (which Taylor disliked).

the "venerable president of Bible society" and lamented the Christianization of America.[32] Scoffing at the "Christian Phalanx" in American culture, Leland called the developing unity among denominations a "horned beast" and refused to join in the ecumenical rush.[33] "Should the many Christian sects in the United States drop their peculiarities, and unite in the manner, and for the purposes, just mentioned, it makes the blood run cold in the veins to think of the horrors that would ensue," he prophesied.[34] In Leland's eyes, church-supported moral and social reform groups were simply replacing the ungodly church-state alliance that had once enveloped the Western world. At the heart of this Constantinian movement was greed instead of benevolence. He observed,

> Religion is become the most fashionable thing among us. Moral societies, Sunday schools—tract societies—Bible societies—missionary societies—and funds to educate and make preachers—are now in the full tide of operation . . . In barbarous times, when men were in the dark, it was believed that the success of the gospel was according to the outpourings of the Holy Spirit, but in this age of light and improvement, it is estimated according to the pourings out of the purse.[35]

Amidst the shouts for morality and missions, Leland only heard materialism. Leland's disdain for the new ecumenism was so strong that he even praised President Andrew Jackson for breaking up the so-called "Era of Good Feelings," convinced that a de-polarized political climate would not bode well for the nation.[36] Welcoming partisanship as a public good, the Jeffersonian Baptist was suspicious of any organization that sought to partner with the church in order to perform something that, he believed, the church could very well perform on its own.[37] Fiercely committed to the independence of the church from the state and the church's unique call to evangelize

32. Leland, "Address at the Dedication of the Baptist Meeting-House in Lanesborough, February 10, 1829," 555.

33. Leland, "Short Sayings," 580; Leland, "Mosaic Dispensation," 670.

34. Leland, "Short Sayings," 581.

35. Leland, "Part of a Speech, Delivered at Suffield, Connecticut, on the First Jubilee of the United States," 523–24.

36. Leland, "Address, Delivered at Dalton, Massachusetts, January 8, 1831," 606; Leland, "Part of a Speech, Delivered at Suffield," 522.

37. Hatch explains, "When the Baptists decided to join the Protestant quest for voluntary association, Leland stepped up his attacks upon missionary agencies and their clerical supporters. For the next fifteen years [1824–1841], he opposed the clerical professionalism at the core of American Protestant denominations" (Hatch, *Democratization of American Christianity*, 96–97).

the nation, Leland nevertheless resolved to defend the rights of voluntary groups, biblical or not: "I have never labored hard to support the creed of any religious society, but have felt greatly interested that all of them should have their rights secured to them beyond the reach of tyrants."[38] Somewhat ironically, Leland believed in the religious liberty of those groups that he believed endangered religious liberty itself. Such a belief was part of the "irony" that Randolph Ferguson Scully has identified in Baptist thinking in the late eighteenth and early nineteenth centuries. By agitating for religious freedom even for Muslims, Baptists like Leland were "actively working to move closer to the center of public culture in the new nation. They believed that the separation of church and state would increase the public profile and influence of Christianity rather than decrease it."[39]

This fierce determination to defend the freedom of *all* religious groups is precisely where Leland pursued his own style of ecumenism. Instead of partnering with denominations *for* religious causes, Leland partnered with other denominations *against* religious oppression. As shown, Leland was even zealous to defend the religious liberty of Muslims and other religions. Freedom of conscience was the bond that united Baptists like Leland with groups such as Roman Catholics, who he once called "marvelous Christians," an appellation few Baptists would ever have bestowed upon "Papists."[40] In a liberty-loving nation, and among a people who generally desired that nation to be Christian, the path to ecumenism was not only ideal, but seemingly inevitable.

John Leland teased, "there is a common saying, 'that a republican government is the best in the world if people only have virtue enough to bear it.' If people had virtue enough, there would be no need of any government."[41] However, at least in practice, most of Leland's Baptist brethren did not subscribe to this kind of thinking. Due to their republican belief that virtue is essential to self-government and that the public good must take priority over self-interest, Baptists eventually adopted the assimilationist, as opposed to Leland's separationist, view of activism. Thomas Baldwin summarized the case for voluntary societies in the new republic when he argued, "however polished and enlightened a people may be, they cannot expect long to enjoy either freedom or prosperity unless they are virtuous."[42] Liberty and lawfulness were inextricable. Freedom and faith went hand-in-hand. In 1808,

38. Leland, "May 15, 1834," 39.
39. Scully, *Religion and the Making of Nat Turner's Virginia*, 107.
40. Leland, "Yankee Spy," 223.
41. Leland, "Miscellaneous Essays," 419.
42. Baldwin, *Sermon, Delivered Before His Excellency Caleb Strong*, 17.

Sylvanus Haynes explained before the Vermont legislature, "although a moral man may not be a religious man; yet a truly religious man will not fail of being a moral man. And if all people were truly religious, what a happy tone it would give to the morals of society . . . how it would remove the grounds of innumerable complaints in our world!"[43] In short, civil—as opposed to state—religion was the most practical way a free people could prevent injustices in their midst. Baptists were slowly loosening the shackles of spiritual tyranny, but they were unwilling to completely doff the externals of religion from their society.

When Richard Furman preached at the Charleston Orphan-House in 1796, he confessed that its purpose was *sine qua non* with the very ideals of the country. "The design of this institution," Furman confessed, "it will be granted, is not of equal magnitude to the emancipation of a nation from the galling yoke of tyranny; the forming a constitution and laws for the wise and just government of a state, or the sending forth of the gospel for the conversion and salvation of mankind. But it is nearly allied to all these interesting subjects, and may be said to embrace them essentially, though on a small scale."[44] Moral and social reformers were not simply improving America; they were embodying American-ness. The United States was not founded as a Christian nation per se, but it was nonetheless a religiously motivated nation, most Baptists believed. Furman also reasoned that the orphan house embodied ecumenical Christianity at its best:

> It has likewise this superior advantage: It unites good men of every denomination in vigorous and common efforts, to promote the best causes—It disposes them to think less of their differences, in things not essential; and to cultivate a friendly intercourse with each other. Whatever may be their different sentiments, in things, either political or religious, compassion, generosity, and charity are common to them all; in the exercise of these they find their delightful employment; here, therefore, they embrace as brethren, and act with harmony. A coalition thus formed, of the wisest and best men in the community; including many of the most finished education, ample fortune, public character, must have a happy effect on the body of the people. The excitements to virtuous and laudable actions, when recommended by such examples, must be deeply felt by all, and will operate with peculiar force on the minds of youth (ever susceptible of favorable impressions) who being thereby called off from vain amusements and dissipating pleasures, will be taught

---

43. Haynes, *Sermon, Delivered Before His Excellency the Governor*, 13.
44. Furman, *Oration, Delivered at the Charleston Orphan-House*, 345.

to engage in pursuits where true glory is to be obtained, and true happiness enjoyed.[45]

In Furman's mind, religious unity was infectious. It improved the national ethic and drew the rest of the country together. Most importantly, it associated Baptists with "the wisest and best men of the community" with "finished education" who could bring respectability to their denomination and help integrate them into the upper echelon of American society. By partnering with other denominations for moral improvement, Baptists were also improving their own social status. In order to secure their place in the new American republic and to earn equality with these groups in the public square, most Baptists believed that education was a denominational necessity.

Education and Political "Respectability"

Scholars have long debated the state of American religion in the maelstrom of the Second Great Awakening. In contrast with Perry Miller's emphasis on "the centripetal power of the Revival," Nathan O. Hatch has famously contended that "centrifugal forces had never been more acute" than during this era.[46] In Baptist life, shades of both theories can be found, as Baptists contributed heartily to the "democratization of American Christianity" as well as to the new ecumenism that defined the early republic. Therefore, the so-called "social control interpretation"—the idea that reform programs were simply a means of control by displaced elite classes—does not properly account for Baptist participation in these groups.[47] Not surprisingly, it also tends to portray Baptists as unsophisticated and uneducated to the point of anti-intellectualist, and this mischaracterization of Baptists has lasted for decades in American religious studies, even among scholars who have challenged the social control model.[48] For instance, Hatch has argued that the "localism and independence" that "confounded" Baptist history between the Revolutionary era and the Jacksonian period, "played out on the fringes of denominational life, is not fully appreciated, given its lack of coherence and

45. Furman, *Oration, Delivered at the Charleston Orphan-House*, 347–48.
46. Hatch, *Democratization of American Christianity*, 63.
47. Griffin, "Religious Benevolence as Social Control," 423–44; Griffin, *Their Brothers' Keeper*; Cole, *Social Ideas of Northern Evangelists, 1826–1860*; Foster, *Errand of Mercy*; Gusfield, *Symbolic Crusade*; Donald, "Toward a Reconsideration of Abolitionists," 19–36.
48. For a brief review of the historiography of this period, see Hirrel, *Children of Wrath*, 3–5.

the penchant for early denominational historians to celebrate the growth of respectability and organizational coherence."[49] While Hatch is correct that early Baptist historiography presents an overly simplified and sanitized depiction of denominational growth, the assumption that rank-and-file Baptists pursued a "quest for localism and independence" at the expense of "respectability and organizational coherence" is a narrative that should also not be pressed too far. The quest for education is an essential piece of the Baptist story in the early republic, not because it competed with revivalism, but because it so often stemmed *from* revivalism.

When given the opportunity, Baptists desired respectability and coherence nearly as much as any other denomination. Education became one of the primary means by which they achieved these ends, before and especially after 1776, and among both rural and especially urban Baptists. For example, planter Evan Pugh of Pee Dee, South Carolina was one of the first beneficiaries of the Baptist education fund by Oliver Hart early in the history of the Charleston Association. Pugh even assisted Hart in attempting to bring together Regular and Separate Baptists in the region.[50] Primitive Baptists in Maryland acknowledged "it is not to Colleges, or to collegial education, as such, that we have any objection. We would cheerfully afford our own children such an education, did circumstances warrant the measure."[51] In New England, Isaac Backus was able "to persuade the more pietistic rural Baptists" that the new college in Rhode Island would not repeat the same godlessness at Harvard and Yale. As Backus well understood, the strongest prejudices on the part of Baptists were not against learning per se, but against the Standing Order and their irreligious establishment.[52] (Ironically, the Hollis Chair of Divinity at Harvard was established in 1721 after Thomas Hollis, a Baptist) The difference is important in understanding how and why Baptists pursued education. Jeremiah Bell Jeter made this distinction when he observed Baptists in Virginia. According to Jeter, Baptists were not anti-intellectualist, but anti-establishmentarian. Reflecting on the revivals of the 1820s, he records,

> This revival was specially important as forming a sort of connecting link between the old and new dispensations of the Virginia Baptists. The fathers preached without salaries, maintained themselves by their secular toils, and trained the churches, most successfully, to give nothing for the support of the

49. Hatch, *Democratization of American Christianity*, 97.
50. Dargan, "Richard Furman and His Place in American Baptist History," 1–3.
51. "Address," *Signs of the Times* 1 (1832) 5.
52. McLoughlin, "Introduction," 11.

gospel. Many of them were opposed, not to learned ministers, but to the training of ministers for their work. They were unfortunately driven to these extremes by their opposition to the colonial religious establishment. As they charged the clergy with preaching from mercenary motives, they deemed it necessary to show their own disinterestedness by preaching without fee or reward. As they maintained that the clergy were men-made preachers, they aimed to demonstrate that they themselves were God-made teachers by preaching without special training for it. With all their excellent qualities and noble works, they erred on these points. These mistakes the progress of knowledge and progress were sure to correct. The new dispensation—the time of missions, Sunday-schools, and ministerial and general education—was co-etaneous with the revival above described. It was not the cause, but an important factor in the change. It would have taken place had the revival not occurred, but certainly not in precisely the same way. It gave a mighty impulse to the Baptist cause in the upper portion of the State—an impulse that was soon felt to its utmost limits—and furnished the first missionaries of the General Association.[53]

Jeter's portrait of Virginia Baptists supports the idea that revival indeed produced certain centripetal effects in American religion, bringing together Baptists from different traditions and providing a "mighty impulse" toward education and organizational coherence. Revivalism and missions, though championed in different ways by different Baptists, should not be placed in opposite corners as if one could not promote the other.[54]

Jeter's account also reveals certain aspects of the Baptist mind. In the early republic, due to the heavy emphasis by Congregationalists and Anglicans upon a learned clergy, many Baptists were virtually incapable of imagining the very concept of education without a political component. As Jeter attests, even in the 1820s, anti-education Baptists were "driven to these extremes by their opposition to the colonial religious establishment," indicating that the strong link between establishment and education was a sour

---

53. Jeter, *Recollections of a Long Life*, 41–42.

54. In South Carolina, Regular and Separate Baptists joined together for the sake of revivalism. In a letter to a Dr. Rippon of London, Richard Furman reported that he had traveled to the Waxhaws and participated in a revival meeting with 11 Presbyterian, 4 Baptist, and 3 Methodist preachers. Although Furman "conceded that there are some incidental evils which attend them," he did "hope the direct good obtained from these meetings will much more than counterbalance the incidental evil" (Richard Furman, "A Letter from Dr. Furman of Charleston, to Dr. Rippon of London," in Foster, *Life and Works of Dr. Richard Furman, D.D.*, 416–17).

legacy that Baptists could still not get out of their mouths. In other words, they opposed education for the reason they opposed organization: religious liberty. In Jeter's hopeful view, however, this aversion was something that "the progress of knowledge and experience [was] sure to correct." The politics of optimism that governed Baptists' approach to disestablishment also framed the way that many Baptists conceived of education. As state-sponsored religion was purged from the earth and "progress" was made, Jeter believed that it was inevitable that education would garner a better reputation among Baptists. Indeed, he was right.

This "progress" also unfolded on the frontier. In Indiana, for instance, a "state-wide educational drive" took place among Baptists, a measure that faced opposition but that culminated in the formation of the Baptist Education Society in 1834, one year after the state convention was established.[55] Even on the "fringes" of the denomination, the Baptist story in the early United States cannot be told as a simple narrative of "incoherence" and decentralization because Baptists continually identified education as a means to unify and legitimize the denomination. Although Hatch briefly recognizes the Baptist "quest for respect" through education, he does not acknowledge the scope of this movement nor does he address the uniquely political ambitions that also drove Baptists to erect and establish their organizations and institutions. By pursuing education for themselves, Baptists were not simply vying for social status. They were in fact seeking the intellectual credentials to participate in the public forum and to engage their fellow citizens in nation-building. For a denomination that generally desired America to be Christian but that also prized something as seemingly precarious as religious liberty, an educated leadership was imperative to achieve the political and social presence they deemed necessary for Baptist views to flourish. In short, Baptists wanted social *and* political respectability. Education was integral to this project. In the proceedings at the Triennial Convention in 1814, the "Institution for Improving the Education of Pious Young Men, Called to the Christian Ministry" submitted that education was "demanded by the improved state of society."[56] As the world was changing in the new republic, Baptists were convinced that they needed to change with it.

To be sure, Baptists had long been stigmatized as an ignorant and unrefined people. In a resolution to the Triennial Convention, the Charleston Association acknowledged that "so large a proportion are held under the power of ignorant prejudices against learning, and of views, habits

---

55. Blake, "Jesse Lynch Holman: Pioneer Hoosier," 45.
56. *Proceedings of the Baptist Convention for Missionary Purposes*, 193.

and passions, which are unfavorable to generous exertion."[57] As previously shown, James Manning once confessed that Baptists were "the poor of the world."[58] This label was not without considerable warrant. For instance, according to the Cayuga Baptist Association, there were only three ministers by 1818 in the state of New York west of the Hudson River with a college education.[59] Moreover, Separate Baptist leaders like Isaac Backus had never been to college.[60] Baptists from urban centers like Boston and Charleston spoke often about the great need for higher learning in their denomination. Indeed, some Baptists seemed opposed to formal education altogether. In 1820, Daniel Parker referred to the fourteenth article of the Triennial Convention on ministerial education and protested, "they believe education essential to the gospel ministry."[61] Under such scrutiny, more sophisticated Baptists like Richard Furman were forced to clarify their true position. "Learning has by some been idolized," Furman conceded, "and it is no wonder that when thus put, in our estimation, into the place of gracious qualifications and the Spirit's influence, it should be rendered impotent, and be as dry beasts. But this furnishes no just reason for its being despised or neglected, in respect of its right use and application."[62]

Pro-mission Baptists also attributed the resistance they encountered to their cause to a lack of education. Once again, Jeremiah Bell Jeter provides a window into Baptist intellectualism when he records his confrontation with an Elder Davis, a man who apparently exercised a "controlling influence" over the Mayo, Strawberry, and Pigg River Associations in Virginia. He writes,

> It is proper that I should give my estimate of the character and abilities of Elder Davis. He was, I doubt not, a good man; but his character, naturally enough, was formed by the circumstances in which he lived. He possessed a vigorous intellect, but his education was poor, he read few books, his knowledge of the world was limited to the narrow sphere in which he lived, and almost all his associates acknowledged his superiority. He fell into a natural mistake. Being the greatest minister of his region, he formed an exalted opinion of his abilities. The deference paid him by his associates made him self-confident, overbearing,

57. Cook, *Biography of Richard Furman*, 190–91.
58. "James Manning to Samuel Stennett, Providence, Nov. 8th, 1783," 315.
59. Belden, *History of the Cayuga Baptist Association*, 31.
60. McLoughlin, *Soul Liberty*, 165.
61. Parker, *Public Address*, 19.
62. Richard Furman, "Circular Letter No. IV," in Foster, *Life and Works of Dr. Richard Furman, D.D.*, 514.

and intolerant. I have never known a man more impatient of contradiction than he was. To differ from him in opinion was to incur his displeasure. He undoubtedly possessed great force of character. He made and left an impression on the community in which he lived, in many respects, I think, unfortunate, but which half a century has not sufficed to erase.

Had Elder Davis received early and careful intellectual culture; had he enjoyed the means of extensive knowledge; had he associated with men of learning and wisdom; had he mingled with the world in its various pursuits; and had he been devoted to earnest and well-directed studies, he would have thought far less of his own abilities, and been held in far higher estimation by his age.[63]

Hardly a better picture of the conflict in the early republic between provincial and cultivated Baptists could be found, and within the context of missions no less.[64] When "the Arminian Skinner" Davis opposed mission groups, Jeter identified him as an "extreme predestinarian," but his primary case against Davis was not so much theological as it was intellectual.[65] According to the somewhat condescending Jeter, Davis had "read few books" and his "education was poor," resulting in his archaic view of missions. Regardless of whether his evaluation was accurate, Jeter touched at the heart of the education issue in Baptist life when he concluded that Davis's "culture had been neglected."[66] By not "associating" with learned men and not "mingling" in the world, Davis was disqualified from making any kind of legitimate argument for or against missions.

A myopic figure like the "Baptist gladiator" Davis who spoke in "coarse, strong language" and shunned differing opinions was yet another reason that Baptists such as James Manning believed colleges and seminaries "added respectability to the Baptist profession."[67] Formal education not only cultivated the life of the mind and raised the level of culture in Baptist circles, but it projected a certain type of refined image that Manning, Jeter, and others believed was a prerequisite for public discourse. For centuries, Baptist churches had passed on historic Baptist principles like religious liberty to future generations. However, by educating the denomination with

63. Jeter, *Recollections of a Long Life*, 95–96.

64. For instance, in *American Baptist Magazine, and Missionary Intelligencer*, Thomas Baldwin expressed his desire "to increase the respectability of the denomination" ("Editor's Address," 6).

65. Jeter, *Recollections of a Long Life*, 92, 95.

66. Jeter, *Recollections of a Long Life*, 92.

67. Manning, "To Thomas Llewelyn, D.D., London," 318.

colleges and seminaries, Baptists were now ensuring that these principles could be defended and maintained in a republic. At Columbian College, both President William Staughton and his wife were committed to this idea. Maria Staughton was anxious "to see the Baptist ministry placed upon a respectable footing, that she was willing to submit to any privation to promote their respectability and their happiness." For her husband, who frequently warned against the evils of infidelity and the value of biblical knowledge, "The character, theological soundness, and public usefulness of the students generally, who received their first touches from his master-hand, are his highest commendation."[68]

Learning and Liberty

For Baptists in the early United States, the issue of education encompassed much more than knowledge itself. The question was not whether knowledge was good or bad, but rather what someone would *do* with their knowledge. John Leland believed that he knew exactly what Baptists would do if they established institutions of higher learning. By his estimate, they had been here before. Referring back to the early church, he explained to a friend in 1828, "after the Christians had gained some standing and lost some of their first love, they erected a College of Alexandria, to recommend Christianity to the carnal world. This project effected the intended object, and soon the law of Christian establishment followed, and the sword was appealed to, to enforce the law." He then deduced, "Here poison was spread into the churches; for, from that day to this, in the greatest part of Christendom, Christianity has been used as a test for civil office—a step to honor—a cloak for insincerity—and a stimulus to persecution."[69] In effect, by seeking to formally educate themselves, Baptists were returning to the third and fourth centuries and recapitulating Constantine's unholy union of church and state, so Leland argued. While most Baptists may not have been able to articulate themselves in such effective (and perhaps exaggerated) terms, many of them believed similarly that education and establishment went hand-in-hand.

However, Leland did not necessarily speak for most Baptists when he expressed his belief that Christianity was not "essential to good government."[70] Indeed, most Baptists believed that Christianity was necessary to produce republican virtue and good governance. If the Christian

---

68. Lynd, *Memoir of the Rev. William Staughton, D.D.*, 161.

69. Leland, "Extracts from a Letter to a Friend," 531.

70. Leland, "Who Has Done the Most Mischief in the World, the Kings-Evil or Priest-Craft?," 489.

ethic and worldview were removed from society, despotism would naturally follow and religious liberty would evaporate. This is why so many Baptists associated Christianity with patriotism and why so many were willing to view Baptist education as a means of preserving their new-found political freedoms. In his address at the opening of Columbian College, William Staughton could not avoid mentioning the fact that the school had been founded in perhaps the most politically auspicious city in the United States: Washington D. C. "From the window of his study," urged Staughton, all the student needed to do was to gaze "on the Mount [Vernon], where dwelt the hero, who, with the eagle of his standard, fought the battles of his country, achieved her liberty, illumined her councils; and, leaving her a legacy of paternal advice and patriotic example, in peace expired."[71] Despite the severe separationism of Baptists like John Leland, God and government were not no easily divorced in most Baptists' minds. Therefore, Baptist education was about training young men in the Scriptures and in virtue, and by extension, in good citizenship.

Sylvanus Haynes articulated the Baptist case for education when he declared, "Ignorance is a dagger to liberty, and an engine of tyranny."[72] For centuries, Baptists had seen what education could do in the wrong hands. However, they had also seen what a *lack* of education could do to perpetuate ignorance and misinformation and servitude. "Here, it is all-important that the people should be enlightened," Thomas Baldwin proclaimed, "as they are the acknowledged source of all power, whether legislative or executive." He insisted, "the more despotic a government is, the more ignorant the people generally are. It is undoubtedly the interest of those in power to keep them so. For were they once so enlightened as to understand the nature of civil liberty, and to act upon any rational system in recovering their usurped rights, it would be impossible to keep them in subjection."[73] With freedom came responsibility. A self-governing nation demanded an educated Baptist denomination. In turn, that Baptists collectively decided to establish so many of their very first colleges and seminaries within the energetic and empowering conditions of the new nation is not a coincidence of history. In Richmond, Virginia, an 1828 article in the *Religious Herald* contended that colleges and schools promoted the "prosperity of the commonwealth."[74] In the words of the Triennial Convention, education was "demanded by the improved state of society." Among these institutions of learning were those

71. Staughton, *Memoir of the Rev. William Staughton, D.D.*, 260.
72. Haynes, *Sermon, Delivered Before His Excellency the Governor*, 12.
73. Baldwin, *Sermon, Delivered Before His Excellency Caleb Strong*, 15.
74. *Religious Herald*, "Influence of Religion on the Laws of Nations," 132.

at Hamilton, New York (1819), Waterville, Maine (1820), Washington, D.C. (1822), Georgetown, Kentucky (1824), and at Newton, Massachusetts (1825). In the ten years following, Richmond College, Wake Forest, Furman University, Mercer University, and New Hampton Institution would also emerge. With a *zeitgeist* of republicanism and inclusiveness, the infant nation was a political, social, and intellectual seedbed for a nascent Baptist denomination with ambitions to evangelize and Christianize America. Although many Baptists still associated education with establishment, just as many seemed to believe that learning was a product of liberty *and* a means to protect it.

As a result, Baptist teachers and administrators inculcated into their students the idea that education, like so many other aspects of Baptist life, should support the cause of religious liberty. Freedom required vigilance, and vigilance required enlightenment. Francis Wayland, one of the founders of Newton Theological Institution (1825) and president of Brown University (1827–1855), submitted that Baptists had always been among the "vanguard" of those who unashamedly promoted the "inalienable rights of conscience." In his *Notes on the Principles and Practices of Baptist Churches* (1857), he asked,

> Such being the facts known to all the world, have we any reason to be ashamed of our fathers? When the very principles for which they suffered are now acknowledged to lie at the very foundation, not only of pure Christianity, but of all civil and religious liberty, shall we hide our light under a bushel, and blush to bear testimony to eternal truth? After having so long stood in the vanguard of that noble host who have contended for apostolic Christianity and the inalienable rights of conscience, now that the victory is half achieved, and our principles are arousing the nations, shall we lay down our arms, furl our banners, and retire ingloriously from the combat? I know not what may be your answer, but I know what would have been the answer of Roger Williams.[75]

For the seasoned educator Wayland, Baptist principles were at the "very foundation" of "all civil and religious liberty." Therefore, having embodied so much of the American spirit, how could they hide their intellectual and spiritual light under a bushel? In addition to more obvious objectives like ministerial training, religious liberty was an important goal in Baptist education because it was the "polar star" of the entire Baptist political project in the early republic.

---

75. Wayland, *Notes on the Principles and Practices of Baptist Churches*, 139.

For instance, when Jonathan Maxcy concluded his Baccalaureate Address to the students at South Carolina College on December 2, 1816, he charged, "Cultivate peace with all men, and support the laws and constitution of your country. I trust and believe that you go from this college with a deep sense of the value of civil and religious freedom. To behold you exerting your talents in support of these, will afford the highest pleasure to those who have conducted your education."[76] Education was for liberty's sake, declared Maxcy. Therefore, educated men should "support" the cause of religious freedom. If the anti-education Baptists of rural America contended that education was contrary to Baptist principles, others like James Manning advocated quite the opposite. Manning, Maxcy's predecessor at the College of Rhode Island, once boasted in a letter in 1783 that the school had been "instrumental in greatly promoting Baptist principles, and the spread of civil and religious liberty throughout New England."[77] Baptist education was good citizenship, Manning asserted. When George Washington visited Providence in 1790, Manning addressed the President inside the library and museum. He maintained, "For the preservation of this freedom, one great object still demands our peculiar attention,—the education of our youth."[78]

Religious liberty was still a precarious and somewhat relative concept in the first decades of the nineteenth century, especially in the Northeast. By 1816, the Massachusetts territory of Maine had such a heavy concentration of Baptists that it was able to allocate state funding for a literary and theological seminary at Waterville (later Colby College) as part of its plural establishment. However, after Maine was separated from Massachusetts in 1820 (as part of the Missouri Compromise), its first legislature passed an act to eradicate the last traces of ecclesiastical taxes for the support of religion. For Baptists, this was a victory in terms of religious liberty but a loss in terms of budget. The "transition from a theological seminary to a college" made it more "difficult to secure for it a more extended patronage, or sympathy, than that of the denomination who had given it being. Besides Baptists, therefore, few, beyond the immediate vicinity of the college, were ready to adopt it as their own." President Jeremiah Chaplain, a graduate of Brown in 1799, encountered some of the most daunting challenges of frontier education that one could ever face. In his eulogy of Chaplain, Robert Everett Pattison considered,

---

76. Maxcy, "Address Delivered to the Baccalaureate of the South-Carolina College," 347.

77. Manning, "To Samuel Stennett, Providence, Nov. 8th, 1783," 314.

78. Manning, *Life, Times, and Correspondence of James Manning, D.D.*, 434.

> Had Mr. Chaplin been welcomed by a portion of the public, not more numerous or wealthy than the Baptists in Maine then were, had there been any distinct and well united body of the inhabitants, who fondly cherished the college as a rich blessing to themselves and their children, to support of which was deemed by them as essential as that of their religious institutions or their civil liberty, around which their sympathies clustered and for the prosperity of which their prayers were offered, there would have been no serious difficulty in the establishment of this college.[79]

The religious ecumenism that Baptists sought in the arena of social and moral reform they often pursued in educational reform. When religious establishment was eliminated, inter-denominational support and religious liberty became even more practical. Pattison's eulogy also attests to how important civil and religious liberty were to early Americans and how critical this ideal was in justifying Baptist education. As Jonathan Maxcy proved and others attested, as the age of theological institutions gave way to an era of state and non-sectarian colleges, religious liberty remained one of the more palatable Baptist distinctives that could be advocated outside the theology department without the accusation of indoctrination. This had the inclusive effect of giving Baptist colleges a "more liberal character," something that Baptists like Chaplin and Pattison desired for the institution.[80]

Daniel Hascall, one of the founders of Hamilton Literary and Theological Institution (established just one year before Waterville), also promoted religious liberty in his theological education. In *The Elements of Theology* (1847), written *For the Use of Families, Bible Classes, and Seminaries of Learning*, he reflected,

> The Bible is his gift to us; so is the preached gospel. And we are also indebted to our fellow-men, who have kindly furnished them to us; to our forefathers, who fled to this country from persecution, that they and we their descendants might enjoy the gospel with civil and religious liberty. We are indebted to the faithful men, who of old died in defense of this gospel, to those who in those days of persecution and ignorance, translated into our language the word of God . . . How shall we repay? We can refund nothing to God, but we may refund to his creatures. We may repay in the same kind as we have received.[81]

---

79. Pattison, *Eulogy on Rev. Jeremiah Chaplin, D.D.*, 12.
80. Pattison, *Eulogy on Rev. Jeremiah Chaplin, D.D.*, 13.
81. Hascall, *Elements of Theology*, 236.

Hascall tethered his faith and his patriotism when he honored his descendants for defending "the gospel with civil and religious liberty" and for liberating them from "the days of persecution and ignorance." From Hascall's vantage point, the Puritans appeared more like Baptists who celebrated the First Amendment than Congregationalists who desired to uphold religious hegemony. Regardless of his slightly revisionist telling of American history, Hascall's account indicates that pro-education Baptists promoted religious liberty as a primary aim of education and of Christianity. For this reason, one might describe the early republic as a period of Americanized education in Baptist life, as Baptists became increasingly convinced that education was not only salubrious for the denomination as a whole, but consistent with the ideals of the nation itself.

As Gregory Wills has shown, Baptists from Massachusetts to Georgia understood religious liberty not merely politically but ecclesiologically, as it enabled them to discipline their churches in accordance with Scripture.[82] In promoting religious liberty, Baptist colleges and seminaries were serving the local church directly. In a 1791 circular letter entitled "The Nature, Business, Power and Government of a Gospel Church," Peter Werden, Stephen Gano, and Justus Hull reminded the Shaftesbury Association that it "must be the prerogative of the church to say, who shall be received as members of the visible church of Christ on earth."[83] In short, Baptists were not anti-intellectual, but anti-establishment. Liberty was essential for the church to be the church, at least as Baptists understood it. Therefore, learning served liberty. After hearing a report on the committee of education in 1839, the Georgia Baptist Association spent time in thanksgiving for the "efforts to promote the interests of education; and in prayer to Him, that he will yet smile more and more upon such efforts."[84]

Rallying around Education

When John Leland indicted the "missionary plan" as a materialistic substitute for authentic Christianity, he quite naturally aimed his invectives at the higher, more educated end of Baptist society. In a treatise entitled *Which Has Done the Most Mischief in the World, The Kings-Evil or Priest-Craft?*, Leland concludes with a short, biting story about James Manning and Sam Niles, a Native American preacher in Charleston, Rhode Island. "Mr. Manning paid Niles a visit," Leland narrated, "and addressed him thus: 'How do

---

82. Wills, *Democratic Religion*, 32–33.
83. Wright, *History of the Shaftesbury Baptist Association*, 31.
84. *Minutes of the Georgia Baptist Association*, 5.

you do brother Niles?' To whom Sam replied, 'Ah, who are you?' Mr. Manning replied, 'I am James Manning, a preacher of the gospel of Christ.' 'Ah,' said Sam, 'do you preach for Jesus Christ or *old ten*?'"[85] The obvious lesson in Leland's "anecdote" was that Baptists like James Manning were more interested in making money than in saving souls. Whether the story was true or fabricated, Manning was the object of Leland's scorn because, as the first president of the first Baptist college in America, he symbolized the gentrification of the Baptist denomination in the early republic. To Leland, a Separate Baptist, this introduced a new form of worldliness in Baptist America. Separate Baptists, after all, had departed from the Congregationalist church precisely due to its lax spirituality, moral decline, and opulence. "Religion and education," he declared, do not "stand on the same ground."[86] With so much money moving around in the denomination, avarice and greed were sure to follow. Leland also took exception with the idea made by some that "schools of learning are the fountains of true piety."[87] If the Baptist fathers went so long without formal education, Leland asked, how did they come about their godliness? Did Manning and others *invent* piety as the so-called "fountains" of it? As an undeniably incisive thinker, John Leland was not anti-intellectualist, but he was certainly anti-elitist.

Although Leland's remarks were often vitriolic and somewhat petty, the idea that education and affluence were often yoked together in Baptist life was not without some degree of truth. Hezekiah Smith, who served as a fellow of Brown University for forty years and missed only three annual meetings during that time, had once provided "crucial" support for the school by soliciting badly needed funds from wealthy planters and merchants in South Carolina and Georgia in 1769 and 1770.[88] Smith, who was easily one of the wealthiest Baptist ministers in New England, was a member of the education committee of the Warren Association and was on the local Haverhill school board. In fact, the first written school report in the history of the town was presented by Smith in 1798.[89] William McLoughlin has labeled Smith, Samuel Stillman, and James Manning the "liberals of the denomination." He explains, "They were on friendly terms with many Congregationalist leaders; they were eager to please and to imitate their manners of dress and behavior; they sought their respect and therefore tried to seem

85. Leland, "Which Has Done the Most Mischief in the World, the Kings-Evil or Priest-Craft?," 495.

86. Leland, "Which Has Done the Most Mischief in the World, the Kings-Evil or Priest-Craft?," 492.

87. Leland, "Miscellaneous Essays," 409.

88. Broome, *Life, Ministry, and Journals of Hezekiah Smith*, 169.

89. Broome, *Life, Ministry, and Journals of Hezekiah Smith*, 102–3.

as sophisticated and urbane as possible."[90] Both Princeton graduates, Smith and Manning had originally studied under Isaac Eaton at Hopewell Academy, the first Baptist preparatory school in America. Eaton had consistently inculcated into young Baptists that they should not "invalidate learning."[91] Among his very first class were David Jones, Samuel Jones, James Manning, John Davis, Hezekiah Smith, David Thomas, Isaac Skillman, and William Williams.[92] These men would help forge the new Baptist denomination in America. In Manning's case, he would eventually establish a Latin school at Warren in the mold of Hopewell.[93]

The cause of education was not restricted to Federalists or college academics, although the probability of a Baptist intellectual presence was greatly increased with the local wealth. In Cheshire, Massachusetts, Rev. Lemuel Covell "gave umbrage" to the more conservative members of his audience by freely expressing his "anti-federalist principles" during an observance day sermon in 1803. Covell was a proud Baptist Republican whose "political sentiments were generally known." Nevertheless, in those days, Cheshire was apparently regarded as a "kind of 'Goshen' among the towns and the people had become wealthy." In such an environment, Covell was "decidedly the champion of the cause of education, and intellectual development," bringing the best teachers into the local school district, overseeing the construction of a town library, and serving as its librarian.[94]

---

90. McLoughlin, *Soul Liberty*, 165. McLoughlin clarifies, "But Manning, Stillman, and Smith were not native New Englanders. They had come to New England from the middle colonies after the Great Awakening. On the whole they took a less radical—a less pietistic—position than did Backus and the Separate Baptists in New England in the 1750s and 1760s. Although these college-educated Baptists from Pennsylvania and New Jersey were willing to sign petitions for alleviation of the ecclesiastical tax laws, to pass resolutions calling for a moral liberal system of toleration, and to raise funds for the purpose of fighting legal battles in the courts against discriminatory actions by sheriffs, constables, and tax assessors, they were not all eager to antagonize the ruling elite in Massachusetts. They preferred to appeal to the Congregationalists' sense of justice and fair play. Hezekiah Smith had once been appointed by the Baptists' Grievance Committee to go to England and deliver a petition to the king, asking him to intervene on the Baptists' behalf, but he found reasons not to go. Samuel Stillman, in whose Boston church John Adams, John Hancock, and Sam Adams sometimes designed to sit and listen to his eloquent sermons, tried his best to prevent Backus and his Separate-Baptist brethren from adopting radical measures. James Manning begged off from activities in Massachusetts because he lived in Rhode Island; besides, he was so concerned for the good reputation of his college among Congregationalists that he never published any sermon or tract on controversial issues" (McLoughlin, *Soul Liberty*, 164–65).

91. Eaton, *Sermon Preached at the Ordination of the Reverend Mr. John Gano*, 1:172.

92. Rogers, *Life, Journal and Works of David Jones, 1736–1820*, 17.

93. McLoughlin, *Soul Liberty*, 275.

94. Brown, *Memoir of the Late Rev. Lemuel Covell*, 136–38.

Regardless of how wealthy these Baptists—Republican or Federalist—became in the early republic, their affluence was not as important as their *influence*, which they threw behind the cause of education. Thomas Baldwin was not only a benefactor of Waterville College, but one of its original trustees. On one occasion, Jesse Mercer donated $750 to Columbian College, where Baldwin was also a trustee. On another occasion, Mercer donated $1000. To Mercer University, he gave $150 for initial expenses, $550 for the land, $1000 for one of the buildings, $400 for another, and a note of $5000, the interest of which assisted faculty salaries.[95] Pro-education Baptists spared no expense to realize their vision of an educated Baptist America. At the inaugural Triennial Convention, Richard Furman did not simply preside over the convention; he also brought forward the "Plan of Education," unveiling an initiative largely born from his own vision for the Baptist denomination.[96] Furman also spoke from the pulpit about the need to educate Baptists in a country that required greater attention to the wheels of democracy. In a sermon in 1800 entitled "On Religious and Civil Duties," he counseled his listeners that a "firm attachment to the constitution, laws and government to our country, is an important duty." Furman believed, like James Manning, that the fate of Baptist education in Rhode Island was intimately tied to the success of the Constitution.[97] Furman later warned, "The libertinism and infidelity which abound in this age, are so dangerous, that great care should be taken by religious parents, to guard the minds of their children against the fatal influence of those evils. Much attention, therefore, should be bestowed on the education of children, and government of families."[98] In an 1804 sermon, he commanded, "Read the best books; converse, as you have opportunity, with the wisest and best men; hear the most pious, well-informed, and faithful preachers. Lay yourself open to information."[99] While John Leland denounced the "maze of laws, like a cobweb" that allegedly subjugated the unlearned, Furman and the leaders of the denomination instead believed that education was a gift to lift Baptists up, not a weapon to keep them down.[100] With the rise of educated leaders in their ranks, Baptists were placing themselves closer to the center of American culture.

---

95. Mallary, *Memoirs of Elder Jesse Mercer*, 238.
96. Cook, *Biography of Richard Furman*, 186, 196.
97. Guild, *Life, Times, and Correspondence of James Manning*, 404.
98. Furman, "Circular Letter No. VII," 547-48.
99. Richard Furman, "Circular Letter No. XI," in Foster, *Life and Works of Dr. Richard Furman, D.D.*, 557.
100. Leland, "Blow at the Root," 239.

Chapter 8

Religious Outsiders No Longer

IF THE POST-REVOLUTIONARY ERA was a reformation and revival for the Baptist church, the Jacksonian period was its political vindication, at least for whites. By the 1820s and 1830s, with exponentially increasing numbers, Baptists were convinced not only that the political winds favored their denomination, but that by embracing religious liberty, the nation itself had validated their sacrifices and beliefs. As Randolph Ferguson Scully has noted, "In letters, petitions, and in the denominational histories that appeared in the early nineteenth century, white Baptists depicted themselves primarily as virtuous non-elites whose political and religious interests were entirely compatible with those of the Revolution and who were dedicated to extending and preserving the Revolutionary legacy."[1] On July 4, 1829, *The Columbian Star and Christian Index* in Philadelphia honored those Baptist patriots during the War of Independence who "seemed to have been aware that freedom of religious inquiry should have a sufficient guaranty." They fought for a country, declared editor W. T. Brantly, in which all denominations and religious persuasions would stand on the "same level" and upon "equal ground." Indeed, he concluded victoriously, "They judged rightly."[2]

Brantly's confidence was common among Baptists of this period, especially since they had begun taking a more direct role in the nation-shaping of the early United States. Baptists, a once marginalized group of dissenters in various parts of the country, had become increasingly active participants in the republic they had helped to establish. At the same time that Baptists were moving closer toward the center of American religious culture

1. Scully, *Religion and the Making of Nat Turner's Virginia*, 104.
2. Brantly, "Character of the Early American Baptist Preachers," 2.

they were also gaining more political power in their respective states and in Washington.[3]

Some Baptists moved back and forth from the farm to the statehouse. In North Carolina in 1822, twenty-five-year-old Baptist layman Alfred Dockery was elected to the House of Commons from Richmond County. Dockery continued to farm when he returned home from his first stint in government, however, in 1835 he also served as a delegate to the state constitutional convention. True to his Baptist principles, Dockery voiced his support for Supreme Court Justice and United States Representative William Gaston in favoring the abolition of the Protestant-only restriction in the constitution, defending the religious liberty of Catholics despite the "persecution and proscription" of the "Romish church." After securing religious liberty for themselves, Baptists had arisen to positions that would determine the liberty of other groups. Dockery even went so far as to contend for the suffrage of free blacks, which the convention rejected. The Baptist layman from Richmond County would soon become a leader in the Whig party, serving six terms in the Senate. Although a staunch Unionist who sided with President Andrew Jackson during the Nullification crisis, Dockery would eventually favor disunion in his own denomination, becoming a founder of the Southern Baptist Convention in 1845 as one of its four vice presidents.[4]

Other Baptists encountered Jacksonian politics more directly, and at the highest level. After Jesse Lynch Holman was appointed a federal judge by President Andrew Jackson in 1835, his opponents charged that he was not actually a friend to the Jackson administration and that he had opposed certain measures during Jackson's presidency. They accused Holman of being "destitute of all the necessary qualifications for the office," and that he was a "fanatic on the subject of religion," perhaps indicating that Holman's Baptist views were a bit too evangelical for many Jacksonians' tastes. In truth, Holman had voted against Jackson in 1824, casting his vote instead for John Quincy Adams during the year of the so-called "corrupt bargain" with Henry Clay.[5] Holman's friend, Peter Brady, had even upbraided Hol-

---

3. According to Gordon S. Wood, this upward trend began in the earliest years of the republic. As the hierarchical society of the eighteenth century "seemed at last to be breaking up," different groups emerged on the political scene. "Farmers, merchants, mechanics, manufacturers, debtors, creditors, Baptists, Presbyterians—all seemed more self-conscious of their special interests than ever before" (Wood, *Creation of the American Republic 1776–1787*, 501).

4. John W. Moore, scrapbook of newspaper columns from the *Biblical Recorder* entitled "Early Baptist Laymen of North Carolina," North Carolina Collection, Wilson Library, University of North Carolina, Chapel Hill.

5. Cheathem, *Andrew Jackson and the Rise of the Democratic Party*, 67–82;

man for his general attitude toward Jackson, an attitude which nearly cost Holman his position. Ultimately, however, after a long trip to Washington to sit down with President Jackson in the White House, Holman clarified his support for the President, and, as previously shown, the institution of slavery.[6] Clearly, not every Baptist was as fawning over "Old Hickory" as John Leland, who frequently extolled Jackson as the "last revolutionary character that will ever be in the U.S" and even compared Henry Clay and John Quincy Adams to Herod and Pilate![7] "When Jackson shall have finished his administration," Leland reflected, "there will be none living, young enough to be president, who had any hand in the revolutionary war. A generation will then take the lead, who never saw the works which were done by Moses and Joshua."[8]

John Leland was thus so satisfied with the work of the seventh president that he could be perhaps considered more Jacksonian than Jeffersonian, insisting in a letter that he was "never better pleased with the measures of government than" under Jackson.[9] On another occasion, Leland opined that he failed to see "any radical difference between the Jeffersonian administration, and the Jacksonian."[10] Nevertheless, Leland's allegiance to the Democratic Party remained unabated, as he celebrated Martin Van Buren, Jackson's successor, as an "unwavering friend of the people."[11] The Virginian even went so far as to call Van Buren "the second Madison" and Jackson "the second Jefferson."[12] Much to his delight, Van Buren's Vice President (1837–41) was Richard Mentor Johnson, a Baptist from Kentucky who defined religious liberty similar to Leland. Johnson's 1829 *Sunday Mail Report*, in which he refused to "compel the people of the United States, by law, to observe the first day of the week," was a shrewd political tract that helped him win the Vice Presidency.[13]

Cheathem, *Andrew Jackson*, 103–7.

6. Blake, "Jesse Lynch Holman: Pioneer Hoosier," 47–49.

7. Leland, "Addressed Delivered at North Adams, on the 4th of March, 1831," 614; Leland, "Address Delivered at Pittsfield, Jan. 8, 1829," 543.

8. Leland, "Short Sayings," 582.

9. Leland, "Letter," 658.

10. Leland, "Huddle of Thoughts," 715.

11. Leland, "Address Delivered at Pittsfield, Jan. 8, 1829," 545.

12. Leland, "Short and Unconnected Sentences," 729.

13. Johnson, *Review of a Report of the Committee*, 19. Johnson was the only Vice President in American history to be elected by the U. S. Senate under the provisions of the Twelfth Amendment of the Constitution. According to Paul E. Johnson "Johnson's *Report* was the classic Jacksonian statement on relations between church and state. It was also a shrewd and powerful political tract, and it helped win Johnson the Vice

As Leland and Johnson and Holman illustrate, even before Andrew Jackson's rise to the presidency, the success of the Baptist denomination was also attended by its various divisions. In November of 1818, Edmund Botsford wrote to a friend from Georgetown, South Carolina,

> What in life are our Baptist brethren about? Some quarreling, some turning Socinians; what next shall we hear? In the midst of all this great work, which God is carrying on, the devil seems to be sowing the seeds of discord and mischief. He seems to have a peculiar spite against us. We have always been set at nought by the world, but this we may always expect; it ought to unite us: instead of which, our Dons are wrangling worse than children.[14]

In the midst of "this great work" of God, not all Baptists were apparently working together. Later in the same letter, Botsford seemed to indicate that he meant political division as well as theological division when he lamented, "We Baptists are like the Arabians, against every man, and every man against us; yea, we exceed, we are against ourselves."[15] The rise of political power in Baptist life did nothing to attenuate the partisan and ideological and racial divisions that had long beset the denomination. In fact, in many ways, it only enhanced these divisions. For instance, in 1822, shortly after the foiled Denmark Vesey slave plot, the predominantly black membership of First Baptist Church of Richmond requested permission of the Dover Association to form "an African Church" and were denied. 700 slaves and free blacks then petitioned the Virginia legislature in 1823 to build an African Baptist Church and were likewise rejected.[16] Even in the same congregations, black and white Baptists in the South were growing farther apart.

Jacksonian politics also divided Baptists on the issue of Native American removal. On one hand, the Baptist Board of Foreign Missions endorsed President Jackson's removal program in the 1820s largely because two-thirds of the members in the denomination lived in the South and West, where Jackson's plan found overwhelming support. On the other hand, as historians have shown, a Jacksonian belief in the voice of the people inspired missionaries like Evan Jones to oppose removal, to march with the Cherokee on the so-called Trail of Tears, and even to serve as chaplain in a Cherokee regiment during the Civil War.[17] Jones, who came to the Cherokee nation

---

Presidency of the United States in 1836" (Johnson, *Shopkeeper's Millennium*, 86).

14. Botsford, "To Dr. Roberts, Georgetown, November 16, 1818," 209.
15. Botsford, "To Dr. Roberts, Georgetown, Dec. 29, 1818," 210.
16. Frey and Wood, *Come Shouting to Zion*, 180.
17. McLoughlin, *Cherokees and Christianity, 1794–1870*, 27, 65, 70.

in 1821 and was superintendent of the Baptist mission from 1824 until his retirement in 1866 (he was active among the Cherokees until his death in 1872), urged the Baptist board to stand against removal. He did not agree with Baptist missionaries like Rev. Duncan O'Briant who signed an oath of allegiance to the state of Georgia and who led his congregation across the Mississippi River in 1832 to start a new mission. Opposition to Jackson's program, he wrote to Lucius Bolles in 1832, was "the decided, constant, unvarying vote of the whole body of the people . . . they have no disposition to remove."[18] Whether for or against President Jackson's decree (and Baptist Governor Wilson Lumpkin's support), a populistic spirit often motivated both parties in the removal controversy. For white Baptists, the question was not whether the voice of the people carried weight, but which people.

As white Baptists assumed a more elevated role in society, they were no longer united by an experience of mutual opposition. In fact, without this shared hardship and a common pursuit of disestablishment, as Richard Johnson proved in the Sunday mail report of 1829, religious liberty itself became more difficult to define. Instead, under the First Amendment, and despite the social caste that inevitably developed along mission and antimission lines, Baptists were held together by organizations and conventions— much like the nation itself. As Harvey T. Cook has observed, "It was only a matter of time when the Baptist people in all the states would feel the same promptings to come together in a general union of representatives of all the states. Whatever stirs the body politic affects in the same way to a less or greater extent all its patriotic parts."[19] In other words, for better or for worse, American politics inexorably shaped Baptist politics. Moreover, the spirit of the age that moved Baptists to forge the Triennial Convention also led them to pursue their own interests and ideologies that threatened their new-found unity.

For example, as the country was wrestling with the tension between states' rights and federal union in the critical decade of the 1830s, Baptists were facing similar questions. The centralization of the denomination, while bringing together Baptists for the cause of missions and education, had exposed the sensitive issue of state rivalries. In 1835, Basil Manly Sr. wrote a letter to James Furman expressing his desire to establish a Southern Baptist Theological Seminary. According to Manly, Baptists in Georgia, North Carolina, Tennessee, and South Carolina "ought to be one in this business," however they were prevented from doing so because each state had first

---

18. Evan Jones to Lucius Bolles, April 26, 1832, American Baptist Missionary Union Papers.

19. Cook, "Biography of Richard Furman," 171.

erected its own theological institution. Schools in Georgia and North Carolina, regretted Manly, had "failed wholly" in their endeavors.[20] Less than a month later, Manly similarly wrote to the editor of the *Southern Baptist and General Intelligencer* that "such an institution must not be confined to a single State," even suggesting a potential location for the seminary along the Tennessee border where every state could have easy access.[21] Only by 1859, fourteen years after the founding of the Southern Baptist Convention in August, Georgia, was the Southern Baptist Theological Seminary eventually established not far from Manly's proposed site in Greenville, South Carolina out of the theology department at Furman University. Manly's son, Basil Manly Jr., was one of the four initial faculty members alongside President James P. Boyce, John A. Broadus, and William Williams. Indeed, state rivalries were overcome, but not without greater sectional divisions. The capability of Baptists to centralize, mobilize, and to assimilate into American culture came just as the American union itself was beginning to fracture. David Marks, a pioneer Free Will Baptist itinerant preacher from western New York, represented most Baptists in the "Burned-Over District" when he complained to Elder Elias Hutchins in North Carolina about the Nullification Crisis in South Carolina. On February 15, 1833, he wrote,

> The course pursued and still persisted in by South Carolina, I think must agitate the public mind in the vicinity of your travels. What is this sad affair about to amount to? In this section of country, the people are generally much incensed against the movements of South Carolina, and a spirit of war is so much awakened, that, I am sorry to say, many seem to thirst for blood, and even are anxious to go to the south to avenge, with the sword, the treasonable movements of the Legislature of that state. While other nations have been in commotion, ours has long enjoyed peace, and has little appreciated the value of its blessings. I fear our sins, our dreadful sins, have provoked the Almighty, and that our nation must receive of the cup of his indignation.[22]

As the nation had "enjoyed peace," Baptists (and Free Will Baptists) had enjoyed significant growth. But the spiritual crests of the Second Great Awakening—perhaps illustrated most violently in western New York—also portended a frightening descent into calamity.[23] The precious unity

---

20. Manly, "Letter to James Furman, Charleston, S.C., February 26, 1835," 97.
21. Manly, "Theological Education in the Southern States," 170–72.
22. Marks, "To Elder Elias Hutchins, February 15, 1833," 312.
23. For an excellent analysis of western New York during this time, see Cross,

of revival was eventually riven by the bellicosity of civil war. However, in the decades before the split of the Triennial Convention in 1845, Baptists amassed a level of political and economic prosperity unprecedented for their denomination.

Greater Wealth and Influence

Thomas S. Kidd and Barry Hankins have aptly labeled Baptists in the colonial period "the ultimate religious outsiders."[24] As most religious historians have also recognized, in their evolution from dissent to the cultural mainstream, the ascendancy of Baptists in American public and political life was dramatic. (In 1983, Martin Marty identified something called the "Baptistification" of America.)[25] For William G. McLoughlin, although Baptists had been marginalized in the seventeenth and much of the eighteenth centuries, it is "not too much to say that the Baptists (especially in the south and west) embodied the basic outlook of the American people for most of the nineteenth century." However, Baptists were "victims of their own success," McLoughlin argues, as they developed their own kind of "second establishment" in American culture.[26] While these kinds of observations of Baptist history are somewhat commonplace in American religious historiography, what has not been as well understood is exactly *how* Baptists became religious insiders. This was an inevitably political process. By the 1830s, the meteoric rise of the Baptists had begun to pry the denomination loose from the cellar of American political life.

The life of Richard Fuller epitomizes the rise of the Baptist denomination into national prominence, illustrating how rank-and-file Baptists themselves did not necessarily have to climb the social ladder for the denomination to gain prestige; sometimes those on the top of the ladder simply became Baptists. After the Revolution, Thomas Fuller and Elizabeth Middleton married and settled in Beaufort, a well-known summer retreat for South Carolina's wealthy planters. Elizabeth, Richard's mother, was a descendant of Arthur Middleton, one of the signers of the Declaration of Independence.[27] For years, Thomas had belonged to the Episcopal church as a "fair and reputable professor." However, in 1803, the year before Richard

---

Burned-Over District.

24. Kidd and Hankins, *Baptists in America*, ix.

25. Marty, "Baptistification Takes Over," 33–36.

26. McLoughlin, *Soul Liberty*, 2–3; McLoughlin, *Cherokees and Christianity, 1794–1870*, 34.

27. Cuthbert, *Life of Richard Fuller, D.D.*, 15.

was born, the elder Fuller had converted to the Baptist faith after a lengthy, heartfelt conversation with a Judge Clay, the head of the bar in Savannah, Georgia (where Clay had been baptized by Rev. Henry Holcombe). Later, on November 6, 1803, Thomas recorded in his diary, "I was baptized in the river with several negroes who had been received the afternoon before. This act has caused some estrangement between my friends and myself."[28] In this solemn act, the aristocratic Fuller had been immersed with the very slaves upon which his wealth and all of South Carolina planter society was built. The egalitarianism of baptism was a hallmark of the Baptist faith.

Nevertheless, the Fullers retained their opulence and afforded the best opportunities for their children. For instance, their son, Dr. Thomas Fuller, became one of the wealthiest cotton planters in South Carolina. Even though Richard's brother kept his membership in the Episcopal church, he "worshipped as frequently in the Baptist church as in his own," indicating both the strength of the Baptist denomination in South Carolina as well as the continued respectability of the Episcopal church in the low country.[29] Richard himself was one of the few Southerners to attend Harvard in the antebellum era, graduating in 1824 despite health trouble.[30] Fuller even traveled to Europe in 1836 for the benefit of his health, indicating a level of wealth unparalleled in most Baptist circles.

After returning from Harvard and practicing law in Beaufort, Richard continued to associate with the Episcopal church in which he had been raised. He also married a wealthy widow whose affairs he attended as her attorney. By all accounts, Richard fit nicely into Southern high society. However, he also exhibited sympathies with Baptist views. As a boy, Fuller had been instructed by W. T. Brantly, pastor of First Baptist Church of Beaufort. Remarkably, when he decided to join the Episcopal church as a young lawyer, he was *immersed* in a local river by the Episcopal rector! Despite the unusual circumstances of his membership, Fuller had several motivations for remaining in the Episcopal church, including the "worldly advantages" that appealed to a young professional such as himself. Also, after his immersion, he was called a "mongrel Baptist" by a fellow Episcopalian, suggesting that Baptists were still perceived as lowly and uncivilized by many in coastal society. In response to the mockery, Fuller delivered to his new brother in

---

28. Cuthbert, *Life of Richard Fuller*, 18, 20.

29. Cuthbert, *Life of Richard Fuller*, 24.

30. According to Michael O'Brien, "between 1820 and 1860, Southerners represented about 9 percent of Harvard students, 11 percent of Yale's, and 36 percent of Princeton's" (O'Brien, *Intellectual Life and the American South, 1810–1860*, 19).

the church a punch to the face![31] The episode did little to quiet the stirrings in Fuller's soul as to the validity of his conversion.

Finally, in the winter of 1831–32, an evangelist named Daniel Baker visited Beaufort. He hosted revival meetings alternately at the Episcopal and Baptist churches, indicating once again that Baptists were emerging from the margins of religious culture. (Between 1776 and 1850, among total Christian adherents in America, the percentage of Episcopalians sunk from 15.7 to 3.5 whereas Baptists increased their share from 16.9 percent to 20.5 percent.[32]) After one of Baker's revival meetings, Fuller converted to the Baptist church, eventually leaving the legal profession in order to become a Baptist preacher and ultimately becoming the third president of the Southern Baptist Convention. By the 1830s, Baptists had reached new heights in their communities, receiving converts from the established church that had once persecuted them. The wealth and influence accumulated by the Baptist denomination was not always an industrious, rags-to-riches story like that of Abraham Lincoln or other Republican figures in the middle of the nineteenth century. Instead, it often descended from above, as lawyers, judges, doctors, and other professionals and businessmen found the Baptist church to be an acceptable theological and social alternative to the high church communities they once called home.[33]

William Hooper of North Carolina was not simply a former Episcopalian; he was an ex-priest! As a professor at the state university in Chapel Hill, Hooper became a Baptist after rejecting the High Church movement of bishop John Stark Ravenscroft. Leaving the security of the state institution to teach at Furman Institute and then to preside over Wake Forest College might have appeared to some like a bit of a risk. But Hooper wrote a friend in 1837 that "in the sphere in which we shall be called to act, more moderate attainments will answer a good purpose and meet the wants of our denomination." Perhaps, he added, we "may raise our people & our ministry to a point from which our successors may raise them to still greater elevation."[34] People from higher walks of life were flocking to the baptismal pool, giving the Baptists a new social texture and even more optimism for the future of

---

31. Cuthbert, *Life of Richard Fuller*, 64–65.

32. Finke and Stark, *Churching of America 1776–1990*, 55.

33. On the frontier, Dr. David Doyle, a medical doctor from North Carolina, was one of the first Baptist preachers in the Missouri Territory (Peck, *Forty Years of Pioneer Life*, 133).

34. William Hooper to James C. Furman, August 8, 1837, James C. Furman papers, Furman University. Cited in Mathews, *Religion in the Old South*, 91–92.

the denomination. In Savannah, United States District Judge Joseph Clay Jr. left the courthouse in order to become a Baptist pastor.[35]

Although prejudices still persisted in the older denominations, Baptists were no longer social interlopers in most regions of the country. As the stories of Fuller and Clay demonstrate, leaders in the courthouse had now come to the meetinghouse. South Carolina in particular was home to some of America's most powerful Baptists. At First Baptist Church of Columbia, the leading lay member, John Clark, was a state commissioner to survey a railroad route to Columbia and repair the State House. In addition to running the most well-known hotel in town, Clark also helped organize the first insurance company in Columbia.[36] James Petigru Boyce, the inaugural president of the Southern Baptist Theological Seminary (who was converted by Richard Fuller), was also from a family of extraordinary affluence. Ker, James's father, was considered to be perhaps the wealthiest man in South Carolina, providing his son with the best education money could buy at Charleston College, Brown University, and Princeton Seminary.[37] Even in the South, black Baptists occasionally amassed wealth and property. Astonishingly, former slave Andrew Bryan of Savannah's First African Baptist Church eventually owned eight slaves! He wrote in 1800, "By a kind Providence I am well provided for, as to worldly comforts, (tho' I have had very little given me as a minister) having a house and lot in this city, besides the land on which several buildings stand, for which I receive a small rent, and a fifty-six acre tract of land, with all necessary buildings, four miles in the country, and eight slaves; for whose education and happiness, I am enabled thro' mercy to provide."[38] Oddly enough, the paternalism that existed among white Baptists could sometimes be found in the black Baptist church as well.

Baptists in the Middle Atlantic also became parvenus, ascending in social status. As Paul E. Johnson has demonstrated in his classic work *A Shopkeeper's Millennium*, the rise of middle-class culture in the famous Rochester revival of 1830–31 was attended largely by successful Baptist businessmen. Prominence within the Baptist church "gained them entry into the town's church-bounded community of respectability." A few years after the revival, a Freewill Baptist minister expressed, "We are treated with much kindness by all classes, and especially by all evangelical Christians."

---

35. Boles, "Henry Holcombe," 391.

36. Wills, *First Baptist Church of Columbia, South Carolina 1809 to 2002* 43.

37. Boyce, *Abstract of Systematic Theology*, ii.

38. Bryan, "Letter from the Negro Baptist Church in Savannah," 50; Kidd and Hankins, *Baptists in America*, 105.

Two months later, a member of Third Presbyterian Church gave him one thousand dollars to build a meetinghouse.[39]

Especially on the frontier, Baptists helped establish new towns and cities where they became men of influence. In Kentucky, farming and land speculation brought Baptist preacher John Taylor considerable wealth. Taylor purchased at least 14,944 acres in Kentucky and 2,051 acres in Indiana. He eventually became one of the founders of Franklin County, Kentucky.[40] Far from the paternalism and rigid class system of New England, Baptists in the west were free to determine their own position in society (or in many cases to leave society altogether). The distillery business of Elijah Craig is but one example of Baptist entrepreneurship.[41] However, Baptists did not all agree on the proper relationship between personal faith and public duty. For instance, from Bullittsburg Church, the first Baptist church in northern Kentucky, Moses Scott served in the Kentucky House of Representatives in 1819 and 1820 as the member from Boone County. However, this did not impress John Taylor, who demurred that "this will be a poor thing in the Day of Settlement with his Lord."[42] The same objections that Taylor registered in opposition to the missions movement he also made against Baptists who sought to fill political office. Taylor's understanding of the Baptist faith included a firm separation of church and state such that *any* accumulation of political influence, whether as a missionary society president or as an elected official, was worthy of suspicion. As his fellow western anti-mission Baptist Daniel Parker urged, "professors of religion" should not be "pleased with the names of honor from the world."[43] However, for many Baptists, religious liberty and civic responsibility were not mutually exclusive. In fact, they believed that one protected the other.

The political and economic rise of white Baptists in American culture in the 1830s is perhaps best captured through the eyes of those who resisted or resented the new wealth in the Baptist denomination. Naturally, the affluence and influence that emerged in Baptist churches produced an imbalance between the powerful and the seemingly powerless, or between the willing and the wary. In 1832, Gilbert Beebe established a Primitive or Anti-Mission Baptist newspaper suitably titled *Signs of the Times* in New Vernon, New York. In addition to addressing theological issues like justification, divine sovereignty, and biblical interpretation, the paper was filled

---

39. Johnson, *Shopkeeper's Millennium*, 126, 117.
40. Taylor, *Baptists on the American Frontier*, 83.
41. Thanks to my friend Casey B. Hough for pointing me to Elijah Craig.
42. Taylor, *Baptists on the American Frontier*, 289.
43. Parker, *Public Address*, 34.

with anti-elitist arguments against the prosperity and power of those in the new wave of benevolent institutions that had emerged across the United States. The periodical began by publishing Maryland Anti-Mission Baptists' Address to the other Old School Particular Baptist Churches in the country. In the Address, they objected to Bible societies, for instance, because "such a monstrous combination, concentrating so much power in the hands of a few individuals, could never be necessary for supplying the destitute with bibles." Such a "concentration of power," they argued, would certainly lead to "the subversion of our liberties."[44] The Primitive Baptists opposed Bible Societies, the American Tract Society, and the Sunday School Union due to the fact "that its vast combination of worldly power and influence lodged in the hands of a *few*, renders it a dangerous engine against the liberties, both civil and religious, of our country, should it come under the control of those disposed so to employ it."[45] For Primitive Baptists, the issue of non-ecclesiastical groups was as much about power as it was about predestination.

The Address from the Old School Particular Baptists is significant not only for what it reveals about the increase of Baptist secular power and the ever-sensitive issue of religious liberty, but also for how Baptists perceived each other in an increasingly public world. According to these anti-mission Baptists, the "leading motive" of missionaries was "not love to souls, but love of fame; hence his anxiety to have something to publish of what he has done."[46] The idea of "famous" Baptists was indeed a new concept in the world, at least on the American side of the Atlantic, and many Baptists did not believe it to be godly or biblical. The result, as Beebe later opined, was "a general amalgamation of the church and the world, by the onward march of Priest-craft."[47]

In 1833, Beebe published a letter in which a Baptist by the name of Charles Polkinhorn recounted his experience at one of the so-called "Antichristian Societies." The account was intended to highlight the alleged greed and hypocrisy of mission Baptists. "You are, no doubt aware," he wrote, "it required the sum of $100 to entitle the Society to representation in the General Convention, we were few in number and had much difficult in raising the amount." Polkinhorn expressed his disgust when "at our meeting for business a letter was read and adopted by the Society, addressed to the Convention setting forth in glowing and extravagant colours our extraordinary success and congratulating the Convention of the Signs of the near

---

44. "Address to the Particular Baptist Churches," 3.
45. "Address to the Particular Baptist Churches," 4.
46. "Address to the Particular Baptist Churches," 5.
47. Beebe, "Signs of the Times," 11.

approach of latter day glory. Indeed, from the letter you would suppose it was breaking in upon us in all its transcendent splendor."[48] The disaffected Baptist's complaint was not just in the high cost of missions, but in its seemingly self-congratulatory and publicized nature. *Signs of the Times* revealed that not every Baptist necessarily adhered to the optimistic postmillennialism that defined the age. By the 1830s, epitomized in Baptists such as William Miller (also in western New York), premillennialism had also found its various spokesmen.[49]

The anti-mission movement among Baptists simply cannot be understood without the elitist movement within Baptist life to which it was responding. Beebe's *Signs of the Times* illustrated repeatedly that theology and evangelism were not always the primary issues at stake in the battle over benevolent societies. In the so-called "benevolent empire," many Baptists saw an actual empire.[50] These voluntary groups afforded Baptists the opportunity to achieve a new kind of status in the United States such that issues of wealth and labor and public image became increasingly prominent in Baptist circles.[51] For example, an 1834 issue of *Signs of the Times* read as follows: "Wealthy people should make it a point to encourage persons at labor. A false shame of being seen at work has been the ruin of many. Times should be changed. People should be proud of being made usefully employed. All honest labor is meritorious."[52] In some ways, the introduction of wealth had begun to change the way that Baptists viewed work itself. The faint echoes of class conflict and wealth distribution can be heard in these kinds of publications, as Baptists reconciled working class values with the implications of their new-found position in society.

However, Anti-mission Baptists were not the only voices in the 1830s decrying the luxury and lavishness in Baptist churches. Sometimes, the missionaries themselves admonished their own supporters. In 1831, Adoniram Judson, the first American Baptist overseas missionary, penned a "Letter on

---

48. Polkinhorn, "City of Washington, Dec. 12, 1822," 47.

49. For an examination of the life and thought of William Miller, see Rowe, *God's Strange Work*.

50. According to George Marsden, "The individuals who made up the interlocking directorship of the 'benevolent empire,' as well as their constituencies, were predominantly Presbyterians and Congregationalists. Dutch Reformed participated frequently also, as did some Baptists and Low Church Episcopalians. Methodists, however, who then appealed to a less-educated class, cooperated relatively little and by the late 1820s came bitterly to regard the 'empire' as a rival" (Marsden, *Evangelical Mind and the New School Presbyterian Experience*, 19).

51. For a look at the impact of voluntary societies on Baptist life in the antebellum era, see Todd, "Southern Yankees," 116–29.

52. *Signs of the Times*, "Integrity," 191.

Ornamental and Costly Attire" to the female members of American churches, namely Baptists. In the letter, Judson addressed those women in the church whose worldliness had begun to negatively influence the Burmese people groups they had been called to reach with the gospel. He exhorted,

> This mission and all others must necessarily be sustained by continual supplies of missionaries, male and female, from the mother country. Your sisters and daughters will continually come out, to take the place of those who are removed by death, and to occupy numberless stations still unoccupied. And when they arrive they will be dressed in their usual way, as Christian women at home are dressed. And the female converts will run around them, and gaze upon them, with the most prying curiosity, regarding them as the freshest representatives of the Christian religion from that land where it flourishes in all its purity and glory. And when they see the gold and jewels pendent from their ears, the beads and chains encircling their necks, the finger rings set with diamonds and rubies, the rich variety of ornamental headdress, "the mantles, and the wimples, and the crisping pins," (see Is. iii, 19, 23) they will cast a reproachful, triumphant glance at their old teachers, and spring with fresh avidity, to repurchase and resume their long-neglected elegances; the cheering news will fly up the Dah-gyne, the Laing-bwai, and the Salwen; the Karenesses will reload their necks, and ears, and arms, and ankles; and when, after another year's absence, I return and take my seat before the Burmese or the Karen church, I shall behold the demon of vanity enthroned in the centre of the assembly more firmly than ever, grinning defiance to the prohibitions of apostles, and the exhortations of us who would fain be their humble followers ... If, on the other hand, you divest yourselves of all meretricious ornaments, your sisters and daughters, who come hither, will be divested of course; the further supplies of vanity and pride will be cut off, and the churches at home being kept pure, the churches here will be pure also.[53]

The new Baptist prosperity among whites had created challenges in the ministry. Fearing a sinful effect upon the Burmese, Judson condemned the extravagance and riches (of women and not men, curiously) that had become "too prevalent in our native beloved land," indicating that Baptists were no longer the "poor of the world" as James Manning had once described them. Instead, Judson believed that the opulence found in Baptist churches actually created a potential spiritual danger to their converts.

---

53. Judson, "Letter on Ornamental and Costly Attire," 479–80.

Certainly, African American Baptists had a unique perspective of white affluence, especially in the South. According to Gregory Wills,

> Yet white Baptists found it impossible to overcome the ideology and the reality of social inequality. The churches expressed the social inferiority of African Americans most visibly in the seating of their meeting houses. Church seating had traditionally reflected social divisions. New England Puritans seated Africans and Indians in galleries or rear seats. Whether Congregationalist or Anglican, churches seated persons of highest social status in the best seats. Advocating a common worship for both races, Baptists assigned the blacks to the worst seats.
> There were limits to this partiality. A white member once complained that "his feelings were hurt in that of Turning the black Brethren and Sisters out from amonts [amongst] us in that Shelters [were] built at the end of the meeting house." One church attempted to split the hair by requesting the deacons to see that "the negroes be not deprived of the seats assigned them; unless there be not otherwise room for the Whites." Yet the seating of the saints revealed the force of inegalitarian social ideology.[54]

The egalitarianism of baptism could not eliminate the caste system of slavery. Even in the church building itself, the wealth and power of white Baptists were unavoidable. Not surprisingly, wealth was often a topic of discussion in the pulpit and in the pew. In the North, in the waning years of his life, Thomas Baldwin put pen to paper in order to compose a series of letters to the young people in his church (Baldwin passed away on August 25, 1825, the same day as Richard Furman). Baldwin made sure to include a warning against seeking the fleeting pleasures of the world. "Can the transitory enjoyments of the mean and sordid pleasures of sense, compensate for the loss of an eternity of real happiness?" he asked the youth. "Earth's highest pleasures can never satisfy an immortal mind. Nor will these pleasures always last. They all perish in the using. Think, then, I beseech you, what your condition will be, when these, poor as they are, shall all forsake you forever."[55] Of all the lessons Baldwin wished to pass on to the next generation of New England Baptists, the frugality of faith and the deceitfulness of riches were two of the most important in his mind.

William McLoughlin's contention that Baptists "embodied the basic outlook of the American people for most of the nineteenth century" is also supported by the fact that many of the nation's most influential political

---

54. Wills, *Democratic Religion*, 63.
55. Baldwin, "Pastoral Letter," 92–93.

leaders in the 1800s were from Baptist parentage. When Baptists weren't claiming political offices for themselves, their children often did so. Abraham Lincoln, as previously shown, was the child of Calvinistic Baptists who traveled west to Kentucky and then Indiana and then Illinois, seeking to carve out a piece of the American frontier for their family.[56] Henry Clay, Lincoln's political hero and founder of the Whig Party, was the son of a Baptist minister who farmed tobacco. John Clay of Hanover County, Virginia pastored Chickahominy Church and was "a plain, but sincere and devout man of God."[57] However, as James C. Klotter has shown, the somewhat stereotypical idea that Clay's father was a lowly, indigent Baptist is not grounded in historical fact. Klotter explains, "In contrast to the image of Rev. John Clay as a poverty-stricken minister of the Old Dominion, in truth Henry's father came from a distinguished family that had been in Virginia almost from the first English settlement. 'Sir John,' as he was called by contemporaries, held sizable landholdings of over 450 acres and owned at least twenty slaves. Most of that estate went to his widow, leaving the family in a comfortable situation."[58] The lives of both Clay and Lincoln were significantly shaped by the fortunes of their Baptist fathers. In fact, through the "Great Compromiser" and the "Great Emancipator" one could easily argue that the economic aspirations of Baptists helped determine the course of not only nineteenth-century American politics, but American history itself.

Establishing Disestablishment

While it is beyond the scope of this work to debate the merits of a so-called Baptist "cultural establishment" into the late nineteenth and early twentieth centuries, the early republic nevertheless served as a kind of gestation period for Baptists into American political culture, as revolutionary and postrevolutionary forces effectively delivered them from persecution (at least in certain states) to marginalization to mainstream. Of course, this process did not occur uniformly from state to state, and, in the cases of Massachusetts and Connecticut, took much longer in some regions than in others. However, even in New England, the dominance of Baptists and their "popular cause" of religious liberty gained demonstrable momentum. For instance, in 1794, John Leland had already observed that in certain pockets

---

56. A similar westward journey was taken by Lewis Craig and his famous "traveling church" to Kentucky in 1781.

57. Tupper, *First Century of The First Baptist Church of Richmond, Virginia 1780–1880*, 55–56.

58. Klotter, *Henry Clay*, 2–3.

of New England Baptists "formed a majority."[59] By the end of the eighteenth century, some Baptists were already bemoaning the fact that certain groups on the frontier had gained an "establishment there in a literary way" by disseminating books and establishing theological institutions, belying their aim to establish their own hegemony in the west.[60] By the second quarter of the nineteenth century, the politics of optimism that had energized Baptists through years of dissent had developed into an increasingly public citizenry who embraced religious liberty as their guiding principle—an *American* principle. As Whitney R. Cross has noted, "A naïve optimism characterized Americans generally in Jacksonian days."[61] Baptists had reason to embrace this optimism more than perhaps any other religious group.

Although Connecticut did not disestablish religion until 1818 and Massachusetts until 1833, signs of a significant cultural and political shift were evident in various ways, including from *within* the state church itself. The establishment was under threat by Congregationalists of the more heterodox sort. Unitarians, "never having been of kin to the Baptists, had no ground for a family estrangement" and began to find common cause with them against the Standing Order. In a rather ironic twist, socially conservative Unitarians united with Baptists against Orthodox Congregationalists for the same reason that Thomas Jefferson and the Enlightenment liberals did. Both groups denied the Trinity, and both sought religious liberty for themselves, but for different reasons. Baptists linked political arms with theological liberals of various stripes throughout the early republic, and this spirit of compromise generally characterized the epoch of history between 1776 and the years leading to the Civil War. One particularly striking example of this compromise was the case of American historian George Bancroft. By the 1820s, Baptists in Worcester, Massachusetts had begun convening in Bancroft's meeting-house, a courtesy which had the effect of softening relations in the area.[62] Like President John Adams, Bancroft was raised in a Unitarian home and was sent to Harvard as a young teenager. George's father, Aaron, a soldier in the Revolution, was a Unitarian clergyman in Worcester, even serving as the president of the American Unitarian Association from 1825 to 1836 (although he remained in the Congregationalist church until his death). However, unlike Adams, Bancroft's Unitarian faith was a bit less static and his politics were not nearly as conservative. As a Jacksonian

---

59. Leland, "Yankee Spy," 227.

60. James Manning, "To the Rev. Dr. Evans, Providence, July 21, 1785," in Guild, *Life, Times, and Correspondence of James Manning*, 357.

61. Cross, *Burned-Over District*, 79.

62. Wayland and Wayland, *Memoir of the Life and Labors of Francis Wayland*, 1:151.

Democrat, Bancroft's populistic and working-class sympathies made him more accommodating to the Baptist cause, especially in New England. With his cousin Samuel at the 1774 Continental Congress, John Adams had retorted that Isaac Backus might sooner expect a change in the solar system than a disestablished Congregationalist church. Half a century later, however, the more democratic and egalitarian George Bancroft seemed willing to help Baptists do exactly that. The age of religious establishment was coming to a close in America, aided greatly by the efforts of the Baptists.

Indeed, the fortunes of Baptists in Worcester changed dramatically in a matter of a few decades. Francis Wayland, who spent a few years in the area before becoming the president of Brown University, would eventually boast a son who would serve as a lawyer and justice of the peace in Worcester. After studying law at Harvard, Francis Wayland III was probate judge in Connecticut in 1864 and became the 54th Lieutenant Governor of Connecticut in 1869–1870 before eventually serving as dean of Yale Law School from 1873 to 1903. At Brown, Francis Wayland II became one of the leading ethicists in the country, famously sparring against Richard Fuller over the issue of slavery in a series of rather civilized paper debates in 1845.[63] In the 1830s, it was noted by faculty and students alike "the interest which Dr. Wayland always manifested in the science of jurisprudence, and his earnest desire that those of his pupils who entered upon the legal profession should be guided by high-minded and generous views of duty."[64] In 1764, Baptists had sought to establish a learned clergy by opening up in Rhode Island their very first college in the colonies. Decades later, due to the new-found power and prestige of the Baptist denomination along with the exigencies of a republican society, Brown University had become an institution in which lawyers and other civil leaders could be trained for their various public duties.[65] With this new emphasis on civic duty, Wayland once urged upon a student, "we can never govern others until we have learned to govern ourselves."[66] Baptists were ready to govern and ready to prepare others to do the same.

---

63. Wayland and Fuller, *Domestic Slavery Considered as a Scriptural Institution*.

64. Wayland and Wayland, *Life and Labors of Francis Wayland*, 240. Kathryn Kish Sklar explains, "The two dominant wings of American Common Sense philosophy—the conservative Evangelical wing represented by Francis Wayland, and the liberal Unitarian wing represented by William Ellery Channing—answered the question of social leadership and moral guardianship in very similar ways" (Sklar, *Catharine Beecher*, 82).

65. This is not to say that future lawyers did not study at Brown University in its earliest days. James Mitchell Varnum, who served in the Revolution as a general in the Continental Army, is one such example. Varnum graduated in the first graduating class in 1769 before studying law under Rhode Island Attorney General Oliver Arnold.

66. Wayland, *Life and Labors of Francis Wayland*, 242.

There are few families that illustrate how quickly white Baptists could insert themselves into the affairs of American politics better than the Galushas. Jonas Galusha's father, Jacob, was a farmer and a blacksmith in the Colony of Connecticut. However, Jonas himself proved a bit more ambitious than his father, fighting in the Revolution as a captain. As a farmer and an inn-keeper, Galusha was elected sheriff of Bennington County, Vermont from 1781 to 1787. He then entered state politics when he became the sixth governor of Vermont (1809–1813). Jonas's wife, Mary, was the daughter of Thomas Chittenden, the first and third governor of the state. Mary's brother, Martin, a Federalist, succeeded Jonas as the seventh governor for only a year before Jonas was again elected to the governorship of Vermont (1815–1820).

Unlike his Federalist brother-in-law, Jonas strongly supported the conflict with Britain in the War of 1812. As a Republican, Galusha shared most of the political shibboleths of his Baptist cohorts, including a Jeffersonian emphasis on religious liberty and an aversion to Old England. In turn, he served as an elector for James Madison in 1808 and for James Monroe in 1820 (and for John Quincy Adams in 1824 and 1828).[67] The relative efficiency with which Jonas Galusha asserted his Baptist Republican views in the fourteenth state and in Washington D. C. is evidence that, outside of the more traditionally religious states like Massachusetts, Connecticut, and Virginia, the early United States was increasingly amenable to Baptist figures and beliefs. Also in Vermont, for example, Dr. Asaph Fletcher, a Baptist, likewise served as an elector for James Monroe in 1816.[68] In the case of Jonas Galusha, Baptists went quite literally from the farm to the governor's homestead. According to Galusha's biographer, "his proclamations for Fasts and Thanksgivings were of unusual length; sometimes, indeed, nearly as long as his messages, indicating that he was more accustomed to thinking and writing upon religious subjects than upon political affairs."[69] Jonas's successive votes for Republicans Jefferson, Madison, Monroe and then for Whig John Quincy Adams in both 1820 and 1824 indicate that Baptists were not as predictable in their voting patterns during the Era of Good Feelings as they had been early on. Even though Jonas was staunchly Republican, he nevertheless voted against Andrew Jackson in 1824 "without any change of his political views," suggesting that the transition from a Jeffersonian to a Jacksonian platform was not as seamless as some like John Leland made it out to be.[70] In addition to the elections in the young republic, the Galusha

---

67. White, *Jonas Galusha, The Fifth Governor of Vermont, a Memoir*, 10.
68. Benedict, *General History of the Baptist Denomination in America*, 488.
69. White, *Jonas Galusha*, 15.
70. White, *Jonas Galusha*, 16.

family would also impact the events leading to the Civil War, as Jonas's son Elon, a Baptist preacher in New York, was an abolitionist whose anti-slavery activities played a role in the fracturing of the Triennial Convention and the birth of the Southern Baptist Convention.[71] Evidenced in the Galusha family, Baptist concepts of liberty were fluid throughout the early national period, as Baptists embraced liberty first for themselves, then for their country, and eventually for others *in* their country.

In some sense, with the passing of the founding fathers, Baptists believed that God had placed upon them a special responsibility to transfer the highest ideals of the nation to the next generation. As torch-bearers of religious liberty, Baptists, the people who had not been chosen to lead the nation in its earliest years, had been ordained to preserve it in the next season of its delicate existence. They had been handed the republican baton, so to speak. After the deaths of John Adams and Thomas Jefferson on the very same day in 1826, and on the fiftieth anniversary of the Declaration of Independence no less, William Staughton, like most Americans, interpreted the coincidence as a sign of divine favor. As Senate chaplain, Staughton preached to Congress in the Capitol building from 2 Samuel 1:23: "Lovely and pleasant were they in their lives—in their death they were not divided; they were swifter than eagles, they were stronger than lions." Comparing Adams and Jefferson to Saul and Jonathan in the Old Testament, Staughton lauded each patriot for his defense of liberty. "Mr. Jefferson was a decided enemy to religious intolerance," he exhorted, "a champion for the inviolable rights of conscience. His correct feelings on this subject, revolted at the idea of the incorporation of Religion with Civil Government."[72] On the other hand, Adams was the "grand sustainer" of the Revolution itself. He was, "in Congress, the same as was Washington in the field, the soul that animated every adventure."[73]

At such a symbolic moment in the early republic, Staughton's praise for the founders was only outdone by his buoyant view of America's future, in which he envisioned a flourishing and free religion. "If, on the face of the earth, there exist a people under peculiar obligations to obey the precepts of Heaven, we are that people," he claimed, proudly revealing his sense of

---

71. Elon Galusha eventually became a follower of the Adventist William Miller. For an examination of the events leading to the formation of the Southern Baptist Convention, including the involvement of Elon Galusha, see Gardner, *Decade of Debate and Division*; Barnes, *Southern Baptist Convention, 1845–1953*; McBeth, *Baptist Heritage*, 382–463; Leonard, *God's Last and Only Hope*, 17–19; Fletcher, *Southern Baptist Convention*, 43–72; Kidd and Hankins, *Baptists in America*, 127–29, 131.

72. Staughton, *Sermon, Delivered in the Capitol of the United States*, 20.

73. Staughton, *Sermon Delivered in the Capitol*, 22–23.

Christian nationalism. "Let temples every where rise in honour of his name, and let them be crowded with grateful, adoring, and holy worshippers."[74] Ultimately, for Staughton, the fate of the United States lay with its piety, not its politics. For this reason, he impressed upon his listeners the importance of character, for "if we sin against Heaven, and in His sight, the sagacity and moral worth of no statesmen can deliver us. The vessel of our commonwealth will be found in an eddy too powerful to escape the tremendous vortex." After warning his countrymen against transgressing the law of God and incurring divine judgment, Staughton boasted, "I rank our Missionary Institutions, our Bible Societies, and our Sunday Schools among the bulwarks of brass which promise our safety."[75] Like other evangelical groups in the infant nation, Baptists had effectively modernized the Puritan idea of a national covenant. Through voluntary and missions groups, Baptists were keeping their solemn oath to God to obey his commands and to pledge themselves to Him. In turn, these groups became the vanguard of the Baptist denomination because they were the means by which religious liberty and their most precious rights as Americans were protected. By establishing benevolence societies and fulfilling their "peculiar obligations" to God and to the world, they were making America prosper. By the time that Adams and Jefferson had passed from their earthly labors and Jacksonian populism had sprung from the soil of republicanism, Baptists had every reason to believe that religious liberty was *sine qua non* with this divine commission. Through the First Amendment of the Constitution and the arduous process of disestablishment that followed, the United States had made freedom of religion its chief moral cornerstone, effectively turning the early republic into a Baptist America.

74. Staughton, *Sermon Delivered in the Capitol*, 28.
75. Staughton, *Sermon Delivered in the Capitol*, 29–31.

Bibliography

Adams, John. "John Adams' Diary, October 14, 1774." In *Letters of Delegates to Congress, 1774-1789: August 1774-August 1775*, 193. Washington: Library of Congress, 1976.

———. *The Works of John Adams, the Second President of the United States, Volume II*. Boston: Little, Brown, and Company, 1865.

Ahlstrom, Sydney E. *A Religious History of the American People*. New Haven, CT: Yale University Press, 2004.

Allen, Carlos R., Jr. "David Barrow's *Circular Letter* of 1798." *The William and Mary Quarterly* 20 (1963) 440–51.

Allen, John. *An Oration, Upon the Beauties of Liberty, Or the Essential Rights of the Americans*. Boston: D. Kneeland, 1773.

Anderson, Courtney. *To the Golden Shore: The Life of Adoniram Judson*. Valley Forge: Judson, 1987.

"Anecdote of an American Negro Slave." In *American Baptist Magazine and Missionary Intelligencer*, 1:20. Boston: James Loring, and Lincoln & Edmands, 1817.

Armitage, Thomas. *A History of the Baptists; Traced by Their Vital Principles and Practices, from the Time of Our Lord and Saviour Jesus Christ to the Year 1889*. New York: Bryan, Taylor, 1889.

———. *A History of the Baptists: Volume 2*. New York: Bryan, Taylor & Co., 1890.

Austin, Joshua. "Statement of Joshua Austin." In *Soul Liberty: The Baptists' Struggle in New England, 1630–1833*, edited by William G. McLoughlin, 217–18. Hanover: Brown University Press, 1991.

Babcock, Rufus. *Forty Years of Pioneer Life: Memoir of John Mason Peck D.D.* Philadelphia: American Baptist Publication Society, 1864.

Backus, Isaac. *An Address to the Inhabitants of New England*. In *Isaac Backus on Church, State, and Calvinism: Pamphlets, 1754–1789*, edited by William G. McLoughlin, 443–46. Cambridge, MA: The Belknap Press of Harvard University Press, 1968.

———. *An Appeal to the Public for Religious Liberty*. In *Isaac Backus on Church, State, and Calvinism: Pamphlets, 1754–1789*, edited by William G. McLoughlin, 309–43. Cambridge, MA: The Belknap Press of Harvard University Press, 1968.

———. *A Door Opened for Christian Liberty*. In *Isaac Backus on Church, State, and Calvinism: Pamphlets, 1754–1789*, edited by William G. McLoughlin, 431–38. Cambridge, MA: The Belknap Press of Harvard University Press, 1968.

———. *A Fish Caught in His Own Net.* In *Isaac Backus on Church, State, and Calvinism: Pamphlets, 1754-1789*, edited by William G. McLoughlin, 167–88. Cambridge, MA: The Belknap Press of Harvard University Press, 1968.

———. *A History of New England with Particular Reference to the Denomination of Christians called Baptists, Volume II.* Newton: Backus Historical Society, 1871.

———. *A Letter to a Gentleman in the Massachusetts General Assembly, Concerning Taxes to Support Religious Worship.* Boston: n.d., 1771.

———. *Government and Liberty Described.* In *Isaac Backus on Church, State, and Calvinism: Pamphlets, 1754-1789*, edited by William G. McLoughlin, 350–65. Cambridge, MA: The Belknap Press of Harvard University Press, 1968.

———. *Policy As Well As Honesty.* In *Isaac Backus on Church, State, and Calvinism: Pamphlets, 1754-1789*, edited by William G. McLoughlin, 371–83. Cambridge, MA: The Belknap Press of Harvard University Press, 1968.

———. *Truth Is Great and Will Prevail.* In *Isaac Backus on Church, State, and Calvinism: Pamphlets, 1754-1789*, edited by William G. McLoughlin, 397–425. Cambridge, MA: The Belknap Press of Harvard University Press, 1968.

Bailyn, Bernard. *The Ideological Origins of the American Revolution.* Cambridge, MA: Harvard University Press, 1967.

———. *Voyagers to the West: A Passage in the Peopling of America on the Eve of the Revolution.* New York: Alfred A. Knopf, 1986.

Baker, Robert A. *The Southern Baptist Convention and Its People, 1607-1972.* Nashville: Broadman, 1974.

Baldwin, Thomas. *A Discourse, Delivered Before the Ancient and Honourable Artillery Company, in Boston, June 1, 1807, Being the Anniversary of Their Election of Officers.* Boston: Munroe & Francis, 1807.

———. "Pastoral Letter." In *Memoir of Rev. Thomas Baldwin, D.D.*, edited by Daniel Chessman, 92–93. Boston: Elder John Peak, 1841.

———. "Editor's Address." *American Baptist Magazine, and Missionary Intelligencer*, 1 (1817) 4.

———. *A Sermon, Delivered Before His Excellency Caleb Strong.* Boston: Young & Minns, 1802.

———. *A Sermon, Delivered February 19, 1795: Being the Day of Public Thanksgiving Throughout the United States.* Boston: Manning & Loring, 1795.

———. *A Sermon, delivered to the Second Baptist Society in Boston, on Lord's Day, December 29, 1799. Occasioned by the Death of General George Washington.* Boston: Manning & Loring, 1800.

Barnes, William Wright. *The Southern Baptist Convention, 1845-1953.* Nashville: Broadman, 1954.

Beebe, Gilbert. "Signs of the Times." *Signs of the Times* 1 (1832) 11.

Belden, A. Russell. *History of Cayuga Baptist Association.* Auburn: Derby & Miller, 1851.

Benedict, David. *A General History of the Baptist Denomination in America, and other parts of the World, Volume I.* Boston: Lincoln & Edmands, 1813.

Bercovitch, Sacvan. *The American Jeremiad.* Madison: The University of Wisconsin Press, 1978.

Blake, I. George. "Jesse Lynch Holman: Pioneer Hoosier." *Indiana Magazine of History* 39 (1943) 25–51.

Bibliography

Bloch, Ruth H. *Visionary Republic: Millennial Themes in American Thought, 1756–1800.* Cambridge: Cambridge University Press, 1985.

Blood, Caleb. *A Sermon Preached Before the Honorable Legislature of the State of Vermont.* Rutland: Anthony Haswell, 1792.

Boles, John B. "Henry Holcombe, A Southern Baptist Reformer in the Age of Jefferson." *The Georgia Historical Quarterly* 54 (1970) 381–407.

Boyce, James Petigru. *Abstract of Systematic Theology.* Escondido: Dulk Christian Foundation, 1887.

Bradford, William. *Of Plymouth Plantation.* In *The American Puritans: Their Prose and Poetry*, edited by Perry Miller, 5–20. New York: Columbia University Press, 1956.

Brantly, W. T. "Character of the Early American Baptist Preachers." *The Columbian Star and Christian Index* 1 (1829) 1–7.

Breen, Patrick H. *The Land Shall Be Deluged in Blood: A New History of the Nat Turner Revolt.* New York: Oxford University Press, 2015.

Broaddus, Andrew. *The Sermons and Other Writings of the Rev. Andrew Broaddus, with a Memoir of His Life*, edited by J. B. Jeter. New York: Lewis Colby, 1852.

Broome, John David, ed. *The Life, Ministry, and Journals of Hezekiah Smith.* Springfield: Particular Baptist Press, 2004.

Broussard, James H. *The Southern Federalists: 1800–1816.* Baton Rouge: Louisiana State University Press, 1978.

Brown, D. C. *Memoir of the Late Rev. Lemuel Covell.* Brandon: Telegraph Office, 1839.

Bryan, Andrew. "A Letter from the Negro Baptist Church in Savannah." In *African American Religious History: A Documentary Witness*, edited by Milton C. Sernett, 49–51. Durham: Duke University Press, 1999.

Bumsted, John M., and Clark, Charles E. "New England's Tom Paine: John Allen and the Spirit of Liberty." *The William and Mary Quarterly* 21 (1964) 561–70.

Burch, Jarrett. *Adiel Sherwood: Baptist Antebellum Pioneer in Georgia.* Macon, GA: Mercer University Press, 2003.

Burkitt, Lemuel, and Read, Jesse. *A Concise History of the Kehukee Baptist Association, From its original rise to the present time.* Halifax: A. Hodge, 1803.

Burleson, William Wade. "Preface." In *The Life and Ministry of John Gano, 1727–1804*, edited by Terry Wolever, 1:3–4. Springfield: Particular Baptist Press, 1998.

Burlingame, Michael. *Abraham Lincoln: A Life, Volume 1.* Baltimore: The Johns Hopkins University Press, 2008.

Burrage, Henry S. *History of the Baptists in Maine.* Portland, ME: Marks, 1904.

Butler, Diana Hochstedt. *Standing Against the Whirlwind: Evangelical Episcopalians in Nineteenth Century America.* New York: Oxford University Press, 1995.

Butterfield, L. H. "Elder John Leland, Jeffersonian Itinerant." *American Antiquarian Society* 62 (1952) 154–252.

Byrd, James P. *A Holy Baptism of Fire & Blood: The Bible and the American Civil War.* New York: Oxford University Press, 2021.

———. *Sacred Scripture, Sacred War: The Bible and the American Revolution.* Oxford: Oxford University Press, 2013.

Cady, John F. *The Origin and Development of the Missionary Baptist Church in Indiana.* Berne: Berne Witness, 1942. Campbell, Jesse. *Georgia Baptists: Historical and Biographical.* Richmond: H. K. Ellyson, 1847.

Carey, Samuel Pearce. *Samuel Pearce: The Baptist Brainerd.* 2nd ed. N.d.: Carey, 1913.

Carwardine, Richard. *Evangelicals and Politics in Antebellum America*. New Haven, CT: Yale University Press, 1993.

———. "Evangelicals, Whigs and the Election of William Henry Harrison." *Journal of American Studies* 17 (1983) 47–75.

Caswell, Henry. *America and the American Church*. London: J. G. & F. Rivington, 1839.

Catron, John W. *Embracing Protestantism: Black Identities in the Atlantic World*. Gainesville: University Press of Florida, 2016.

Cheathem, Mark R. *Andrew Jackson and the Rise of the Democratic Party*. Knoxville: The University of Tennessee Press, 2018.

———. *Andrew Jackson: Southerner*. Baton Rouge: Louisiana State University Press, 2013.

Chessman, Daniel, ed. *Memoir of Rev. Thomas Baldwin, D.D., Late Pastor of the Second Baptist Church in Boston*. Boston: John Peak, 1841.

"Church and State." *Signs of the Times* 1 (1833) 64.

Cist, Charles. *The Cincinnati Miscellany, or Antiquities of the West, Vol. I*. Cincinnati: Caleb Clark, 1845.

Cole, Charles C., Jr. *The Social Ideas of Northern Evangelists, 1826–1860*. New York: Columbia University Press, 1954.

Cook, Harvey T. "A Biography of Richard Furman" (Greenville, 1913). In *Life and Works of Dr. Richard Furman, D.D.*, edited by G. William Foster Jr., 65–248. Harrisonburg, VA: Sprinkle, 2004.

Cook, Richard B. *The Early and Later Delaware Baptists*. Philadelphia: American Baptist Publication Society, 1880.

Cooper, William J., Jr. *The South and the Politics of Slavery, 1828–1856*. Baton Rouge: Louisiana State University Press, 1978.

Cornell, Saul. *The Other Founders: Anti-Federalism and The Dissenting Tradition in America, 1788–1828*. Chapel Hill: University of North Carolina Press, 1999.

Cost, Jay. *James Madison: America's First Politician*. New York: Basic, 2021.

Crocker, Henry. *History of the Baptists in Vermont*. Bellows Falls, VT: P.H. Gobie, 1913.

Cross, Barbara M., ed. *The Autobiography of Lyman Beecher, Volume 1*. Cambridge, MA: The Belknap Press of Harvard University Press, 1961.

Cross, Whitney R. *The Burned-Over District: The Social and Intellectual History of Enthusiastic Religion in Western New York, 1800–1850*. New York: Harper & Row, 1965.

Cunningham, Noble E. *The Jeffersonian Republicans in Power: Party Operations, 1801–1809*. Chapel Hill: The University of North Carolina Press, 2013.

Curry, Thomas J. *The First Freedoms: Church and State in America to the Passage of the First Amendment*. New York: Oxford University Press, 1986.

Cuthbert, James Hazzard. *Life of Richard Fuller, D.D.* New York: Sheldon & Company, 1878.

Cutler, William Parker, and Cutler, Julia Perkins, ed.*Life, Journals and Correspondence of Rev. Manessah Cutler, LL.D.* Cincinnati: Robert Clarke, 1888.

Dagg, John L. *Autobiography of Rev. John L. Dagg, D.D.* Harrisonburg, VA: Gano, 1982.

Danbury Baptist Association. "From the Danbury Baptist Association." *The Papers of Thomas Jefferson, Volume 35, 1 August to 30 November 1801*, edited by Barbara B. Oberg, 407–9. Princeton: Princeton University Press, 2008.

Dargan, E. C. "Richard Furman and His Place in American Baptist History." In *Life and Works of Dr. Richard Furman, D.D.*, edited by G. William Foster, Jr., 35–60. Harrisonburg, VA: Sprinkle, 2004.

Den Hartog, Jonathan J. *Patriotism and Piety: Federalist Politics and Religious Struggle in the New American Nation*. Charlottesville: University of Virginia Press, 2015.

———. "The War of 1812." In *America and the Just War Tradition: A History of U.S. Conflicts*, edited by J. Daryl Charles and Mark D. Hall, 74–96. Notre Dame, IN: University of Notre Dame Press, 2019.

Dexter, Franklin Bowditch, ed. *The Literary Diary of Ezra Stiles: Mar. 14 1776–Dec. 31 1781*. New York: Charles Scriber's Sons, 1901.

Dictionary of American Biography. Charles Scribner's Sons, New York, 1936.

Disosway, Gabriel Poillon. *The Earliest Churches of New York and its Vicinity*. New York: James G. Gregory, 1865.

Donald, David H. *Lincoln Reconsidered*. New York: Alfred A. Knopf, 1956.

Drayton, William Henry. "A Letter from Freeman of South Carolina, to the Deputies of North America." In *Documentary History of the American Revolution, 1764–1776*, edited by R. W. Gibbes, 11–38. New York: D. Appleton, 1855.

Dreisbach, Daniel L. *Thomas Jefferson and the Wall of Separation Between Church and State*. New York: New York University Press, 2002.

Dunlevy, A. H. *History of the Miami Baptist Association*. 1869.

Durst, Dennis L. "The Reverend John Berry Meachum (1789–1854) of St. Louis: Prophet and Entrepreneurial Black Leader Educator in Historiographical Perspective." *The North Star: A Journal of African American Religious History* 7 (2004) 1–24.

Dwight, Timothy. *Travels in New England and New York*. 4 vols. New Haven, CT: S. Converse, 1821–1822.

Edwards, Morgan. *Materials Towards a History of the Baptists in Delaware State, Volume III*. Philadelphia: J. B. Lippincott Company, 1885.

Elder, Robert. *Calhoun: American Heretic*. New York: Basic, 2021.

———. *The Sacred Mirror: Evangelicalism, Honor, and Identity in the Deep South, 1790–1860*. Chapel Hill: The University of North Carolina Press, 2016.

Elkhorn Baptist Association. "Circular Letter." Minutes of the Elkhorn Association of Baptists, Began and Held Agreeable to Appointment, at David's Fork Meeting-House, State of Kentucky, the 2d Saturday in August, 1807.

Elliot, Jonathan. *The Debates in the Several State Conventions, Vol. 1*. Philadelphia: J. B. Lippincott, 1891.

Elton, Romeo. "Memoir." In *The Literary Remains of Jonathan Maxcy, D.D.*, edited by Romeo Elton, 9–28. New York: A. V. Blake, 1844.

Esbeck, Carl H. "Disestablishment in Virginia, 1776–1802." In *Disestablishment and Religious Dissent: Church-State Relations in the New American States, 1776–1833*, edited by Carl H. Esbeck and Jonathan J. Den Hartog, 139–80. Columbia: University of Missouri Press, 2019.

Esbeck, Carl H. and Den Hartog, Jonathan J. "Introduction: The Task, Methodology, and Findings." In *Disestablishment and Religious Dissent: Church-State Relations in the New American States, 1776–1833*, edited by Carl H. Esbeck and Jonathan J. Den Hartog, 3–23. Columbia: University of Missouri Press, 2019.

"Extract of a Letter to the Editor, dated March, 1814." *The Massachusetts Baptist Missionary Magazine*, Volume 3. Boston: Manning & Loring, and Lincoln & Edmands, 1811.

Fea, John. *The Bible Cause: A History of the American Bible Society*. Oxford: Oxford University Press, 2016.

Feldman, Noah. *The Three Lives of James Madison: Genius, Partisan, President*. New York: Picador, 2017.

Field, Peter S. *The Crisis of the Standing Order: Clerical Intellectual and Cultural Authority in Massachusetts, 1780–1833*. Amherst: University of Massachusetts Press, 1988.

Finke, Roger, and Stark, Rodney. *The Churching of America 1776–1990: Winners and Losers in Our Religious Economy*. New Brunswick: Rutgers University Press, 1992.

Fitzmier, John R. *New England's Moral Legislator: Timothy Dwight, 1752–1817*. Bloomington: Indiana University Press, 1998.

Fletcher, Jesse H. *The Southern Baptist Convention: A Sesquicentennial History*. Nashville: Broadman & Holman, 1994.

Foster, Charles I. *An Errand of Mercy: The Evangelist United Front, 1790–1837*. Chapel Hill: University of North Carolina Press, 1960.

Foster, Douglas A. *A Life of Alexander Campbell*. Grand Rapids: Eerdmans, 2020.

Foster, G. William, Jr., ed. *Life and Works of Dr. Richard Furman, D.D.* Harrisonburg, VA: Sprinkle, 2004.

Frazier, Gregg L. *God Against the Revolution: The Loyalist Clergy's Case Against the American Revolution*. Manhattan: University Press of Kansas, 2018.

Frey, Sylvia R., and Betty Wood. *Come Shouting to Zion: African American Protestantism in the American South and British Caribbean to 1830*. Chapel Hill: The University of North Carolina Press, 1998.

Fristoe, William. *A Concise History of the Ketocton Baptist Association*. Staunton: William Gilman Lyford, 1808.

Fuller, A. James. "A Song of Mercy and Judgment: The Piety of Basil Manly, Sr. (1798–1868)." In *Soldiers of Christ: Selections from the Writings of Basil Manly, Sr., and Basil Manly, Jr.*, edited by Michael A. G. Haykin et al., 1–24. Cape Coral: Founders, 2009.

Furman, Richard. *America's Deliverance and Duty*. In *Life and Works of Dr. Richard Furman, D.D.*, edited by G. William Foster Jr., 391–408. Harrisonburg, VA: Sprinkle, 2004.

———. *Death's Dominion Over Man Considered. A Sermon, Occasioned by the Death of the Honorable Major General Alexander Hamilton*. In *Life and Works of Dr. Richard Furman, D.D.*, edited by G. William Foster Jr., 231–48. Harrisonburg, VA: Sprinkle, 2004.

———. *Exposition of the Views of the Baptists, Relative to the Coloured Population of the United States, in a Communication to the Governor of South Carolina*. Charleston: A. E. Miller, 1823.

———. *Humble Submission to Divine Sovereignty: The Duty of a Bereaved Nation* (Charleston, 1800). In *Life and Works of Dr. Richard Furman, D.D.*, edited by G. William Foster Jr., 367–87. Harrisonburg, VA: Sprinkle, 2004.

———. *An Oration, Delivered at the Charleston Orphan-House* (Charleston, 1796). In *Life and Works of Dr. Richard Furman, D.D.*, edited by G. William Foster, Jr., 343–63. Harrisonburg, VA: Sprinkle, 2004.

———. *Rewards of Grace Conferred on Christ's Faithful People: A Sermon, Occasioned by the Decease of the Rev. Oliver Hart, A.M. Pastor of the Baptist Church at Hopewell.*

In *Life and Works of Dr. Richard Furman, D.D.*, edited by G. William Foster Jr., 317–42. Harrisonburg, VA: Sprinkle, 2004.

———. *Unity and Peace: A Sermon* (Charleston, 1794). In *Life and Works of Dr. Richard Furman, D.D.*, edited by G. William Foster Jr., 288–316. Harrisonburg, VA: Sprinkle, 2004.

Gano, John. *Biographical Memoirs of the Late Rev. John Gano*. New York: Southwick and Hardcastle, 1806.

Gano, Stephen. *A Sermon on the Death of General George Washington*. Providence: John Carter, 1800.

Gardner, Robert G. *A Decade of Debate and Division: Georgia Baptists and the Formation of the Southern Baptist Convention*. Macon, GA: Mercer University Press, 1995.

Gaustad, Edwin S. *Roger Williams*. New York: Oxford University Press, 2005.

Grenz, Stanley. *Isaac Backus, Puritan and Baptist: His Place in History, His Thought and Their Implications for Modern Baptist Theology*. Macon, GA: Mercer University Press, 1983.

Griffin, Clifford S. "Religious Benevolence as Social Control." *Mississippi Valley Historical Review* 44 (1957) 23–41.

———. *Their Brothers' Keeper: Moral Stewardship in the United States, 1800–1865*. New Brunswick: Rutgers University Press, 1960.

Guild, Reuben Aldridge, ed. *Chaplain Smith and the Baptists: Life, Journals, Letters, and Addresses of the Rev. Hezekiah Smith, D. D., of Haverhill, Massachusetts, 1737–1805*. Philadelphia: American Baptist Publication Society, 1885.

———. *Life, Times, and Correspondence of James Manning*. Boston: Gould and Lincoln, 1864.

Gusfield, Joseph. *Symbolic Crusade; Status Politics and the American Temperance Movement*. Urbana: University of Illinois Press, 1963.

Guthman, Joshua. *Strangers Below: Primitive Baptists and American Culture*. Chapel Hill: The University of North Carolina Press, 2015.

Hamburger, Philip. *Separation of Church and State*. Cambridge, MA: Harvard University Press, 2004.

Harris, Waldo P. *Georgia's First Continuing Baptist Church*. Appling, GA: Kiokee Baptist Church, 1997.

Harriss, Samuel. "Address of the Committee of the United Baptist Churches of Virginia, assembled in the city of Richmond, 8th August, 1789, to the President of the United States of America." In *The Writings of the Late Elder John Leland*, edited by L. F. Greene, 52–54. New York: G. W. Wood, 1845.

Hart, Oliver. *America's Remembrancer, with Respect to her Blessedness and Duty*. Philadelphia: Dobson, 1791.

Haselby, Sam. *The Origins of American Religious Nationalism*. New York: Oxford University Press, 2015.

Hatch, Nathan O. *The Democratization of American Christianity*. New Haven, CT: Yale University Press, 1989.

Haykin, Michael A. G., et al., eds. *Soldiers of Christ: Selections from the Writings of Basily Manly, Sr., and Basil Manly, Jr.* Cape Coral, FL: Founders, 2009.

Harsch, Lloyd. "Who Dat Say Dey Gonna Teach Dem Saints?: Baptist Beginnings in New Orleans to the Founding of the Baptist Bible Institute," *Journal for Baptist Theology and Ministry* 17 (2020) 183–214.

Hart, D. G. *John Williamson Nevin: High Church Calvinist*. Phillipsburg: P&R, 2005.

Hascall, Daniel. *The Elements of Theology, or, The Leading Topics of Christian Theology.* New York: Lewis Colby & Co., 1847.

Haynes, Lemuel. "Liberty Further Extended." In *Black Preacher to White America: The Collected Writings of Lemuel Haynes, 1774-1833*, edited by Richard Furman, 17-23. Brooklyn: Carlson, 1990.

Haynes, Sylvanus. *The Bible Method of Supporting the Gospel Ministry, Exhibited, Illustrated, and Defended.* Exeter: Josiah Richardson, 1819.

———. *A Sermon, Delivered Before His Excellency the Governor.* Randolph: Sereno Wright, 1809.

Heimert, Alan. *Religion and the American Mind: From the Great Awakening to the Revolution.* Cambridge, MA: Harvard University Press, 1966.

Hirrel, Leo P. *Children of Wrath: New School Calvinism and Antebellum Reform.* Lexington: The University Press of Kentucky, 1998.

Holcombe, Henry. "Address to the Friends of Religion." *Georgia Analytical Repository* (September-October, 1802) 215-35.

———. *The First Fruits, in a Series of Letters.* Philadelphia: Ann Cochran, 1812.

———. *A Sermon, Occasioned by the Death of Lieutenant-General George Washington, Late President of the United States of America* (Savannah, 1800). In *Political Sermons of the American Founding Era, 1730-1805*, edited by Ellis Sandoz, 2:1399-414. Indianapolis: Liberty Fund, 1991.

Holifield, E. Brooks. *The Gentlemen Theologians: American Theology in Southern Culture, 1795-1860.* Durham: Duke University Press, 1978.

———. *Theology in America: Christian Thought from the Age of the Puritans to the Civil War.* New Haven, CT: Yale University Press, 2003.

Hollis, Daniel Walker. *University of South Carolina, Volume 1: South Carolina College.* Columbia: University of South Carolina Press, 1951.

Holton, Woody. *Unruly Americans and the Origins of the Constitution.* New York: Hill and Wang, 2007.

Hopkins, Samuel. *A Dialogue Concerning the Slavery of the Africans.* Norwich: Judah P. Spooner, 1776.

Horn, James. *1619: Jamestown and the Forging of American Democracy.* New York: Basic, 2018.

Howe, Daniel Walker. *The Political Culture of the American Whigs.* Chicago: Chicago University Press, 1979.

———. *What Hath God Wrought: The Transformation of America, 1815-1848.* New York: Oxford University Press, 2007.

Howell, Robert Boyle C. *The Early Baptists of Virginia.* Philadelphia: The Bible and Publication Society, 1857.

———. *The Terms of Communion at the Lord's Table.* Philadelphia: American Baptist Publication Society, 1846.

Irons, Charles F. *The Origins of Proslavery Christianity: White and Black Evangelicals in Colonial and Antebellum Virginia.* Chapel Hill: University of North Carolina Press, 2008.

Isaac, Rhys. "Evangelical Revolt: The Nature of Baptists' Challenge to the Traditional Order in Virginia, 1765-1775." *The William and Mary Quarterly* 31 (1974) 345-68.

Jefferson, Thomas. "Letter from Thomas Jefferson to Messrs. Nehemiah Dodge, Ephraim Robbins, and Stephen S. Nelson, a committee of the Danbury Baptist association in the state of Connecticut, January 1, 1802." The Papers of Thomas Jefferson (Manuscript Division, Library of Congress), Series 1, Box 89, December 2, 1801–January 1, 1802.

———. *Notes on the State of Virginia*. Boston: Lilly and Wait, 1832.

Jeter, Jeremiah Bell. *A Memoir of Abner W. Clopton, A.M.: Pastor of Baptist Churches in Charlotte County, Virginia*. Richmond: Yale & Wyatt, 1837.

———. *The Recollections of a Long Life*. Richmond: The Religious Herald Co., 1891.

Johnson, Paul E. *A Shopkeeper's Millennium: Society and Revivals in Rochester, New York, 1815–1837*. New York: Hill and Wang, 2004.

Johnson, Richard Mentor. *Review of a Report of the Committee, To Whom Has Referred the Several Petitions on the Subject of Mails on the Sabbath*. Boston: Peirce and Williams, 1829.

Jones, Charles C. *The Religious Instruction of the Negroes, in the United States*. Savannah: Thomas Purse, 1842.

Jones, Daniel P. *The Economic and Social Transformation of Rural Rhode Island, 1780–1850*. Boston: Northeastern University Press, 1992.

Jones, David. *A Journal of Two Visits Made to Some Nations of Indians on the West Side of the River Ohio, in the Years 1772, 1773*. Burlington: Isaac Collins, 1774.

———. "Indian Affairs." *Philadelphia Aurora* (December 20, 1811).

———. "The Old Indian School Must Be Abandoned." *Philadelphia Aurora* (November 24, 1812).

———. "The Old Indian School Must Be Changed." *Philadelphia Aurora* (November 4, 1812).

Joslin, J., et al. *A History of the Town of Poultney, Vermont, From its Settlement to the Year 1875, with Family and Biographical Sketches and Incidents*. Poultney: J. Joslin, B. Frisbie, F. Ruggles, 1875.

Judson, Adoniram. "Letter on Ornamental and Costly Attire." In *A Memoir of the Life and Labors of the Rev. Adoniram Judson, D.D.*, edited by Francis Wayland, 479–80. Boston: Phillips, Sampson, and Company, 1853.

Juster, Susan. *Disorderly Women: Sexual Politics and Evangelicalism in Revolutionary New England*. Ithaca: Cornell University Press, 1994.

Karp, Matthew. *This Vast Southern Empire: Slaveholders at the Helm of American Foreign Policy*. Cambridge, MA: Harvard University Press, 2016.

Kidd, Thomas S. *American History*. Nashville: B&H Academic, 2019.

———. "A Baptist Abolitionist Appeals to Thomas Jefferson." https://www.thegospelcoalition.org/blogs/evangelical-history/baptist-abolitionist-appeals-thomas-jefferson/.

———. *God of Liberty: A Religious History of the American Revolution*. New York: Basic, 2010.

———. *Thomas Jefferson: A Biography of Spirit and Flesh*. New Haven, CT: Yale University Press, 2022.

Kidd, Thomas S., and Hankins, Barry. *Baptists in America: A History*. New York: Oxford University Press, 2015.

King, Joe. *A History of South Carolina Baptists*. Columbia: The General Board of the South Carolina Baptist Convention, 1964.

Klotter, James C. *Henry Clay: The Man Who Would Be President*. New York: Oxford University Press, 2018.

Koester, Nancy. *Harriet Beecher Stowe: A Spiritual Life*. Grand Rapids: Eerdmans, 2014.

Leland, John. "Address to the Association of the Sons of Liberty, Cheshire, March 4, 1813." In *The Writings of the Late Elder John Leland*, edited by L. F. Greene, 373–75. New York: G. W. Wood, 1845.

———. "Address at a Democratic Meeting Held at Cheshire, August 28, 1834." In *The Writings of the Late Elder John Leland*, edited by L. F. Greene, 651–56. New York: G. W. Wood, 1845.

———. "Address at the Dedication of the Baptist Meeting-House in Lanesborough, February 16, 1829." In *The Writings of the Late Elder John Leland*, edited by L. F. Greene, 547–56. New York: G. W. Wood, 1845.

———. "Address Delivered at the Request of the Republican Committee of Arrangements, at Pittsfield, on the Anniversary of American Independence, July 4, 1824." In *The Writings of the Late Elder John Leland*, edited by L. F. Greene, 501–7. New York: G. W. Wood, 1845.

———. "Address Delivered at Pittsfield, Jan. 8, 1829." In *The Writings of the Late Elder John Leland*, edited by L. F. Greene, 541–46. New York: G. W. Wood, 1845.

———. "A Blow at The Root: Being a Fashionable Fast-Day Sermon, Delivered at Cheshire, April 9, 1801." In *The Writings of the late Elder John Leland*, edited by L. F. Greene, 235–55. New York: G. W. Wood, 1845.

———. "The Book of Job." In *The Writings of the Late Elder John Leland*, edited by L. F. Greene, 706–8. New York: G. W. Wood, 1845.

———. "An Elective Judiciary." In *The Writings of the Late Elder John Leland*, edited by L. F. Greene, 285–300. New York: G. W. Wood, 1845.

———. "Events in the Life of John Leland." In *The Writings of the Late Elder John Leland*, edited by L. F. Greene, 9–40. New York: G. W. Wood, 1845.

———. "Free Thoughts on War." In *The Writings of the Late Elder John Leland*, edited by L. F. Greene, 454–68. New York: G. W. Wood, 1845.

———. "The Government of Christ a Christocracy." In *The Writings of the Late Elder John Leland*, edited by L. F. Greene, 273–82. New York: G. W. Wood, 1845.

———. "Letter to Hon. R. M. Johnson, June 9, 1834." In *The Writings of the Late Elder John Leland*, edited by L. F. Greene, 648–50. New York: G. W. Wood, 1845

———. "The Mosaic Dispensation." *The Writings of the Late Elder John Leland*, edited by L. F. Greene, 665–70. New York: G. W. Wood, 1845.

———. "Parts of a Speech, Delivered at Suffield, Connecticut, on the First Jubilee of the United States." In *The Writings of the Late Elder John Leland*, edited by L. F. Greene, 517–26. New York: G. W. Wood, 1845.

———. *The Rights of Conscience Inalienable*. In *The Writings of the Late Elder John Leland*, edited by L. F. Greene, 179–92. New York: G. W. Wood, 1845.

———. "Short Essays on Government, and the Proposed Revision of the Constitution of Government for the Commonwealth of Massachusetts." In *The Writings of the Late Elder John Leland*, edited by L. F. Greene, 473–79. New York: G. W. Wood, 1845.

———. "Short Sayings." In *The Writings of the Late Elder John Leland*, edited by L. F. Greene, 572–82. New York: G. W. Wood, 1845.

———. "Speech Delivered in the House of Representatives of Massachusetts, on the Subject of Religious Freedom, 1811." In *The Writings of the Late Elder John Leland*, edited by L. F. Greene, 353–58. New York: G. W. Wood, 1845.

———. "Transportation of the Mail." In *The Writings of the Late Elder John Leland*, edited by L. F. Greene, 564–66. New York: G. W. Wood, 1845.

———. "The Virginia Chronicle." In *The Writings of the Late Elder John Leland*, edited by L. F. Greene, 92–124. New York: G. W. Wood, 1845.

———. "The Yankee Spy." In *The Writings of the Late Elder John Leland*, edited by L. F. Greene, 215–29. New York: G. W. Wood, 1845.

———. "Which Has Done the Most Mischief in the World, The Kings-Evil or Priest-Craft?" In *The Writings of the Late Elder John Leland*, edited by L. F. Greene, 484–95. New York: G. W. Wood, 1845.

Leonard, Bill J. *God's Last and Only Hope: The Fragmentation of the Southern Baptist Convention*.Grand Rapids: Eerdmans, 1990.

Lepore, Jill. *The Name of War: King Philip's War and the Origins of American Identity*. New York: Vintage, 1998.

———. *These Truths: A History of the United States*. New York: W. W. Norton & Co., 2018.

Liele, George. "An Account of Several Baptist Churches." In *African American Religious History: A Documentary Witness*, edited by Milton C. Sernett, 44–48. Durham: Duke University Press, 1999.

Lindman, Janet Moore. *Bodies of Belief: Baptist Community in Early America*. Philadelphia: University of Pennsylvania Press, 2008.

Looney, J. Jefferson. *The Papers of Thomas Jefferson: Retirement Series*. 18 vols. Princeton: Princeton University Press, 2005–2022.

Lynd, Samuel W., ed. *Memoir of the Rev. William Staughton, D.D.* Cincinnati: Lincoln, Edmands, & Co., 1834.

Madison, James."The Federalist No. 37." In *The Federalist: A Commentary on the Constitution of the United States*, edited by Robert Scigliano, 221–29. New York: The Modern Library, 2001.

———. "To Edward Livingston, July 10, 1822." In *Letters and Other Writings of James Madison, Vol. III, 1816–1828*. New York: R. Worthington, 1884.

———. "To George Eve, 2 January 1789." https://founders.archives.gov/documents/Madison/01-11-02-0297.

Mallary, Charles D., ed. *Memoirs of Elder Edmund Botsford*. Charleston: W. Riley, 1832.

———. *Memoirs of Elder Jesse Mercer*.New York: John Gray, 1844.

Malone, Dumas. *Jefferson the President: First Term, 1801–1805*. Charlottesville: University of Virginia Press, 2006.

Manly, Basil, Sr. "On the Emancipation of Slaves." In *Soldiers of Christ: Selections from the Writings of Basil Manly, Sr., and Basil Manly, Jr.*, edited by Michael A. G. Haykin, Roger D. Duke, and A. James Fuller, 61–68. Cape Coral: Founders, 2009.

———. "Theological Education in the Southern States." *Southern Baptist and General Intelligencer* n.d. (1835) 170–72.

Manning, James. "To Samuel Stennett, Providence, Nov. 8th, 1783." In *Guild, Life, Times, and Correspondence of James Manning, and the Early History of Brown University*, edited by Reuben Aldridge, 315. Boston: Gould and Lincoln, 1864.

Marsden, George M. *The Evangelical Mind and the New School Presbyterian Experience: A Case Study of Thought and Theology in Nineteenth-Century America*. Eugene, OR: Wipf & Stock, 2003.

Marshall, Abraham. "The Lazy Student's Apology." In *Daniel and Abraham Marshall: Pioneer Baptist Evangelists to the South*, edited by Thomas Ray, 204–5. Springfield: Particular Baptist, 2006.

———. "A Sermon, on II Kings VI. 6 'The Iron Did Swim.'" In *Daniel and Abraham Marshall: Pioneer Baptist Evangelists to the South*, edited by Thomas Ray, 195–203. Springfield: Particular Baptist, 2006.

Marty, Martin. "Baptistification Takes Over." *Christianity Today* n.d. (1983) 33–36.

Mason, Matthew. *Slavery and Politics in the Early American Republic*. Chapel Hill: The University of North Carolina Press, 2006.

Mathews, Donald G. *Religion in the Old South*. Chicago: The University of Chicago Press, 1977.

Maulden, Kristopher. *The Federalist Frontier: Settler Politics in the Old Northwest, 1783–1840*. Columbia: University of Missouri Press, 2019.

Maxcy, Jonathan. "An Address, Delivered to the Candidates for the Baccalaureate of Rhode Island College, at the Anniversary Commencement, September 2, 1801." In *The Literary Remains of Rev. Jonathan Maxcy, D.D.*, edited by Romeo Elton, 317–27.New York: A. V. Blake, 1844.

———. "An Address, Delivered to the Graduates of Rhode Island College, at the Anniversary Commencement, in the Baptist Meeting-House in Providence, September 5, 1798." In *The Literary Remains of the Rev. Jonathan Maxcy*, edited by Romeo Elton, 309–14. New York: A. V. Blake, 1844.

———. "A Discourse, Delivered in the Chapel of South Carolina College, July 4th, 1819, at the Request of the Inhabitants of Columbia." In *The Literary Remains of the Rev. Jonathan Maxcy, D.D.*, edited by Romeo Elton, 279–95. New York: A. V. Blake, 1844.

———. "A Discourse Designed to Explain the Doctrine of the Atonement." In *The Atonement: Discourses and Treatises by Edwards, Smalley, Maxcy, Emmons, Griffin, Burge, and Weeks*, edited by Edwards A. Park, 87–110. Boston: Congregational Board of Publication, 1859.

———. "An Oration Delivered at the First Congregational Meeting House, in Providence, on the Fourth of July, 1799." In *The Literary Remains of the Rev. Jonathan Maxcy, D.D.*, edited by Romeo Elton, 383–94. New York: A. V. Blake, 1844.

———. "An Oration Delivered Before the Providence Association of Mechanics and Manufacturers, at the Annual Election, April 13, 1795." In *The Literary Remains of the Rev. Jonathan Maxcy, D.D.*, edited by Romeo Elton, 351–66. New York: A. V. Blake, 1844.

———. "An Oration Delivered in the Baptist Meeting House in Providence." In *The Literary Remains of the Rev. Jonathan Maxcy, D.D.*, edited by Romeo Elton, 367–77. New York: A. V. Blake, 1844.

McBeth, H. Leon. *The Baptist Heritage: Four Centuries of Baptist Witness*. Nashville: Broadman, 1987.

McClymond, Michael J. *The Devil's Redemption: A New History and Interpretation of Christian Universalism, Vol. 1*. Grand Rapids: Baker Academic, 2018.

McCoy, Isaac. *History of Baptist Indian Missions*. Washington: William M. Morrison, 1840.

———. *Remarks on the Practicability of Indian Reform, Embracing their Colonization*. New York: Gray and Bunce, 1829.

McLoughlin, William G. *The Cherokees and Christianity, 1794–1870: Essays on Acculturation and Cultural Persistence*, edited by Walter H. Conser Jr. Athens: The University of Georgia Press, 2008.

———. *Isaac Backus and the American Pietistic Tradition*. Boston: Little, Brown and Company, 1967.

———, ed. *Isaac Backus on Church, State, and Calvinism: Pamphlets, 1754-1789*. Cambridge, MA: Harvard University Press, 1968.

———. *Soul Liberty: The Baptists' Struggle in New England, 1630-1833*. Hanover: Brown University Press, 1991.

Meachum, John Berry. *An Address to all the Colored Citizens of the United States*. Philadelphia: King and Baird, 1846.

Meacham, Jon. *Thomas Jefferson: The Art of Power*. New York: Random, 2012.

Menikoff, Aaron. *Politics and Piety: Baptist Social Reform in America, 1770-1860*. Eugene, OR: Pickwick, 2014.

Mercer, Jesse. "African Colonization." *The Christian Index* (15 June 1837).

———. *History of the Georgia Baptist Association*. Washington: n.d., 1838.

———. "Ten Letters, Addressed to the Rev. Cyrus White, in reference to the Scriptural View of the Atonement." Washington, GA, 1830.

Merrill, Daniel. *Balaam Disappointed: A Thanksgiving Sermon, Delivered at Nottingham-West, April 13, 1815*. Concord: Isaac & W. R. Hill, 1815.

Messer, Asa. "An Address, Delivered to the Graduates of Brown University, at the Commencement, September 4, 1811." In *The Literary Remains of the Rev. Jonathan Maxcy, D.D.*, edited by Romeo Elton, 415-20. New York: A. V. Blake, 1844.

———. "A Discourse, Delivered in the Chapel of Rhode Island College, to the Senior Class, on the Sunday Preceding Their Commencement, 1799." In *The Literary Remains of the Rev. Jonathan Maxcy, D.D.*, edited by Romeo Elton, 423-34. New York: A. V. Blake, 1844.

Miller, Nicholas P. *The Religious Roots of the First Amendment: Dissenting Protestants and the Separation of Church and State*. New York: Oxford University Press, 2012.

Minutes of the Georgia Baptist Association, held at Williams' Creek, Warren County, Georgia, on the 12th, 13th, and 15th of Oct. 1838. Washington: Christian Index, 1838.

Minutes of the Shaftesbury Association. Bennington, VT: n.d., 1792.

Morgan, Edmund S. *American Slavery, American Freedom: The Ordeal of Colonial Virginia*. New York: W. W. Norton & Company, 1975.

———. "Ezra Stiles and Timothy Dwight." *Massachusetts Historical Society, Proceedings* 72 (1957-1960) 101-17.

Morris, B. F. *Christian Life and Character of the Civil Institutions of the United States, Developed in the Official and Historical Annals of the Republic*. Philadelphia: George W. Childs, 1864.

Morris, B. F., ed. *The Life of Thomas Morris: Pioneer and Long a Legislator of Ohio, and U.S. Senator from 1833 to 1839*. Cincinatti: Moore, Wilstach, Keys & Overend, 1856.

Najar, Monica. *Evangelizing the South: A Social History of Church and State in Early America*. New York: Oxford University Press, 2008.

Nelson, William H. *The American Tory*. Boston: Beacon, 1964.

Nettles, Thomas J. "Richard Furman." In *Baptist Theologians*, edited by David Dockery and Timothy George, 140-64. Nashville: Broadman, 1990.

Nichols, Joel A. "Georgia: The Thirteenth Colony." In *Disestablishment and Religious Dissent: Church-State Relations in the New American States 1776-1833*, edited by Carl H. Esback and Jonathan J. Den Hartog, 225-48. Columbia: University of Missouri Press, 2019.

Noll, Mark A. *America's God: From Jonathan Edwards to Abraham Lincoln*. New York: Oxford University Press, 2002.

———. "Missouri, Denmark Vesey, Biblical Proslavery, and a Crisis for *Sola Scriptura*." In *Every Leaf, Line, and Letter: Evangelicals and the Bible from the 1730s to the Present*, edited by Timothy Larsen, 97–122. Downers Grove, IL: IVP Academic, 2021.

———. *Princeton and the Republic (1768–1822): The Search for a Christian Enlightenment in the Era of Samuel Stanhope Smith*. Vancouver: Regent College, 1989.

O'Brien, Michael. *Intellectual Life and the American South, 1810–1860: An Abridged Edition of Conjectures of Order*. Chapel Hill: The University of North Carolina Press, 2010.

Osgood, David. *The Wonderful Works of God Are To Be Remembered*. In *Political Sermons of the American Founding Era, 1730–1805*, edited by Ellis Sandoz, 2:1217–34. Indianapolis: Liberty Fund, 1998.

Park, Edwards A. ed. *The Atonement: Discourses and Treatises by Edwards, Smalley, Maxcy, Emmons, Griffin, Burge, and Weeks*. Boston: Congregational Board of Publication, 1859.

Parker, Daniel. *A Public Address to the Baptist Society, and Friends of Religion in General on the Principles and Practice of the Baptist Board of Foreign Missions for the United States of America*. Vincennes: Stout & Osborn, 1820.

Parkinson, William. *A Sermon, Delivered in the Meeting House of the First Baptist Church, in the City of New York*. New York: John Tiebout, 1812.

Particular Baptist Committee at Black Rock Meeting House. "Address to the Particular Baptist Churches of the 'Old School' in the United States." *Signs of the Times* 1 (1832) 5.

Paschal, George Washington. *History of North Carolina Baptists, Vol. II*. Raleigh: North Carolina Baptist State Convention, 1955.

Patterson, James A. *James Robinson Graves: Staking the Boundaries of Baptist Identity*. 2nd ed. Knoxville: The University of Tennessee Press, 2020.

Pattison, R. E. *Eulogy on Rev. Jeremiah Chaplin, D.D.* Boston: William D. Ticknor & Co., 1843.

Pendleton, James Madison. *Reminiscences of a Long Life*. Louisville: Press Baptist Book Concern, 1891.

Perdue, Theda, and Michael D. Green. *The Cherokee Nation and the Trail of Tears*. New York: Penguin, 2007.

Pitts, Walter F., Jr. *Old Ship of Zion: The Afro-Baptist Ritual in the African Diaspora*. New York: Oxford University Press, 1993.

Polkinhorn, Charles. "City of Washington, Dec. 12, 1822." *Signs of the Times* 1 (1833) 47.

Poore, Benjamin Perley, ed. *The Federal and State Constitutions: Colonial Charters, and Other Organic Laws of the United States*. Washington, DC: Government Printing Office, 1878.

Porterfield, Amanda. *Conceived in Doubt: Religion and Politics in the New American Nation*. Chicago: The University of Chicago Press, 2012.

Proceedings of the Baptist Convention for Missionary Purposes; Held in Philadelphia, in May, 1814. Philadelphia: Ann Coles, 1814.

Ray, Thomas. *Daniel and Abraham Marshall: Pioneer Baptist Evangelists to the South*. Springfield: Particular Baptist Press, 2006.

Religious Herald. "The Influence of Religion on the Laws of Nations." *Religious Herald* (August 22, 1828) 132.

Richey, Russell E. *Early American Methodism.* Bloomington: Indiana University Press, 1991.

Riley, Padraig. *Slavery and the Democratic Conscience: Political Life in Jeffersonian America.* Philadelphia: University of Pennsylvania Press, 2016.

Robinson, David, ed. *William Ellery Channing: Selected Writings.* New York: Paulist Press, 1985.

Rogers, James A. *Richard Furman: Life and Legacy.* Macon, GA: Mercer University Press, 2001.

Rowe, David L. *God's Strange Work: William Miller and the End of the World.* Grand Rapids: Eerdmans, 2008.

Rowland, Lawrence S., Jr., et al. *The History of Beaufort County, South Carolina: Volume 1, 1514-1861.* Columbia: University of South Carolina Press, 1996.

Saillant, John. *Black Puritan, Black Republican: The Life and Thought of Lemuel Haynes, 1753-1833.* New York: Oxford University Press, 2003.

Schaff, Philip. *America: A Sketch of Its Political, Social, and Religious Character.* New York: C. Scribner, 1855.

Scully, Randolph Ferguson. *Religion and the Making of Nat Turner's Virginia: Baptist Community and Conflict, 1740-1840.* Charlottesville: University of Virginia Press, 2008.

Sellers, Charles. *The Market Revolution: Jacksonian America, 1815-1846.* New York: Oxford University Press, 1991.

Semple, Robert Baylor. *A History of the Rise and Progress of the Baptists in Virginia.* Richmond: Pitt & Dickinson, 1894.

Sherwood, Adiel. *Strictures on the Sentiments of the Kehukee Association.* Milledgeville: Camak & Ragland, 1828.

Signs of the Times. "Address to the Particular Baptist Churches of the 'Old School,' in the United States." *Signs of the Times* 1 (1832) 3.

———. "Integrity." *Signs of the Times* 2 (1834) 191.

Sklar, Kathryn Kish. *Catharine Beecher, A Study in American Domesticity.* New York: W. W. Norton, 1973.

Sobel, Mechal. *Trabelin' On: The Slave Journey to an Afro-Baptist Faith.* Princeton: Princeton University Press, 1988.

Smith, Craig Bruce. *American Honor: The Creation of the Nation's Ideals during the Revolutionary Era.* Chapel Hill: The University of North Carolina Press, 2018.

Smith, Eric C. *John Leland: A Jeffersonian Baptist in Early America.* New York: Oxford University Press, 2022.

———. "'Oh That All Bigotry was Rooted Out of the Earth!': The Evangelical Catholicity of Oliver Hart and the Regular Baptists." *Southeastern Review* 7 (2016) 86-107.

———. *Oliver Hart and the Rise of Baptist America.* New York: Oxford University Press, 2020.

Smith, Miles, IV. "South Carolina." In *Disestablishment and Religious Dissent: Church-State Relations in the New American States 1776-1833,* edited by Carl H. Esback and Jonathan J. Den Hartog, 181-202. Columbia: University of Missouri Press, 2019.

Smithers, Gregory D. *The Cherokee Diaspora: An Indigenous History of Migration, Resettlement, and Identity.* New Haven, CT: Yale University Press, 2015.

Snyder, Robert Arthur. "William T. Brantly (1787–1845): A Southern Unionist and the Breakup of the Triennial Convention." Louisville: The Southern Baptist Theological Seminary, PhD diss., 2005.

Spangler, Jewel L. *Virginians Reborn: Anglican Monopology, Evangelical Dissent, and the Rise of the Baptists in the Late Eighteenth Century*. Charlottesville: University of Virginia Press, 2008.

Spencer, John H. *A History of Kentucky Baptists*. Cincinnati: J. R. Baumes, 1885.

Staudenraus, P. J. *The African Colonization Movement*. New York: Columbia University Press, 1961.

Staughton, William. *Sermon, Delivered in the Capitol of the United States*. Washington: Columbian Office, 1826.

Stiles, Ezra. *The United States Elevated to Glory and Honor*. New Haven, CT: Thomas & Samuel Green, 1783.

Stillman, Samuel. *A Sermon Preached Before the Honorable Council, and the Honorable House of Representatives of the State of Massachusetts-Bay, in New England, at Boston, May 26, 1779*. Boston: T. and J. Fleet, 1779.

———. *Select Sermons on Doctrinal and Practical Subjects*. Boston: Manning & Loring, 1808.

———. *Thoughts on the French Revolution*. Boston: Manning & Loring, 1795.

Stowe, Harriet Beecher. *The Key to Uncle Tom's Cabin*. London; Clarke, Beeton, and Co., 1853.

Stout, Harry S. *American Aristocrats: A Family, a Fortune, and the Making of American Capitalism*. New York: Basic, 2017.

———. *The New England Soul: Preaching and Religious Culture in Colonial New England*. New York: Oxford University Press, 2012.

Tate, Gayle T. "Free Black Resistance in the Antebellum Era, 1830 to 1860." *Journal of Black Studies* 28 (1998) 213–22.

Taylor, Alan. *American Republics: A Continental History of the United States, 1783–1850*. New York: W. W. Norton, 2021.

Taylor, J. B. *Biography of Elder Lott Carey*. Baltimore: Armstrong & Berry, 1837.

Taylor, John. *Baptists on the American Frontier: A History of Ten Baptist Churches of which the Author has been Alternatively a Member*. Edited by Chester Raymond Young. Macon, GA: Mercer University Press, 1995.

Thompson, C. Bradley. *America's Revolutionary Mind: A Moral History of the American Revolution and the Declaration That Defined It*. New York: Encounter, 2019.

Todd, Obbie Tyler. "Baptist Federalism: Religious Liberty and Public Virtue in the Early Republic." *The Journal of Church and State* 63 (2021) 440–60.

———. "The Populist Puritan: Jonathan Edwards and the Rise of American Populism." In *Jonathan Edwards within the Enlightenment: Controversy, Experience, and Thought*, edited by John T. Lowe and Daniel N. Gullotta, 137–52. Gottingen: Vandenhoeck & Ruprecht, 2020.

———. "The Sainted Furman: Richard Furman as America's Most Influential Baptist." *The Southern Reformed Theological Journal* (2020) 99–120.

———. "Southern Yankees: Southern Baptist Clergy in the Antebellum North (1812–1861)." *Themelios* 47 (2022) 116–29.

Tomek, Beverly C. *Colonization and its Discontents: Emancipation, Emigration, and Antislavery in Antebellum Pennsylvania*. New York: New York University Press, 2011.

Torbet, Robert G. *A Social History of the Philadelphia Baptist Association: 1707—1940*. Philadelphia, 1944.

Townsend, Leah. *South Carolina Baptists, 1670–1805*. Florence: The Florence Printing Company, 1935.

Tupper, H. A. *The First Century of The First Baptist Church of Richmond, Virginia 1780–1880*. Richmond: Carlton McCarthy, 1880.

———. *Two Centuries of the First Baptist Church of South Carolina 1683–1883*. Baltimore: R. H. Woodward and Company, 1889.

Turner, John G. *They Knew They Were Pilgrims: Plymouth Colony and the Contest for American Liberty*. New Haven, CT: Yale University Press, 2020.

Tyler-McGraw, Marie. *An African Republic: Black and White Virginians in the Making of Liberia*. Chapel Hill: The University of North Carolina Press, 2007.

Van Horne, William E. "Revolutionary War Letters of the Reverend William Van Horne." *The Western Pennsylvania Historical Magazine* 53 (1970) 105–38.

Washington, George. "Farewell Address." In *The Papers of George Washington*, September 19, 1796. http://gwpapers.virginia.edu/documents/washingtons-farewell-address/.

———. "To the Corporation of Rhode Island College." In *Life, Times, and Correspondence of James Manning*, edited by Reuben Aldridge Guild, 435. Boston: Gould and Lincoln, 1864.

———. "To the United Baptist Churches of Virginia, May 1789." https://founders.archives.gov/documents/Washington/05-02-02-0309.

Wayland, Francis. *The Death of Ex-Presidents in Occasional Discourses*. Boston: J. Loring, 1833.

———. *Notes on the Principles and Practices of Baptist Churches*. New York: Sheldon, Blakeman, & Co., 1857.

Wayland, Francis, and H. L. Wayland. *A Memoir of the Life and Labors of Francis Wayland, Vol. I*. New York: Sheldon & Company, 1868.

Wayland, Francis, and Richard Fuller. *Domestic Slavery Considered as a Scriptural Institution*. New York: Lewis Colby & Co., 1847.

White, Pliny H. *Jonas Galusha, The Fifth Governor of Vermont, a Memoir*. Montpelier: E. P. Walton, 1866.

Wigger, John. *American Saint: Francis Asbury and the Methodists*. New York: Oxford University Press, 2009.

Wilentz, Sean. *The Rise of American Democracy: Jefferson to Lincoln*. New York: W. W. Norton & Co., 2005.

Williams, Daniel. "A New Era in Their History: Isaac McCoy's Indian Canaan and the Baptist Triennial Convention." *The Confluence* (Spring/Summer 2016) 57–61.

Wills, Gregory A. *Democratic Religion: Freedom, Authority, and Church Discipline in the Baptist South, 1785–1900*. New York: Oxford University Press, 1997.

———. *The First Baptist Church of Columbia, South Carolina, 1809 to 2002*. Nashville: Fields, 2003.

Wilson, James Grant, and John Fiske, eds. *Appleton's Cyclopaedia of American Biography*, New York: D. Appleton and Co., 1888.

Wimberly, Dan B. *Cherokee in Controversy: The Life of Jesse Bushyhead*. Macon, GA: Mercer University Press, 2017.

Wolever, Terry, ed. *The Life, Journal and Works of David Jones, 1736–1820*. Springfield: Particular Baptist Press, 2007.

———. *The Life and Ministry of John Gano, 1727–1804*, Vol. I. Springfield: Particular Baptist Press, 1998.

Wood, Gordon S. *The Creation of the American Republic: 1776–1787*. Chapel Hill: The University of North Carolina Press, 1998.

———. *The Radicalism of the American Revolution*. New York: Vintage, 1993.

Wood, Peter H. *Black Majority: Negroes in Colonial South Carolina from 1670 through the Stono Rebellion*. New York: W. W. Norton & Company, 1974.

Woodson, Hortense C. *Giant in the Land: The Life of William B. Johnson*. Springfield: Particular Baptist Press, 2005.

Wright, Stephen. *History of the Shaftesbury Association, from 1781 to 1853*. Troy: A. G. Johnson, 1853.

Yarnell, Malcolm B., III. "Early American Political Theology." In *First Freedom: The Beginning and End of Religious Liberty*, edited by Jason G. Duesing et al., 49–79. Nashville: B&H Academic, 2016.

Zvesper, John. *Political Philosophy and Rhetoric: A Study of the Origins of American Party Politics*. London: Cambridge University Press, 1977.

Index of Subjects

abolitionism, 4, 48, 103, 106, 107, 116–18, 143
Alien and Sedition Acts, 77, 87
American Revolution, xiv, 1, 4, 5, 18, 20, 21, 22, 24, 33, 35, 36, 41, 44–46, 48, 49, 52, 53, 59, 93, 123, 129, 133, 137, 138, 155, 160, 187, 193, 205
An Appeal to the Public, 21
Anglicans, 18–20, 97, 167, 174, 201
Anti-Federalists, 12, 93, 185

Balkcom case, 12
Baptists
    American, 24, 47, 142, 149, 159–60
    anti-mission, xiii, 139, 140–46, 149, 197–99
    black, xiii, xvii, 3, 4, 5, 104–5, 108, 147, 190, 194, 196, 201
    Calvinist, xiii
    English, 22, 24, 27, 47, 48, 138, 142, 145, 146–47, 149–52, 159, 167
    Free Will, xiii, xvii, 192, 196–97
    General, xiii, 167
    Hard Shell, 139
    Landmark, xiii, xvii, 68
    Missionary, xiii, 141, 142, 144, 145, 150, 151, 161, 176
    Native American, xvii, 127, 183–84
    Particular, xiii, 198
    Primitive, xiii, 66, 139, 145–46, 165, 173, 197–99
    Regular, xiii, 21, 59, 151, 167, 173, 174n54
    Separate, xiii, 2, 18, 22, 36, 39, 59, 77, 166, 168, 173, 174n54, 176, 184
    Six-Principle, 97
    Two-Seed-in-the-Spirit, xiii
    United, xiii, 56, 59
    white, 2, 7, 12, 14, 24, 41, 112, 127, 129, 187, 191, 197, 205
Baptist Missionary Society, 145, 150, 159
Bastille, 154
Battle of Lexington, 36
Battle of New Orleans, 69, 70, 158
Bill for Establishing Religious Freedom, 67, 68
Bill of Rights, 67, 68, 74, 129
Boston Tea Party, 35

Calvinism, xiii, 10, 27, 30, 143, 151
Cambridge Platform, 51
chaplaincy, 8, 23, 45, 68, 79, 91, 93, 94, 108, 123, 190, 206
Charleston Confession, 92
civil disobedience, 24, 35, 37
Civil War, 191, 193, 203, 206
colonization, 5, 107–9, 116, 125–26
Congregationalists, 18, 23, 28, 31, 36, 37, 40, 41, 42, 45, 74, 85, 113, 127, 138, 141, 145, 146, 152–53, 165, 166, 168, 174, 183, 184, 201, 203, 204
conscience, 2, 3, 22, 29, 38, 42, 47, 57, 71, 72, 76, 79, 80, 93, 94, 114, 129, 170, 180

Index of Subjects

Continental Congress, 37, 38, 54, 85, 91, 204
Constitution, 1, 2, 53–54, 56, 58, 59, 67, 68, 74, 75, 76, 78, 79, 84, 91–96, 109, 113, 186, 207
corrupt bargain, 188

debt, 69, 77, 78, 161
Declaration of Independence, 10, 44, 73, 91, 94, 193–94, 206
deism, 13, 14, 15, 48, 63, 67, 80, 85, 86, 89, 90
Democratic Party, xvii, 110, 188, 204

economy, 161
education, 2, 57, 84, 96–101, 131, 140, 141, 142, 147, 151, 172–86
Elkhorn Association, 61
emancipation, 109, 113, 118, 120, 127
Enlightenment, 15, 63, 143, 203
Episcopalians, 20, 31, 39, 49, 50, 130, 163, 165, 194–95, 199n50
Era of Good Feelings, 106, 169, 205
establishment/disestablishment of religion, 7, 9, 10, 11, 14, 16, 19, 20, 31, 35, 38, 39, 47, 91, 95, 96, 113, 130, 163, 174, 181, 191, 202–7
evangelism, 31

farming, 1–2, 161
First Amendment, xvi, 6, 7, 11, 54, 68, 85, 91, 183, 191, 207
Federalist Papers, 58, 91
Federalists, xv, xvii, 2, 14–15, 23, 24, 25, 32, 58, 62, 63, 64, 65, 69, 70, 72, 76, 78, 80, 82–101, 134, 140, 153, 155, 156, 157, 158, 165, 168, 185–86, 205
Fourth of July, 4, 12, 87, 93, 112
France, xiv, 14, 15, 46, 84, 86–88, 133, 149–51, 154, 156
Freemasonry, 8
Friends of Humanity, 118, 128

Glebes, 19

Hartford Convention, 25, 69, 70, 101, 153

Independents, 22, 167

Jay's Treaty, 70, 131, 153
Jews, 31, 79

King Philip's War, 120

Liberty Party, 116
Louisiana Purchase, 69
loyalism, 4, 17, 38, 40, 41, 42, 161

Manifest Destiny, 133
Memorial and Remonstrance, 67
Methodists, 1, 11, 25, 26, 135, 150, 167, 199n50
Missouri Compromise, 109, 181
Munster, Germany, 16, 164
Muslims, 31, 32, 79, 170

Native Americans, 1
nationalism, 136–53
nativism, 87, 143
New Divinity, 97
Northwest Ordinance, 115
Notes on the State of Virginia, 6–7, 63
Nullification Crisis, 110, 153, 188, 192

office-holding, 32–33, 76–77

pacificism, 156
populism, 146, 191, 198, 204, 207
poverty, 22, 24
Presbyterians, 22, 39, 45, 105, 163, 164, 167, 168, 197, 199n50
Protestantism, 29, 36, 130, 146, 163, 188

Quebec Act, 37

religious tests, 31, 32, 74, 78
Republicans, xv, xvii, 2, 7, 8, 12, 13, 14, 15, 18, 23, 24, 60–81, 96, 101, 117, 132, 134, 135, 154–55, 157, 158, 161, 185–86, 205
revivalism, xiii, 25, 26, 52, 66, 75, 141, 145, 164, 167, 172–74, 192–93
Revolution of 1800, 12, 66
The Rights of Conscience Inalienable, 71–72

Index of Subjects

Roman Catholicism, 7, 14–15, 27, 30, 37, 143, 164, 170, 188

Sabbath, 8, 30, 155
Saybrook Platform, 51
secession, 69
Sons of Liberty, 156
Southern Baptist Convention, 99, 110, 126, 127, 188, 192, 195, 206
Southern Baptist Theological Seminary, 98, 110, 144, 191, 192, 196
Standing Order, 2, 18, 22, 36, 39, 41, 46, 50, 61, 65, 78, 96, 141, 145, 153, 168, 173, 203
States' Rights, 69, 153, 191
suffrage, 76, 117, 188
Sunday Mail Prohibition, 9

taxes, xiii, xv, 10, 12, 16, 24, 34, 36, 37, 38, 39, 43, 70, 77, 78, 103, 146, 181
Three-Fifths Compromise, 3, 113–14
temperance, 137, 141, 152
Trail of Tears, 126–27, 137, 190
Treaty of Ghent, 69, 70, 158

Treaty of Paris, 48
Triennial Convention, 22, 101, 108, 110, 125, 127, 138–39, 140, 145, 146, 149, 150, 153, 159–60, 175, 176, 179, 186, 191, 193, 206
Truth is Great and Will Prevail, 34, 42

Unitarians, 23, 66, 85, 203
Universalists, 48, 143, 166

Valley Forge, 94
Virginia Statute for Religious Freedom, xiv-xv, 10–11

War Hawks, 53, 156
War of 1812, 1, 8, 46, 53, 62, 68, 69, 85, 137, 153–62, 205
Warren Association, 17–18, 24, 37, 38, 85, 184
Wealth of Nations, 12
Westminster Confession, xv
Whig Party, xvii, 147, 148, 188, 202
Worcester v. Georgia (1832), 127, 152

XYZ Affair, 154

Index of Names

Adams, John, 13, 15, 38, 39, 40, 58, 66, 77, 84, 85, 87, 90, 134, 153, 203–4, 206–7
Adams, John Quincy, 115, 188–89, 205
Adams, Samuel, 38, 39, 54, 204
Alden, Noah, 24, 74
Allen, John, 43, 103
Angel, John, 44
Armitage, Thomas, 23
Arnold, Benedict, 90
Asbury, Francis, 11
Augustine, 132
Austin, Joshua, 22

Backus, Isaac, xv, 2, 7, 18, 21, 22, 23, 24, 27, 29, 30, 34, 35–39, 42–43, 46–47, 50–51, 72, 74, 76, 78, 79–80, 82, 85, 103, 106, 121, 122, 173, 176, 204
Bailyn, Bernard, 15,
Baldwin, Thomas, 3, 18, 23, 33, 51, 58, 60–62, 76, 77, 79, 80, 101, 102, 128, 131, 135, 136, 140–41, 158, 159, 168, 170, 179, 186, 201
Bancroft, George, 203–4
Barrow, David, 117–19
Beebe, Gilbert, 197–98
Blood, Caleb, 30, 95
Bonaparte, Napoleon, 70, 133, 150
Botsford, Edmund, 149–50, 167, 190
Boyce, James P., 192, 196
Bradford, William, 35
Bradford, William (Plymouth), 51
Brantly, W. T., 140, 156, 187, 194

Broaddus, Andrew, 108, 130, 131
Broadus, John A., 192
Brown, Amasa, 155, 161–62
Brown, John and Nicholas, 97, 103
Brown, Moses, 105
Brown, Obadiah, 9, 108
Bryan, Andrew, 20–21, 196
Bunyan, John, 152
Burgess, Allison, 107
Burr, Aaron, 58, 115
Bushyhead, Jesse, 113, 127, 137
Butler, Elizur, 127
Butler, Ezra, 34
Byrd, James P., 39, 112

Calhoun, John C., 106, 110, 156
Calvin, John, 27, 29
Carey, Lott, 5, 11–12, 108
Carey, William, 145, 149, 159, 161
Carwardine, Richard J., 147
Chandler, James, 41
Chaplin, Jeremiah, 181–82
Chase, Philander, xiv
Caswall, Henry, xiv
Clay, Henry, 188–89, 202
Coke, Thomas, 150
Colgate, William, 108
Constantine, 26, 178
Cook, Harvey T., 25, 191
Cook, Joseph, 151
Cook, William, 42
Cornwallis, Charles, 44, 91
Covell, Lemuel, 185
Craig, Elijah, 197
Craig, Lewis, 202n56

Index of Names

Crane, William, 108

Dagg, John L., 155
Dargan, E. C., 20
Den Hartog, Jonathan J., 67, 83, 85
Dessaussure, Henry William, 139
Dockery, Alfred, 188
Drayton, William Henry, 37, 45
Dreisbach, Daniel, 83
Dwight, Timothy, xv, 84, 88, 98, 138–39, 140–41, 144, 168

Eaton, Isaac, 185
Edwards, Jonathan, 26, 29, 97, 98, 165
Edwards, Morgan, 41, 83, 91, 161
Elder, Robert, 155
Eliot, Andrew, 37
Esbeck, Carl H., 67
Eve, George, xiv
Ewing, John, 48

Fea, John, 143
Fletcher, Asaph, 11, 167, 205
Fletcher, Samuel, 17
Fossett, Peter, 115
Foster, Benjamin, 97
Franklin, Benjamin, 15, 94, 143
Frazier, Gregg L., 42
Fuller, Andrew, 145, 151–52
Fuller, Richard, 193–96, 204
Furman, Richard, 9, 15, 19, 20, 21, 32, 44, 45, 48, 50, 52, 55, 58, 61, 88, 98, 99–101, 110–12, 130, 139–40, 149, 155, 160–61, 163, 164, 167, 171, 176, 186, 191

Galusha, Jonas, 108, 205–6
Galusha, Elon, 206
Gano, Joanna, 8
Gano, John, 8, 23, 95, 124
Gano, John Stites, 124–25, 133–34
Gano, Sarah, 49
Gano, Stephen, 8, 49, 95, 108, 115, 133, 183
George, David, 5
Greene, Nathanael, 15
Grenz, Stanley, 8
Grimke, John F., 139

Hamburger, Philip, 83
Hamilton, Alexander, 15, 58, 77
Hancock, John, 54
Hankins, Barry, 17, 47, 75, 103, 193
Hart, Oliver, 19, 20, 45, 83, 92, 93, 97, 99, 101, 151, 167
Harrison, William Henry, 125, 148
Hascall, Daniel, 182–83
Haselby, Sam, 138–41
Hatch, Nathan, 79, 83, 140, 172–73, 175
Haynes, Lemuel, 36
Haynes, Sylvanus, 24, 25, 29, 75, 78, 171, 179
Helwys, Thomas, 27
Henry, Patrick, xiv, 10, 54, 55, 67
Hitchcock, Enos, 45
Holcombe, Henry, 10, 14, 86, 88, 93, 95–96, 101, 156–57, 165, 194
Hollis, Thomas, 37, 173
Holman, Jesse Lynch, 116, 149, 188–90
Holmes, Obadiah, 39
Hooper, William, 195
Hopkins, Samuel, 36, 165
Howe, Daniel Walker, xvii, 7, 165
Howell, R. B. C., 144
Hull, Justus, 183
Hume, David, 90
Hutchinson, Anne, 39

Isaac, Rhys, 19

Jackson, Andrew, 70, 71, 88, 110, 113, 116, 124, 125–27, 137, 158, 169, 188–91, 205
Jefferson, Thomas, xv, 2, 3, 5, 6, 10, 11, 12, 13, 15, 18, 33, 54, 55, 57, 58, 63, 65, 66, 67, 68, 69, 72, 82, 84, 85, 88, 90, 107, 115, 118–20, 133, 134, 136, 146, 154, 161, 189, 203, 206–7
Jenckes, Daniel, 97
Jeter, Jeremiah Bell, 106, 108, 158, 161, 162, 173–77
Johnson, Richard, 9, 189–91
Johnson, William B., 99, 110, 112, 149, 164
Jones, Charles C., 105

Index of Names

Jones, David, 1–2, 8, 45–46, 47, 53, 68, 79, 123–24, 126, 127, 136, 138, 155, 156, 185
Jones, Evan, 127, 137, 190–91
Jones, Horatio Gates, 53
Judson, Adoniram, 145, 146, 152, 159, 199–200
Judson, Ann, 146

Karp, Matthew, 106
Kidd, Thomas S., 17, 47, 75, 83, 103, 193
King George III, 16, 37, 41
King Louis XVI, 87

Laurens, Henry, 15
Lee, Richard, 17
Leland, Aaron, 34
Leland, John, xiv, xv, 2, 6–7, 9, 18, 22, 24, 26, 28–29, 31, 32, 33, 34, 43, 49, 52, 53, 54, 58, 60, 64–68, 70, 72, 73, 75–81, 82, 96, 97, 113–14, 120, 122, 131–34, 149, 151, 153, 156–58, 161, 168–70, 178–79, 183–84, 186, 189–90, 202–3, 205
Lepore, Jill, 94
Liele, George, 4, 41
Lincoln, Abraham, 115, 118, 195, 202
Lincoln, Thomas, 115
Lindman, Janet Moore, 103
Locke, John, 29, 30, 80, 90, 112, 113, 122–23
Lumpkin, Wilson, 124, 126, 127, 191
Luther, Martin, 27

Madison, James, xiv, 10, 18, 35–36, 44, 54, 55, 61, 67, 68, 69, 75, 78, 91, 124, 155, 156, 158, 189, 205
Manly Sr., Basil, 109–10, 112, 191–92
Manning, James, 1, 12, 22, 23, 24, 25, 27, 40, 41, 46, 48, 57, 83, 85, 87, 91, 95, 96, 98, 106, 129, 133, 138, 154, 163, 165, 168, 176–77, 181, 183–86, 200
Marshall, Abraham, 21, 63, 72
Marshall, Daniel, 20, 21
Marshall, John, 127
Marty, Martin, xvi, 193
Mathews, Donald G., 3

Maxcy, Jonathan, 12–13, 23, 29, 30, 31, 53, 55, 58, 66, 87, 88, 92, 97, 98–99, 112, 121, 134, 135, 140, 151, 154, 165–66, 181–82
Maxcy, Levi, 12
McCoy, Isaac, 125–28
McLoughlin, William G., xv, 10, 12, 17, 21–22, 34, 46, 47, 86, 121, 167–68, 184, 193, 201
Meachum, John Berry, 147–48
Menikoff, Aaron, 9, 108, 155
Mercer, Charles Fenton, 107
Mercer, Jesse, 11, 13, 32–33, 46, 108, 151–52, 186
Mercer, Silas, 8
Merrill, Daniel, 16, 17, 28, 32, 50, 65, 70, 78, 154–56
Messer, Asa, 52, 90
Miller, Nicholas P., 34
Miller, Perry, 172
Miller, William, 199
Monroe, James, 44, 107, 124, 205
Moore, Matthew, 41
Morgan, Edmund, 103
Morris, Thomas, 115

Newton, Isaac, 90
Noll, Mark A., xviii, 110

O'Sullivan, John L., 133

Paine, Thomas, 43, 90
Parker, Daniel, 141, 145, 146, 149, 176, 197
Parker, Isaiah, 29
Parkinson, William, 24, 31, 68, 157–59
Pearce, Samuel, 99, 100
Peck, John Mason, 26, 58, 118, 146–49
Pendleton, James Madison, 68
Phelps, Elnathan, 44
Pinckney, Charles Cotesworth, 15, 20, 61, 88, 164n7
Price, Richard, 165–66
Priestley, Joseph, 165–66
Pugh, Evan, 173

Rabun, William, 108, 152
Reeve, James E., 127

Rice, Luther, 145, 159
Richey, Russell E., 135
Rippon, John, 47, 48
Rogers, William, 93, 101, 159
Rutledge, Edward, 15
Rutledge Jr., John, 139

Schaff, Philip, xvi
Scully, Randolph Ferguson, 170, 187
Semple, Robert, 108, 131
Sharp, Henry, 41
Shays, Daniel, 77
Shephard, Jonathan, 45
Sherwood, Adiel, 52, 54, 141–44
Skillman, Isaac, 185
Smith, Adam, 11
Smith, Ebenezer, 102
Smith, Elias, 140–41
Smith, Eric, xv, 64, 68
Smith, Hezekiah, 23, 45, 49, 83, 90, 91, 100, 103, 153, 167, 184–85
Smith, John, 115
Stafford, Seth, 95
Staughton, Maria, 178
Staughton, William, 22, 46, 100, 101, 150, 159, 178, 179, 206–7
Stiles, Ezra, 40, 41, 168
Stillman, Samuel, xv, 13, 23, 23, 66, 74, 79, 83, 86–87, 93, 100, 103, 129, 131, 166, 167–68, 184
Stowe, Harriet Beecher, 112
Strong, Caleb, 102
Stuart, Moses, 141

Tallmadge, Matthias B., 160–61

Tarrant, Carter, 63, 118
Taylor, John, 48, 141, 146, 155, 168, 197
Teague, Colin, 108
Tennent, William, 45
Thompson, C. Bradley, 93, 122–23
Turner, Nat, 5–6, 112

Van Buren, Martin, 71, 189
Van Horne, William, 45, 94, 95, 100
Vesey, Denmark, 111, 190

Ward, William, 159
Washington, George, 3, 14, 15, 48, 54, 55–58, 60, 63, 64, 74, 75, 86, 90, 91, 95, 150, 181, 206
Watts, Isaac, 155
Wayland, Francis, 60, 62, 180, 204
Welch, James E., 146
Werden, Peter, 75, 183
Whitefield, George, 97
Whiteside Jr., William, 137
Williams, Roger, 16, 27, 50, 83, 120–21
Williams, William, 185
Williams, William, 192
Wills, Gregory, 183, 201
Winchester, Elhanan, 165–66
Winsor, Samuel, 97
Winthrop, John, 132
Witherspoon, John, 91
Witt, Daniel, 162
Woods, Henry A., 18
Worcester, Samuel A., 127

Index of Scripture

Genesis
3:15	64

Exodus
1	9:4

Numbers
23:23	92

Deuteronomy
28:43–44	77

2 Samuel
1:23	206

2 Kings
6:6	63

Psalms
46:9	68
52:7	90

Isaiah
10:27	22–23
52:7	158
66:1–5	78

Matthew
12:42	7
22:21	129
24:5–29	131
24:6–8	86
28:18–20	159

Mark
12:17	32

Luke
19:14	78

Romans
13	157

Galatians
5:1	129

2 Thessalonians
2:7	8

1 Timothy
6:1	

1 Peter
2:16	3

www.ingramcontent.com/pod-product-compliance
Lightning Source LLC
Chambersburg PA
CBHW050851230426
43667CB00012B/2243